MURDER & MAYHEM IN THE FOURTH CORNER

True Stories of Whatcom, Skagit & San Juan Counties' Earliest Homicides

T. A. WARGER

Chuckanut Editions

Village Books

1200 11th Street

Bellingham WA 98225

360-671-2626

Research and writing by T. A. Warger

Illustrations by Jake Reller & Brian Young

Cover concept by Vladimir Verano

Cover and page design by Emily Zimmerman

Village Books Publishing Team Jessica H. Stone & Candee Blanc

ISBN 978-0-692-18088-4

LCCN 2014953622

Printed in Bellingham WA, USA

Also by T. A. Warger

Books

Murder in the Fourth Corner

More Murder in the Fourth Corner

Images of America: Mount Baker (with John D'Onofrio)

Big Ole: A Timber Mill Whistle in Bellingham

Documentary Films

The Mountain Runners (with Brian Young)

Shipyard (with David Lowrance)

Author's Note

As I was reading Lottie Roeder Roth's *History of Whatcom County*, published in 1926, I came across this passage under "Crime Record" on page 547. Her timely writing coincides with the period of my murder series, during the time of settlement through the Great Depression. I found her observations as to why crime and violence were prevalent in Whatcom County interesting and so am reprinting them here:

"The criminal record in any community never forms a pleasing subject and may be passed over lightly although it cannot be altogether overlooked, as some of the criminal cases were chief subjects of interest throughout the county at the time of their occurrence. In considering conditions in Whatcom County, especially after the boom days had come and gone, three things must be borne in mind; first, that there were hundreds of disappointed, almost desperate men stranded here when the tide of fortune turned; second, that the proximity of the international border has always tempted to crime and, third, that the county was pursuing the same 'wide open' policy towards vice that was adopted by all the West at that time and that there was no restraint upon the passions of men except where they expressed themselves in actual violence. Bearing these three things in mind, the criminal record of Whatcom County is remarkable only for its cleanness [*sic*]."

Foreword

I first met Todd Warger in February of 2015 when I presented at the Whatcom Museum on the subject of my newly published book, *The Wages of Sin*, which focuses on the Great Sedro-Woolley Bank Robbery of 1914. Todd had just published the second edition of Murder in the Fourth Corner, and with a shared interest in historical crime in the Pacific Northwest, I knew I had found a kindred spirit. See, for those of us who have this type of calling, researching and publishing a book on local crime isn't a recipe for a spot on the *New York Times*' Bestseller List. Hours spent in research come with one guarantee: your time will never be fully compensated monetarily. And yet, here we both are continuing along with this labor of love.

For some of us, finding an incomplete story in recorded history produces an itch that simply has to be scratched. As with any local news event, the story rarely gets covered by the news media in a way we consider being complete. There's always more to the story. There's always a backstory that hasn't yet been told about the people involved. There's always more that can be done to honor those who had a part in the events.

And so when scratching that itch, our compensation for hundreds upon hundreds of research hours comes in a few forms. First, the satisfaction of recording the factual events of our local history in a way that is thorough and complete; satisfaction that the story hasn't only been half written or half reported, but that the facts have been exhaustively researched and cross-referenced. Second, the joy of telling about another human being whose story may have been lost in history; honoring their spirit or their sacrifice, or their influence on the local community that no doubt came in the form of tragedy.

And finally, for true crime writers, our job is done when we know that events in history are compiled in a way that they can be read and understood; that they're recorded and remembered, and that the lessons of history are learned. Because when history passes without the honor of lessons learned, the result is often that history repeats. And when it comes to local crime, that's history we'd rather not see repeat.

It is a special honor to introduce you to this third edition of *Murder in the Fourth Corner* and the intriguing events thoroughly researched and reported by our region's finest local crime writer, Todd Warger. Enjoy these fascinating stories that for better or worse have earned a place in our region's history.

Rustan Robertson

Acknowledgments

I would like to thank Chuckanut Editions for taking an interest in publishing the third installment to this series, and preserving local history. To all those who contributed in making this book possible, I thank you sincerely for all your efforts. Jessica Stone and Candee Blanc are a fantastic publishing team to work with. Emily Zimmerman, cover and page design, thank you for the hard work, and in continuing in Vladimir Verano's cover concept. And, thanks to Andrew Shattuck McBride for making *Murder & Mayhem* look good.

I wish to thank Daryl C. McClary for contributing information about the murder of George Lanterman.

Brian Young, for designing the maps for this edition. Heather Britain at Whatcom Superior Court. Alison Costanza, Washington State Archives Northwest Regional Branch, and Ruth Steele, Center for the Pacific Northwest Studies. Maggie Cogswell, research assistant at the Washington State Archives in Olympia. Jeff Jewell, Whatcom Museum photo archivist and historian. Elaine Walker at the Anacortes Museum archives. Mari Densmore, Skagit County Historical Museum. Patterson Smith, owner of Detective Magazines Archives.

Laura Nelson Jacoby, many thanks for sharing your grandfather Galen Biery's photo collection.

For my mother, Cynthia Warger

In my life time, I have murdered 21 human beings. I have committed thousands of burglaries, robberies, larcenys, arsons and last but not least I have committed sodomy on more than 1,000 male human beings. For all of these things I am not the least bit sorry. I have no conscience so that does not worry me. I don't believe in Man, God nor devil. I hate the whole damed human race including myself [sic].

— Carl Panzram, 1891-1930

Mama, put my guns in the ground
I can't shoot them anymore.
That long black cloud is comin' down
I feel I'm knockin' on heaven's door.

— Bob Dylan, 1941- Present
"Knockin' On Heaven's Door" 1973

Table of Contents

PART I - Whatcom County

PART II - Skagit & San Juan Counties

Part I
Whatcom County

Chapter 1
Mrs. Thomas' Potato Patch

Where is Gunilda Thomas? The question ran rampant throughout the Fairhaven district without the slightest clue. She lived alone in a roughshod house on what was known as the "far-side" of Happy Valley. Her home was quite literally at the end of the road, with its back nestled into brush and woods, where the only border into the wild was her potato garden. The nearest neighbor was blocks away, if there had been blocks. Being so far out from town neighbors watched closely over one another. But no one had seen the woman, neither at home or in town since July 19, 1908. Various appointments came and went without cancellation, and it was now well into September. No one had seen hide nor hair of her, that is, except her "abusive"

Happy Valley, 1912. Gunilda Thomas' home was nestled along the hillside, hidden within the tree line. Neighbors were spread far apart. Courtesy of Laura Jacoby's, Galen Biery collection

ex-husband, James K. Thomas. Thomas claimed she had traveled south toward Tacoma. He assumed she was visiting their daughter, Ethel, at the Chehalis State Training School. With no word or letters from the woman, speculation ran high. By the first week of September, both Bellingham Police Captain Alexander L. Callahan and Whatcom County Prosecutor Virgil Peringer were receiving calls from concerned citizens to investigate.

Police Chief Hiram Cade and Prosecutor Peringer were indeed suspicious, as the couple had been at odds for years. They were drunkards. Both physically and mentally abusive toward one another. Because of her shattered home life, their fourteen-year-old daughter had become a rebellious adolescent. Officers had been out to the dwelling more times than they could count. And the couple had been in the courtroom so many times, Peringer was on first name basis.

Knowing of Gunilda's protective obsession for her daughter, Chief Cade wrote to see if the state training school knew anything of her mother's whereabouts. In the meantime, Peringer asked about Thomas; discovering at the time of Gunilda's disappearance he was flush with cash and had for several days been on an extreme drunken binge. After recovering from this spree of drunkenness, he nervously told others that his ex-wife was away and he was taking care of her place. On Thursday, September 24, Chief Cade received a reply from C. A. Loomis in Chehalis stating that Ethel had not heard from her mother since July.

LEFT: Bellingham Chief of Police Hiram Cade, received numerous calls from concerned individuals that Gunilda Thomas was missing. File photo: *Bellingham Herald*

RIGHT: Whatcom County Prosecutor Virgil Peringer, defended Gunilda Thomas several times against her husband. File photo: *Bellingham Herald*

Build Up to a Crisis

Gunilda Paulson (27) and James K. Thomas (36) were married in Tacoma, August 12, 1892, moving to Fairhaven about 1898. Thomas was born in New York in 1856 to William and Cynthia (Crosby or Moore). He had three sisters and two brothers. One sister, Delphine "Della" Thomas, would marry John Calvin Dyer in 1900, becoming the "Landlady" of the Monogram Annex Hotel apartments on the 404 block of Harris Avenue in Fairhaven. At age 19 (1875), Thomas was living in Wasioja, Minnesota, before moving to Minneapolis five years later. He presumably followed his sister Delphine to Washington, who by all accounts was the smarter sibling. Delphine had also lived in Minnesota at the time of her brother and no doubt took mercy and cared for her brother.

Gunilda Paulson[1] was born in Norway about 1865 to John and Anna. She had two brothers and two sisters. Gunilda, with her sisters, immigrated to America living in Stony Brook, Grant County, Minnesota by 1885. Although distance separated her and Thomas in Minnesota, it is probable the two crossed paths.

After the death of his wife Cynthia, William Thomas moved into Happy Valley to be closer to his daughter. William purchased three lots of property in the Carter Addition where he lived at 2322 Happy Court.[2] William also acquired six lots in the East Fairhaven Addition far away from town providing a plot for his son and his newlywed to build a home on. James Thomas would never be a wealthy individual, lacking ambition and wit. He was lazy and preferred the bottle to steady employment. He worked odd jobs when in need, and other times worked in his sister's hotel dining room, but never held a steady position. Thomas' sister and father most likely financed the family. James did manage to build a crude home, and two years from the month of their marriage in August 1894, Gunilda gave birth to a daughter, Ethel.

Unfortunately, the marriage was an unstable joining. In 1905, Whatcom County Sheriff Andrew Williams served papers to Thomas; Gunilda wanted a divorce. They had been separated for the most part, with Thomas still sleeping in the house and becoming brutally hostile toward her. A poorly scribbled handwritten note by her attorney was found in Gunilda's civil case file, describing some of the abuse states: "May 20 club 3 ft long across arm and

[1] AKA: Gunilda, Gunnilda, Grenalda, Guinalda, Grunelda, and Jennilda. Gunilda will be used in this story, the name she signed on her divorce complaint.
[2] Corner of 21st and Happy Court.

legs. I'll treat you so mean you will hate me, about June 15th. 23d September left her." [*sic*][3]

In the written complaint before Judge Jeremiah Neterer, Gunilda states that although they continued to live together, she remained a "dutiful wife, was economical, and managed his household affairs with frugality." The complaint goes on to state that although Thomas was physically able to earn a living for himself and family, over the past two years he has refused to work and provide. Gunilda had been compelled to work out of the home, take in washing and "do anything that was respectable to make an honest livelihood." She had been the object of charity with neighbors providing her with food and clothing.

Far worse were her claims of abuse. During their marriage, Thomas had disregarded his wedding vows and obligations, had been guilty of cruelty and abusive language. Gunilda told Judge Neterer, her husband slapped her face, and on several occasions, had violently thrown her to the floor without cause. He had threatened to kill her, and had in the presence of Ethel used vile, abusive and obscene language accusing her of infidelity. "James Thomas," Gunilda claimed "impaired her heath, peace of mind and destroyed her happiness and her life made a burden." Gunilda wanted custody of Ethel and half the property.

In February 1906, Gunilda won her case, receiving custody of Ethel, decreed all six lots of the East Fairhaven Addition including the house, and the sum of $7.50 monthly for the support of Ethel. Gunilda was both relieved of her burden and eager to start her new life. Unfortunately, Thomas didn't seem affected by the verdict. He at first compiled, but by November 1907 the two were back in court with Thomas in arrears in the sum of $60.00. He was reprimanded and ordered to pay back-support. The following ten months would be the most horrific that Gunilda Thomas could imagine, and a period of emotional turmoil for Ethel.

Investigation

On Friday, September 25, 1908 Bellingham Police Captain Alexander L. Callahan went out to investigate Gunilda Thomas' home. He took with him Detective Thomas Nugent and officer A. S. Crosslin. Virgil Peringer, doing his own investigating, went along expecting the worst. The men took the trolley running out into Happy Valley and walked the rest of the way toward the East

---

[3] Law offices of Frye and Healy, Lighthouse Block. CPNWS Whatcom Civil Case #7435

Fairhaven Addition. Crosslin, the lesser authority of the group, knocked several times on Gunilda's door, receiving no answer. Crosslin then looked through the windows and walked around the home finding no one about. It was known, according to neighbors, that James Thomas had been working or snooping around the property for weeks. This was apparent, as all the fruit on the trees were harvested and the garden picked clean. There were chicken coops, but no chickens running about. Regrouping at the porch, Nugent used one of a ring of skeleton keys he carried to gain entry and the four men were soon inside. The house had three rooms on the first floor. The bedroom, curtained off, was also the living room, and opened direct into the kitchen with humble furnishings. The walls were hung with magazine prints and apparel. A smaller bedroom in the rear, containing a steamer trunk once filled with freshly laundered clothes, was now tossed over the room. The house had been ransacked. Nugent went up into the attic where there was only a single room; that too had been turned over. The windows were boarded up and very dark, so he went back downstairs to rejoin Peringer. The house itself was messy from a lack of proper care, but it was nevertheless tossed upside down with drawers pulled, clothes strewn about and cupboards emptied.

Crosslin called the others to come into the bedroom area at once. The officer showed the men a pillowslip and bed sheets stained in blood. Pulling these away the men were puzzled to discover a large section of the mattress fabric cut away and a blanket hastily sewn in its place. The men stared at one another in confusion. Callahan gripped the poorly stitched blanket and tore it away with a swift yank. Inside, the mattress was saturated with dried blood. The bed springs were thick with heavy clots of blood clinking to the coils. Crosslin looking on the floor noted large dried bloodstains on the rug near the bed. About the place were all the woman's clothes. Her shoes still tucked under the bed. But where was Mrs. Thomas?

TOP LEFT : Detective Thomas Nugent.
Courtesy of Whatcom Museum

TOP RIGHT: Officer A. S. Crosslin.
File photo: *Bellingham Herald*

BOTTOM RIGHT: Bellingham Police Captain
Alexander L. Callahan.
File photo: *Bellingham Herald*

Captain Callahan was convinced that the ex-husband knew something of her whereabouts. He and Detective Nugent, while walking back from the far-side of Happy Valley, decided to stop at William Thomas' home at Happy Court, where James had lived since his divorce. The others took the trolley back to Bellingham. Nugent knocked and knocked on the door, but neither father nor James answered. Looking up toward the upper-floor windows James was spotted spying from behind a curtain. Callahan ordered him to come down at once and open up or he would smash the door in. Thomas complied, opening the door slowly, acting nervous and confused by the police presence. When asked about his ex-wife he claimed to know nothing, but that she left town and gave him the key to her house. Callahan knew Thomas was guilty of something and arrested him on the spot. Questioning failed to bring anything to light, other than James admitting that on July 19, the night of her disappearance, he ate dinner with Gunilda. After his statement, he refused to talk further about his former wife. It was decided to hold him overnight and to return to Gunilda's the following morning to conduct a comprehensive search of the premises.

At 7 o'clock Saturday morning, September 26, Callahan, Crosslin, Detective Nugent and Prosecutor Peringer again arrived on the far-side of Happy Valley. They searched throughout the interior and beneath the house, but discovered no clues. Next the men cut down saplings from the backyard and sharpened the ends. Then the men proceeded to probe the soil around the garden for soft spots where the ground may have been disturbed.

Around noon, Detective Nugent spied a pile of dead potato vines piled up between two stumps. These he cast off and Nugent soon discovered the ground beneath soft. He was confident that he was onto something. Probing the ground with his pole it sunk fast releasing a pungent stench that nearly bowled him over. Nugent excitedly informed the others, "We definitely have something here, boys." With shovels cutting into the earth, the men started to dig and soon discovered that a hole of about two feet deep or more had been filled in, as a pile of weeds were mixed in with the dirt. The deeper they dug the stronger the wretched odor became.

The diggers stopped momentarily, stared at one-another, and then worked with renewed feverish energy. They next discovered a buried log. This looked suspicious and they removed it. The ground underneath was even softer. The spades soon struck a blanket, and the officers were given a shock by their unearthing. Although they had expected to make a ghastly find under the blanket they were not prepared for the sight of the soupy rotting flesh and bare bones from the lower limbs of a human body. Satisfied that they had found Mrs. Thomas, they quit digging and started for Fairhaven, where a telephone call was placed to Coroner Henry Thompson, and to the undertaking parlors of W. H. Mock & Son on Elk Street.[4] No further work would be done until the coroner arrived. Mrs. Thomas' potato patch was now a crime scene.

The murder was one of the most ghastly ever committed within the city. A year prior had witnessed the brutal slaying of Addie Roper of Blaine.[5]

---

[4] State Street
[5] See chapter one of *More Murder in the Fourth Corner.*

That homicide was so heinous it numbed the community. Addie had been beaten, raped, gagged, axed and burned. Coroner Henry Thompson arrived with George Mock at the shallow grave and with the assistance of officers went through the meticulous process of removing Gunilda's remains from the ground. Thompson looked at the pile of potato vines Nugent tossed aside, then gazed at the partial exposed corpse between two stumps in the woman's own garden. He shook his head, stating to no one in particular, "Do you ever get tired of this? I sure do."

The body was still fairly intact, held together by her clothing, but the flesh had fallen away and her features were gone. The skeleton had fallen apart in places. Persons who had known Gunilda identified her by her hair and the gold-fillings in her teeth. Isaac Johnson, who had known the woman for years, was called upon and was positive in his identification. He recognized her dark auburn hair, and the way she wore it. She parted it in the middle, looped it up in the back and tied it with a ribbon. "It always had a tendency to curl," he said. The clothing was also recognized, as she had dressed all the time for work, but around her were wrapped a bathrobe and two blankets.

The most diabolical feature of the whole affair was the building of a furnace grave for the reception of the body. Under the remains had been laid a layer of paper and fine wood. Up the side of the grave extended a chimney to give the blaze a draft. There was evidence of the fire having been started, but it had not burned as planned, for the body was untouched by the flames, although the clothing was scorched in spots. The flue was faulty and did not draw as intended. The chilling part was that the flesh appeared smoked, giving the body a mummified appearance.

After the remains had been removed, Thompson viewed them on the spot as he feared what was left of Gunilda would disintegrate during transportation. He noted two small wounds over the heart, indicating that she may have been shot twice. Matted blood in the hair indicated that she had been struck about the head, but the skull was not visibly fractured that he could tell. If the body survived the wagon trip intact he would make a closer examination at the undertaking parlors of W. H. Mock & Son.

Thompson decided since too little was left of the remains to give a determinate examination, and under the belief the murderer was in custody, no inquest would be necessary. In late afternoon Gunilda's flesh, bones and clothing were placed in a rough wooden box and taken away. Detective Nugent stayed behind and dug further in the grave hoping to recover a weapon, but found none.

Captain Callahan held back informing James Thomas of the discovery. He had been held in solitary confinement at the city jail and was devoid of any news or visitors. Callahan and Chief Cade wanted to "sweat" a confession out him without his knowledge of the discovered body. Callahan hope to break down Thomas. He and Nugent would ask Thomas about a rumored $500 hidden away on the property. Although the woman worked hard daily, money had not been found. Since the woman's disappearance, Thomas was known to have plenty of cash. He drank considerably. His ex-wife's house had fourteen empty whisky bottles lying about. The place was ransacked, and he admitted staying there. The hidden bloodstains and blood-soaked mattress; the fact that he had money, but didn't work; that he took her chickens to his place and canned all the fruit from her orchard; that he refused to open up his door when the officers came to question him; the police claimed these were all circumstances pointing to his guilt. If he was not guilty, why did he not report her missing? That's when Callahan would inform the prisoner that a body had been found in her garden; that someone had tried to burn her. Callahan would then ask why Thomas had not come across the newly dug grave in the garden, which he claimed to have worked daily.

Murder in Happy Valley! Mrs. J. K. Thomas Murdered.
Bellingham Herald, September 26, 1908

Meanwhile, word was getting out that something was stirring in Happy Valley. Rumors and gossip were rampant on the streets and in the barrooms of Fairhaven and Bellingham. James Thomas was arrested and his ex-wife was missing, the conclusions seemed obvious. The *American Reveille* jumped on the story before its competitors with the front-page story, "Foul Play Feared on the South Side." The feature accompanied another story of foul play, the arrest of Beck's Theatre and hotel trusted employee, M. G. Brown for embezzlement. More disturbing for a contemporary reader was the quarter-front page advertisement offering free tickets for the Beck's Theatre's smash hit, "The Clansman" which promised seventy-five players on stage.

The Trouble with Ethel

After all the bitter infighting, abuse, cruelty and a brutal divorce, the pair never really separated. Thomas hung around the house much of the time with Gunilda not approving—but permitting it. Thomas would continue inflicting abuse upon Gunilda. When he desired, Thomas would go to the little house and force himself on his ex-wife, fulfilling his sexual needs. Suffering the most from this dysfunctional existence was their young adolescent daughter, Ethel, who grew up in the oppressive atmosphere of her feuding parents. In the midst of this, Gunilda became obsessively attached to Ethel. Attached in the sense that she feared her daughter would one day leave her mother; finding herself suddenly alone. This proved a problem, as Ethel struggled to be free. In return she desperately fought back for her own survival. As Gunilda tried holding her daughter down, she was forced to fight an additional conflict with Thomas who now refused to pay child support. Gunilda now had to take her ex-husband to court for back support. Thomas was ordered by the court to pay her, and he seethed for revenge.

Thomas didn't have to wait long. At about this time 14-year-old Ethel started to rebel, escaping from her isolated home as much as possible. She would run away whenever the opportunity arose to explore the curiosities of the city. The act would lock her into a deep-heated conflict with her mother. Her daytime inquisitiveness soon waned, as she became seduced by the nightlife of the seedier parts of Bellingham. Sneaking out at night, she would be gone until the morning hours. Word soon got back to the parents that Ethel was running with foul middle-aged men, whom entertained more than a casual interest in her. Dragged back home from her excursions, Ethel soon discovered new hideaways. These were entertainment places more appropriate toward people of color.

After the 1907 court decision, Ethel became the cause of further argument between Thomas and his ex-wife. It's possible Thomas thought he could avoid future child support if his daughter were out of the picture. James Thomas came to the conclusion his ex-wife could no longer handle their daughter. He wanted her sent away to the Chehalis State Training School, a reform school for juveniles who were abandoned, orphaned or petty criminals. Thomas claimed Gunilda was deeply infatuated with the girl, an obsessive nature that was causing all her domestic problems. He argued, for the good of the girl, she needed to be taken from her mother and placed into a setting of proper care.

The record lacks detail of events over the winter and spring of 1908, but the conflict escalated to a point where Gunilda tried to take her daughter across the border into Canada at Christmas to avoid arrest. A court statement by E. M. Day cited that the association of the child with the "low mother, who was much of the time under the influence of liquor, and the negligence shown by the mother who permitted her child to go about the streets of Bellingham and other places, visiting places that were improper for any child budding into womanhood, and associating with vicious young and middle age men…"

In a court hearing that followed, Gunilda slapped Sheriff Andrew Williams in the face when he tried to take Ethel. James Thomas got his way, Ethel was sent to Chehalis to the wails of her screaming mother.

Thomas Cracks

A "work-over" gained no useful information from Thomas. Chief of Police Cade suggested allowing a *Bellingham Herald* reporter into the cell to interview the prisoner. Cade hoped Thomas would slip and say something incriminating and useful to them. Cade pointed out that Thomas was going nowhere and being a drunken simpleton he would surely break with time in isolation.

"Yes, I know what they suspect me of," said Thomas to a *Herald* reporter, "and I wish to God I knew where the woman is." Thomas reiterated that he had not seen Gunilda since the evening of July 19, and while she was angry with him for having Ethel sent to the state training school, they had no open quarrel. "She told me then that she was going away, and I guessed that she would go either to Tacoma or Chehalis, so that she could be near Ethel…she was always rather secretive in her manner, being happiest when she told people the least of her affairs. She talked of her cousin in California…but never mentioned any particular place, and I never asked her, so, she may be down there."

Thomas told the reporter they had trouble from the time they were married, and had many quarrels over Ethel. "She was crazy about the girl. She fought like a tiger when I wanted to have the girl placed in proper hands. You remember," he said, "how she took the girl across the line about Christmas time and how she slapped Sheriff William's face in the courtroom while Ethel was before the judge? When she went away I thought she was going to be near Ethel. The police tell me that she is not in Chehalis; so, I don't know where the woman is."

Thomas continued, "While at dinner on the last day I saw her, she told me to care for her chickens and her house. I came at 5 o'clock that evening and she was still there...I did not see her go. I have not heard from her since, and I do not know where she is now." He added he took all the vegetables, pears, raspberries and plums down to his house and canned them.

The reporter thought it funny that she did not pack her trunk with her clothes when she left. Thomas thought for a moment before saying, "I think she left in a hurry and failed to have them ready in time."

Later that evening Captain Callahan stopped by Thomas' cell and asked if he was all right, being treated well or needing food. Thomas indicated he was well. "Oh, and by the way," said the captain, "we found your ex-wife buried in her potato patch." Dropping the bombshell to a blank-faced Thomas, Callahan walked out of the cell room.

That same Saturday evening, Coroner Thompson, Dr. C. E. Martin, Chief Cade, Crosslin, Detective Nugent and George Mock examined the body. Mock did his best to clean Gunilda up. It was clearly shown one bullet had struck the woman on the side of the head, although it probably did not enter the brain. Part of the zygoma arch (cheekbone) was carried away and the orbital bone shattered. A second bullet had without question gone through the body, as a hole indicated at least one, if not two bullets had gone through the body in the region of the heart. One of the undergarments beneath her back was saturated with blood. Coroner Thompson and Dr. Martin thought it queer that the body's decomposition occurred so rapidly even though it was in a shallow grave two months. The fact the underground incinerator failed to cook the body may have had something to do with it.

Although Thomas was not immediately shaken when Callahan told of finding the body, by Sunday his nerve was going fast. The jailer said he sang and whistled nervously the greater part of the night. About midnight he began to weaken. When Callahan looked in about that hour before leaving for home, Thomas begged to be allowed to tell his side of the story. The captain told him it could wait until morning. Callahan figured that if Thomas showed no surprise or concern for a confession, then the police must know all. The more Thomas sweated, the more he would talk, thought Callahan. Then, the captain placed his hat on his head, bidding his prisoner a good night.

Callahan was correct, morning found James Thomas all the more eager to talk. So great was his desire he could hardly wait for Chief Cade and Detective Nugent to get Court Stenographer O. H. Lamoreux. He talked without hesitation. Thomas stated the killing was done in self-defense. So little inquiries were made about the absence of Gunilda at first that Thomas thought he was perfectly safe. He declared he did not think anyone would ever find her body.

After telling his tale, Thomas felt much relieved. He blamed whiskey for his downfall. He stated if he had not been drinking he would not have killed her. He insisted that he shot her in self-defense. Gunilda fired first, declaring she kept a gun. Callahan stated no weapon was found at the crime scene. Thomas said after the killing he sold both the guns, his own and hers.

After the fatal shooting, Thomas claimed he had little memory of events as "alcohol had drowned his mind." He claimed to have picked the body up and laid her out on the bed. He then lay beside her bleeding corpse, and fell into a deep slumber.

Several days later, fearing that the body would be detected, and he blamed, Thomas went back to the house to dispose of the body. The remains were beginning to stink. He picked up her body, carried it into the garden and placed it in a hole beside a stump that had been dug by Gunilda in her efforts to burn it out. He used it for a grave and buried the body. For six weeks he claimed to have visited the grave nearly every day.

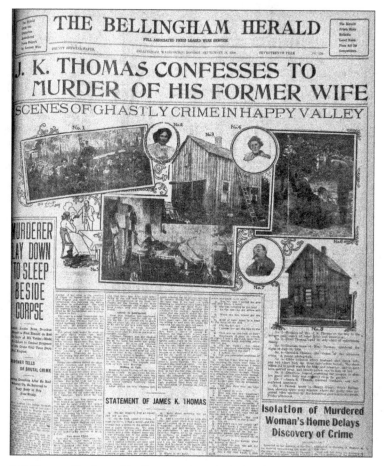

J. K. Thomas Confesses. The front page is covered with photographs and artwork, sensationalizing the crime. *Bellingham Herald*, September 28, 1908

Edited Confession:

Q: (Nugent) "Just go ahead and tell us, Jim."

A: "On the 19th, about 5 o'clock, I went up there; I had a bottle, and the woman had a bottle in the house; we had a quart between us. We were drinking more or less until about 12 o'clock, and a little dispute came up; I said, 'All right, I will go home.

"As I backed towards the door and opened the door and started out she pulled a gun from under her clothes where she kept it. I gave it to her three years ago. She aimed and shot. I pulled a gun from my pocket and fired once or twice…I heard her say, My God, I am gone. I dropped my gun. I didn't wait to put it in my pocket. I went in and picked her up off the floor and laid her on the bed, and I must have dropped over and went to sleep, because I found myself at 9 o'clock in the morning beside her in bed. Knowing not what to do, I covered her with bedclothes and went to town and got full of booze. I don't think I went back for two days. I went back and opened the door and picked her up and carried her down into the garden. I rolled her in a blanket and laid her down aside of a big stump and thrown some dirt over her, and I covered her up in the vines…had her all covered up in good shape."

Grilling Thomas made him alter his story further. He claimed at the time of the argument they were both in bed, she with most of her clothes off. "She was accusing me of a woman and I was accusing her of a man. I says, if that is the case I will get up and go home, and started to open the door and was backing out, and she says, "Well." She says "You better"—she always had her gun under her pillow, and as I was stepping back she pulled her gun and shot. Of course she missed—she must have. I always have my gun in my pocket…I pulled my gun and shot twice, I think. She was standing by the bed and kind of went right down in a heap at the head of the bed."

Thomas was asked if she didn't have her corsets off, for which he could not say as he was "pretty well boozed up, so was she." Nugent offered that she appeared fully dressed; her skirts were all on, her underclothes, corsets and everything. James said he dressed her later to look proper.

In regard to the money, Thomas couldn't say where it was, as he found none, but only three dollars. He admitted he looked through the trunk, drawers, closets etc, but turned up empty. Chief Cade pointed out he was spending a lot of cash on booze the past few months for a non-working man. Cade probed if the argument was over money, and after Gunilda not giving him any he shot her. Thomas protested this was not the case.

Cade asked if there were any attempt to burn the body, as there were cinders at the bottom of the hole. Thomas claimed that is where she had been burning out a stump. The hole was already there. He simply had thrown some dirt over it. Cade didn't believe the convenience of a pre-dug hole that was still burning. "There is nothing that you know of that would make the body decay rapidly—didn't put anything on the body?"

"No," claimed Thomas. "The *Reveille* came out and said I was an unwelcome visitor. I furnished her eggs, milk, and butter ever since April, cut her wood and spaded her garden and planted her peas, cleaned out her strawberries and been doing all the work."

Cade interjected how he did all this work for her, but it was she who dug her own grave and that she was burning out a stump. Thomas simply continued that she was a hard worker. "She went out into the woods and helped me saw down trees; she always used to do that through the years. As far as beating her, we never had trouble, only the *Reveille* says several times."

Q: "Do you remember how many times you have either been arrested or she has had you arrested since your trouble started here four years ago you might say?"

A: "I think Ethel had it figured up nine times."

Cade then surprised others in the room by asking if he thought his brother-in-law, John Dyer, suspected something wrong before he (Cade) took hold of the case? Dyer, besides being a blacksmith, was a Bellingham reserve officer who had been doing special duty on the south side. Thomas claimed, "One day I met him in the morning. I think it was about three weeks ago. He says, "There is a suspicion that you killed Gunilda," and he says, "They are going to investigate." That was the substance of it, further than that he personally never spoke to me."

After the confession, Cade and Callahan conferred. They heard the confession, but didn't believe a large extent of it. There were many holes. Thomas didn't deny killing her, but was it the true story? Was the shooting premeditated? Where are the guns? Where was the proof of self-defense or proof that Gunilda ever had a gun or fired a gun? Was there money in the house?

Chief Cade took John Dyer off the police force on account of the close connection with the case. Cade deemed it best to have him removed at least for the time being. He believed Dyer was not implicated in the crime, but Cade knew the man suspected something and didn't come forward. For the "good of the service" he was temporarily removed.

The following day the *Bellingham Herald* published all the gory details of the murder case. They outlined a history of the lengthy feud between the married couple, the troubled daughter and gave the reader a chilling visual of the crime scene enticing *thrill seekers* to the murder house:

"For the officers, who have worked on more than one murder case," declared to the *Herald*, "it is the most brutal murder they have ever been detailed to ferret out."

"The cabin stands far from any other habitation, but affords a view of the Happy Valley beyond. Deserted in solitude of the forest slashing surrounding the scene of the murder...the place was visited by curiosity seekers all day Sunday... The darkened rooms of the cabin in their adjacent property and the tangled growth of the forest around the tall stubs of the burned fir trees in the old clearing inviting enough, for a murder at the best. In their desolation are mute reminders of the gaunt, tall woman who called the place home."

Thomas Nugent relived the day with a *Herald* reporter. He told how they wandered about in the garden and prodded in the loose ground near an apple tree, but the whole potato patch had been dug over and there was nothing to go by:

"I pushed a stick in the loose ground, and it went down to easy for quite a distance, and then struck something hard. We know now that it was that little log, or fence post. Callahan scraped all the potato vines from the spot, and I put a stick in this hole near the stump and it went all the way down to the skull in the grave, and the stench soon let us know that what we wanted was right there. All that was left of the woman was that skeleton there now."

Brutal Crime! Morbid thrill seekers dressed in their Sunday best pose for a photograph at the potato patch grave. Hundreds of people would descend on the murder site, many seeking souvenirs. *American Evening* and *Morning Reveille*, September 28, 1908

On account of the confession, the authorities would have liked the case out of the way. But Thomas would make a fight of it and prove self-defense. His attorney, James B. Abrams, already had foundation for it in the confession. Thomas was the only one present when he killed Gunilda, so it would be difficult to establish premeditation. However, the police claimed he had threatened to kill his ex-wife on several occasions, and it was known he sought legal counsel as to his rights to claim his former wife's property. Thomas was told he had no rights to it. Later, he suggested securing the release of Ethel from the state training school. This looked strange to authorities, as it was through his own instigation she was committed. It was a thin-veil to use his daughter as a pawn against his ex-wife.

On Tuesday morning, September 29, 60-year-old William visited his son's cell. It was a sorrowful meeting. James tried to be cheerful. While at liberty, he was able to get plenty of strong drink to hold up his spirits, now he had no such relief and was beginning to show the effects of the strain. In the Superior Court that morning Prosecuting Attorney Peringer had a warrant issued for his arrest, charging Thomas with murder in the first-degree. Judge Jeremiah Neterer, before whom the information was sworn, declined to fix bail, so Thomas would be held until the trial was set.

Also that Tuesday, Ethel Thomas arrived from Chehalis for the final burial of her mother set for Thursday. Ethel would stay with her Aunt Maria Edwards. Thomas had deeded his home in Happy Court to Maria for a dollar. Gunilda's home would go to her daughter. Ethel, under the law, had the right to name her own guardian, and the Edwards agreed to act in that capacity and adopt the child as their own.

On Monday, October 5 a plea of "Not guilty," was entered by Thomas when arraigned on the charge of murder in the first-degree. Appearing for the prisoner, Abrams was to notify the court before Saturday whether he would be ready to go to trial in November. If not, Thomas would wait until the next term in January. Peringer wanted the trial in November, so he might credit it as his last criminal trial before leaving office in January. Deputy Prosecutor George Livesey had secured the Republican nomination for the office of prosecuting attorney and would soon replace Peringer. On October 9, all parties agreed to have a jury called in December to try the case.

Trial

As a trial date was being determined, the remote home of Gunilda Thomas become the target of looters. It was discovered on October 15, when Mrs. D. P. Day, of the Associated Charities, Patrolman Doty, and an expressman, went into the place to salvage items for Ethel and pack anything useful for charity. The house was found ransacked beyond the plundered condition previously known. What few valuables left in the home were either taken or found broken on the floor.

A distressed Mrs. Day stated to local papers her disgust of such vandals, and that the place looked as though someone had gone in and, after picking out the valuables, piled the rest in the center of each room. The old clothes were found not worth taking. Ethel had asked Day to bring back a few mementos, including a coat, but she found none of these. Her mother's trunk and all the valuables of which Ethel wanted were gone.

The trial started on the morning of December 7. Nine out of the first ten men examined as jurors passed for cause. Both Peringer and Abrams agreed that twelve men would be chosen before nightfall. Every prospective juror was asked as to whether or not he had conscientious scruples against inflicting capital punishment, and only one had been released.

James Thomas was brought into courtroom a few minutes before the case was called. The *Herald* said, "…he looks sleek and fat and seems to worry but little over the outcome. In fact, he has evidently been benefited so far as physical appearances go by his confinement." At his side sat his sister Maria Edwards, both sitting alongside Attorneys Abrams and C. H. Shamel. Prosecuting Attorney Peringer and Deputy Prosecutor Livesey sat opposite of the table. Neither side subpoenaed Ethel Thomas as a witness, as it was not believed she could shed any light on the murder. Nor would she make an appearance on her own.

TOP LEFT : Whatcom Deputy Prosecutor
George Livesey.
File photo: *Bellingham Herald*

RIGHT: Judge Jeremiah Neterer.
File photo: *Bellingham Herald*

BOTTOM LEFT: Attorney James Abrams.
File photo: *Bellingham Herald*

In a statement, Peringer merely told of the crime to which Thomas had confessed. The information charging Thomas with murder in the first-degree was read and then the examination by the twelve whom would have to decide the fate of James K. Thomas was started.

From the trend of the questions asked by Abrams and Shamel in the examination of the jurors, it appeared as though their defense would be based on mental irresponsibility brought on by intoxication. They would attempt to show Thomas was drunk and not capable of acquiring motive or malice and that he simply shot his wife while in a drunken stupor. Thomas, in his confession, laid the foundation for self-defense by saying that the woman shot at him first, but it was believed his counsel would not use it as Thomas shot and killed Gunilda in her own house, where he had no right to be at the hour of midnight.

On December 8, a hundred spectators were present in the courtroom when the trial started despite a heavy downpour of rain. Among the spectators were said to be many women. At the side of the prisoner sat William Thomas, his aged father. The blood-stained mattress, blankets and quilts from the dead woman's home were on display and would be presented as exhibits for the state.

The morning session was characterized by fierce attacks upon Detective Thomas Nugent by the defense. Claims were made that Nugent had "sweated" and threatened Thomas to "come through" with his confession. Abrams claimed that Nugent threatened to arrest Delphine Dyer, sister of the prisoner unless he confessed, charging her with accessory to murder. He claimed, Nugent said, if he confessed he promised that the state would make it right with him for saving the county a great deal of expense in a trial. In a thundering voice, Abrams demanded the confession could not be admitted to the jury for the reason it was obtained under threats, duress and the holding out of promises to the defendant.

The use of "threats" was referred to frequently until at last the court demanded counsel be more specific. It was brought out the threat to arrest his sister and the use of language "you better confess" constituted the greater part of the "sweating." It was also claimed the sisters had been refused the privilege of seeing Thomas, and that no legal adviser was permitted to see him. Denying council alone should be enough to throw the case out, fought Abrams.

Detective Nugent strenuously denied the use of threats. After an extended argument regarding the confession and testimony by Nugent, Judge Neterer in the afternoon overruled the objections of counsel to have the confession thrown out. The confession was introduced to the jury.

The following day, Wednesday December 9, the courtroom was filled with even more spectators who followed the testimony in newspapers with interest. Peringer put forth the state's evidence: the confession of the prisoner to the murder, the testimony of witnesses to show the woman had not been seen after July 19, and that her body was found where Thomas admitted he had buried it. Detective Nugent, A. S. Crosslin, Captain Callahan, Sheriff Andrew Williams,

Dr. C. E. Martin and Gunilda Thomas' friends, James Robertson and William Erlick all testified that the body found buried in the potato patch was that of Mrs. Thomas. No further attempt would be made to show that the body found was not that of Gunilda Thomas.

Sheriff Williams was the first witness called by the state. His testimony reflected his visits to the troubled home and his exchanges with the deceased woman. He told the jury the tearful stories told by Gunilda regarding Thomas' habits and his actions towards her. Following Williams, George Mock was called to the stand, and testified as to the position, general condition and appearance of the body prior to and after its removal to his undertaking parlors.

With the conclusion of the cross-examination of Captain Callahan, the state rested at 11:35 a.m. Callahan's testimony closely paralleled that of Detective Nugent. Peringer signified to the court that all the evidence on behalf of the prosecution had been given. Following a short recess, Attorney Abrams interposed a motion that the jury be instructed to bring in a verdict of not guilty, on the grounds the alleged crime had not been proven. Nothing had been introduced to show the defendant was guilty of any of the lesser crimes charged in the information and corpus delicti[6] had not been established. Again, Peringer stated that corpus delicti was established by James Thomas' own confession.

This was promptly overruled. Court adjourned until 1:30, when, without the usual preface of an opening address to the jury, Abrams started his defense. Abrams would attempt to show that Thomas was drunk at the time and had no malice and he probably shot in self-defense, as he claimed. Witnesses would show the woman had made threats against Thomas.

The *Reveille* reflected on the proceedings, with the consensus that the prosecution's case was undoubtedly weak in establishing any evidence directly bearing on the crime charged against Thomas. No one doubted a strong chain of circumstantial evidence had been woven around him, supported by his "alleged" confession. The *Reveille* felt the prosecution's evidence pointed strongly toward his guilt, while, on the other hand, the defense had so far produced nothing that would establish his innocence.

The first witness for the defense was Maria Edwards (sister). From the nature of the questions asked and the objections interposed by Peringer and Livesey it was believed counsel would seek a drunken defense; that he was in fear of his divorced wife who had threatened to shoot him.

---

[6] Body of the crime.

Maria Edwards testified as to the drinking habits of her brother prior to his arrest. She stated her brother was in the habit of drinking heavily, although maintaining he was habitually quiet and peaceable when under the influence of liquor. She testified she had went to her brother about twenty times since the divorce for the purpose of assisting in caring for him during his periodic states of intoxication. She further testified Thomas and his wife seemed on the best of terms, except when Gunilda was under the influence of liquor.

Thomas' sister Delphine also testified to her brother's habits, agreeing with her sister. Ten witnesses in all were examined during the course of the afternoon session, all providing the same line of testimony, that James Thomas was a drunk, but not of a quarrelsome disposition, but the reverse. "James was known to become quiet and sleepy, said Delphine, "until he had consumed enough liquor to cause him to sink into a comatose state and remain so for several days…"[7]

Neighbor Nellie McGinnis gave the strongest testimony for the defense when she stated Gunilda had threatened to take the life of her former husband:

"I have seen Mrs. Thomas go by my house several times quite drunk. On the occasion of Ethel being sent to the reform school she came to my house about eight or nine o'clock in the morning and asked me if I was going to testify against Ethel so that she would be committed to the school. During the course of the conversation she mentioned her husband and told me that she had a gun and was going to shoot him. I told her that she had better not do that, but she said she would. This was during the latter part of October in 1907."

On cross-examination Peringer pushed McGinnis further regarding Thomas' visits, to which she stated: "I knew Thomas was in the habit of going up to his former wife's home. She had been complaining to me about that and she accused him of getting drunk and coming up there for an illegitimate purpose, and said if he did not stop doing so and troubling her that way she would shoot him."

At 4:30 p.m. the defense had exhausted their list of witnesses for the day and court was adjourned.

Shortly after ten o'clock the following morning came the only surprise of the trial when the defense announced the closing of testimony, without putting Thomas on the stand. It was understood from the opening of the trial Thomas would go on to refute the confession he made to police, but the evidence was

---

[7] *American Reveille*, December 10, 1908.

completed without his testimony.

On Thursday, December 10, closing arguments began with hope that the fate of the prisoner would rest with the jury before night. In a well-delivered speech lasting over an hour and a quarter, Deputy Prosecuting Attorney George Livesey opened the argument for the state. He talked earnestly to the jury and "not only the men who are to decide the fate of Thomas, but the spectators listened with rapt interest" to his summation of the evidence.

Livesey once again outlined the case. He re-told how Mrs. Thomas went missing, the investigation, finding the body in the potato patch, and the confession. He made clear to the jury Thomas was an unwelcome visitor at the woman's home, going there only to gratify his lusty passions. She had resisted and refused to submit and he killed her. Raising his voice and waving his arms to the jury, Livesey bellowed, "...there is no doubt but that Thomas had deliberately planned to murder the woman...the jury could only bring in one verdict as a result of the testimony – murder in the first-degree."

The evidence of the defense, claimed Livesey, merely showed Thomas when drunk was good-natured, and when real drunk became prostrate. "The defense?" he declared, "there was none. It consisted merely of drunkenness."

As for self-defense, he insisted Thomas had no right in the home of the woman; that according to his own confession he was standing in the doorway when she shot at him and missed. He could have run away and did not need to kill Gunilda.

C. H. Shamel followed Livesey, for the defense. After a preliminary talk, he argued corpus delicti had not been established. The body found had not been proven to be that of Mrs. Thomas, and due to the absence of better evidence there must be a reasonable doubt in the minds of the jurors as to whether Thomas killed his former wife or not. In such a case they would have to free the prisoner. Shamel then took up the legal points involved in the case and explained each at length to the jury, stressing premeditation and arguing Thomas was drunk and therefore could not plan in advance the murder.

After final arguments by Shamel and closing remarks for the defense by Attorney Abrams, Peringer made the final argument for the state. Then, Judge Neterer gave his instructions to the jury.

Verdict

The jury was more lenient than expected, handing in a verdict of murder in the second-degree on Monday, December 21. When asked if he had anything to say why sentence should not be pronounced upon him, Thomas replied, "Nothing your honor." Judge Jeremiah Neterer had no desire to go over the details of the horrible crime. After making a few remarks he pronounced sentence and dismissed the prisoner. Judge Neterer imposed life imprisonment at hard labor in the State Penitentiary at Walla Walla, then denied motion for a new trial. Neterer unsympathetically told the prisoner that he was fortunate in that the jury did not return a verdict of murder in the first-degree, as expected.

Thomas showed little emotion. "He had evidently prepared for the worse," said the *Herald*, "aside from a tightening of the lips, moved not a muscle, nor even blinked an eye lash. He was cool and collected throughout the time he was in the courtroom and walked out again with a steady step as he was led back to his cell."

William Thomas and James' sisters were in the courtroom when the verdict was read. The father showed little emotion at the hard blow delivered on his son, but the sisters wept during the greater part of the time.

James K. Thomas entered the State Penitentiary walls as prisoner No. 5340. His convict entrance medical examination reported a man of 55 years of age, standing at five foot-eleven, 210 pounds, balding with dark grey hair and grey eyes. The record claimed Thomas to be a drunk, used tobacco and had gonorrhea.

On Wednesday, January 20, 1909, Ethel Thomas returned to Bellingham after being released from the Chehalis State Training School. The circumstance being that the young girl was suffering from pulmonary tuberculosis. She took up residence with her Aunt Maria Edwards. Ethel would not improve, dying with a few family members at her bedside on Saturday April 17. Ethel was fourteen. She was buried at Bayview Cemetery. A few months later on July 27 appraisers for Gunilda Thomas' estate filed an inventory in the county clerk's office showing a value of $300. The indebtedness was $108.

James K. Thomas, (Top) prisoner No. 5340 at the Washington State Penitentiary at Walla Walla. Courtesy of the Washington State Archives, Olympia

Aftermath

An extraordinary piece of evidence was discovered in June 1913, but never came to light until July 1914. H. D. Ramsey was hired to tear down and remove Gunilda's residence as vandals were using it as a flophouse. The wood was to be repurposed at Delphine Dyer's Monogram Annex Hotel. Ramsey was removing a green door casing and examining a splintered area to see if it were repairable, when he noticed a battered bullet buried in the casing. Ramsey was sure it was a .38 and by picking away the slivers was able to remove the bullet without damaging it. Ramsey showed it to Thomas' brother-in-law, John Dyer, who was working at the site as well. Ramsey was excited stating "this proves what Jim said, that Mrs. Thomas was shooting at him from her bed at the time…" Dyer quickly retorted to Ramsey "Don't say anything about this because if you do Maria and Dell (the sisters) will just keep hammering on that, so don't even mention it." Dyer then took the bullet.

Dyer afterward gave up the slug. In examining the wood casing he had saved, it was determined the bullet had traversed in an upward direction lodging under the splinters, made by the slanting entrance of the bullet. The evidence, information and Ramsey's affidavit was placed in the hands of the courts, a copy forwarded to the governor's office along with a copy to the warden. It was inserted into the prisoner's file on July 19, 1915, but never reviewed.

Another item of interest appeared in James Thomas' pardon records from a Hugh M. Cary of Sac City, Iowa dated Jan 14, 1915.

What truth lies within is a matter of conjecture:

"Dear Sisters Dyer and Edwards,

I expect that I knew about as much about Jim and maybe more than anybody else but you sisters. The deadly trouble began between Jim and ex-wife when Ethel began to run around at night. One night my wife and I met Ethel on the North Side going to the Jap dance and I tried to make her go back to her pa's with us but she would not and I came home and went and told Jim where his girl was; he was so mad that he took one of your sisters and went over and got her and then Ethel's mother took sides against Ethel's father. So her pa had Ethel sent to a reform school. The Court was to blame for your Br. going up to Jim's ex-wife's because of the alimony that Jim was to pay. He had to take it to his wife, so when I spoke to James and told him he had not better go near her house he would tell me he had too [*sic*]. But he had no intention of harming her in the least; but he did not intend to let her harm him; so the night he killed her he went up there to talk to her about Ethel and his upcoming wedding. I and wife was invited to his wedding when it should come off, the time was not set just when they would get married so they talked over what they would do with Ethel and then he told her that he was going to get married and that's then the fire flew, and she said he would never get out of her house alive. So the only chance he had was to pretend that he was not going home tonight, so he said he would go upstairs to Ethel's bed, intending when she was asleep in her bedroom he would slip down the stairs and slip out, but she was expecting him to do just that thing so she laid down on her bed without undressing and soon began to snore, so Jim thought that was his chance so he slipped down stairs and got to the door and as he opened the door she shot but the bullet went over his head and out through the open door but he wheeled around and shot her before she was able to shoot again, but his aim was good. But what he should have done was to have jumped out of the door and run. He was ready for her if he had to. But here James made the mistake of his life, that made Jim so crazy he did not know what to do so he did the worst thing possible. He could have cut her up and carried her away out in the brush and buried her so no one would of found her. But no, he was crazy. He put her where she could be found the most handy. He should have been tried for insanity. He is to be pitied..."

After four years of exemplarity conduct, petitions and letters sent to Governor Marion Hay pleading for an early release, James K. Thomas was given a conditional pardon on August 3, 1917. Thomas moved in with his sister Delphine at her Monogram Annex Hotel working as a waiter in the hotel's dining room. At other times he worked as a barber, no doubt a trade he learned in prison. Thomas died at his sisters on December 23, 1930 at 74 years, although the Washington State Bureau of Identification had Thomas still alive on January 15, 1940. Delphine, the sister who staunchly stood by her brother, died March 20, 1943 at 83.

Chapter 2
David Long's Domestic Woe

David H. Long lay silent on the cold earth beneath his son-in-law's rented double-cottage at 1015 Forest Street, just under the kitchen floorboards where he cocked his neck upward straining to hear the conversation above.[8] This wasn't the first time he wiggled into the cramped crawl space to eavesdrop on his family. Long was not in favor of his young daughter, Ida, marrying Norman Humes, but was overruled by his wife Susan. All in town knew it wasn't Ida whom Humes was enamored with, but her mother. Long was rather naïve to the fact of a

Looking down from Sehome Hill, north toward New Whatcom, September, 1890. The label to the right indicates the site of the double-murder at 1015 Forest Street. Keeslingville, the home of David Long, is in the distance. Courtesy of Whatcom Museum

[8] Some newspapers at the time misprinted the address as 1055 Forest.

45

potential rival, and only recently awakened to the fact of his wife's infidelity.

Ida was considered "dimwitted," for lacking the intelligence of a normally developed girl of her age. And her father, feeling guilty for allowing the lengthy drama to have continued for so long decided it was time to act and defend his only child. It was eight o'clock in the evening on Wednesday, December 2, 1891 and all hell was about to break loose.

The Long Family

David Long stood 5 feet 6 inches in height; thickset, blue eyes and he wore a heavy light colored mustache. He was noted for boisterous talk when agitated, and renowned in New Whatcom[9] for regularly carrying his holstered Colt .45 revolver at his hip. Long was forty-one-years old at the time of the heinous crime, which many had seen coming. Born in Freeport, Illinois in 1850, David Long would later move to Iowa, then from Iowa to Granby, Missouri and then to Arkansas. Long returned to Granby, where he met and married eighteen-year-old Susan Russell.

Susan Evaline Russell, daughter of James and Elizabeth Russell, was born August 14, 1858 in Morgan County, Illinois. She was second to the youngest of four brothers and a sister. By 1870 Susan lived in Marion, Newton County, Missouri where she would eventually meet Long. The couple would live in Missouri long enough to give birth to their only child, a daughter, Ida A. Long in August 1876. The family would relocate to Dallas, Texas, where Long became a cattle-puncher and from there to Whatcom in 1888. All the while, Long would insist he and Susan lived happily together. But the last year was anything but happy.

When David Long moved his family to Whatcom he purchased a small house on what was then known as Keeslingville, at Holly and Thirteenth Street.[10] Calvin Keesling purchased this section from the Edward Eldridge donation claim. He worked for a time as a teamster and farmer before being hired

---

[9] The Longs came to present day "Bellingham" at a pivotal period in the city's history, as it was on the road to consolidation from four separate townships. By February 1891, the former Whatcom and Sehome were consolidated into New Whatcom. Fairhaven and Bellingham will come into the fold later. For the purposes of this story, New Whatcom and Sehome (past tense) will be used and Whatcom upon the arrival of the Long family.

[10] Keeslingville was located along Front Street (Eldridge Ave.) to the south—North Street to the north—bordered by Spruce and West Streets. Calvin Keesling was chairman of the board of commissioners. Keesling died September 1890. This little enclave was eventually annexed by New Whatcom in June, 1892 with a vote of 294 to 25.

on building plank roads for the town of Whatcom.[11] Susan Long was said to be a "comely woman" who possessed an ugly disposition, greatly exasperating her husband. Their daughter, Ida, would eventually be described within the local newspapers of 1891 as "a child of little intellect, with small features and small round face, black hair and eyes and a dark olive complexion. Small at 16-years of age she was mistaken to look barely thirteen." The *Fairhaven Herald* would later say she exhibited, "squirrel teeth which are always exposed."

In January 1891 David Long took his family to a gathering at the Salvation Army barracks where a talk was given. Sitting behind Long's young teenage daughter was a handsome red headed 21-year-old gentleman who gave his name as "Reddy" Norman Griffin. They talked for a time, Griffin claiming to be a schoolteacher. After the meeting the four walked back to Keeslingville together, although Griffin lived in the opposite direction in Sehome. David and Susan walked ahead, allowing Griffin and Ida to get acquainted.

The two saw one another a few more times before Griffin said he had to go to Skagit county for work, but would write. One day, Ida received a letter and was confused taking it to her father. Long immediately was suspicious as the note was illegible for the hand of a teacher, and it was signed "Humes" not Griffin as he stated was his name. When he returned and was confronted by Long, Humes admitted it was his real name. From that day forward Long no longer trusted Norman Humes, but his wife said there was nothing wrong with Ida having a friend, since she had few.

Little is known of Norman Humes, other than he was born to Earl and Christie Ann (McDonald) about 1870 in Nova Scotia. Earl was born 1849 in Stormont, Ontario, before moving to St. Patrick Channel, Victoria county in the Maritimes where he was employed as a cooper. Until 1881, Norman also resided in Victoria, before coming to Washington. He had been in Whatcom about two years working on a pile driver building the G Street wharf, and more recently had employment at the Cornwall mill.

As spring wore into summer, Long was tiring of seeing Humes at his home when returning from work. Long was becoming evermore wary of the relationship, as Ida was only fifteen, still in school and seemingly getting too involved with the older man. His worries may have been compounded by the fact that Ida possessed little intellect, and Long feared she may easily be taken advantage of by Humes' influence. It was further unnerving to have

---

[11] New Whatcom Directory, 1891, claims occupation "miner."

his wife constantly defending the romantic relationship. Susan's defense of Humes bewildered Long.

It wasn't long before rumors spread throughout New Whatcom of Humes having relations with Susan. Townsfolk thought it inconceivable Long was so ignorant of such shenanigans taking place under his own roof. All the while, Long was focused on just keeping Humes out of his home and away from his only offspring rather than seeing the larger picture of what was happening. Neighbors watched as Long left each morning for work, and around lunchtime, Humes appeared. By August, Ida had turned sixteen. Long took a firm stand and put his foot down; Humes was to keep away from his home and daughter. His action had the opposite effect. Susan became hostile toward her husband and she and Ida would leave the house in the evening to meet with Humes.

The marriage grew cold. Susan became antagonistic toward her husband, but maintained her "wifely duties." David Long grew irritated and jealous, but whenever he became enraged and violent toward his wife, he would shrink back in fear of her leaving him, as she was known to do.

About this time, Long had an idea to both improve himself, and hopefully prove to Susan he had the potential of being his own man. By the late 1880s electricity was coming to the area. At first, electrical power was primarily being used for mills, trolleys and to power companies that could afford the massive generators. But, it was becoming mainstream for city street lighting; Fairhaven priding itself amongst the first at the time. The January 1891 *Bellingham Bay Reveille* boasted a contract with the Bellingham Bay Electric Light Company for twenty-four new electric lights. That same week a new dynamo for the company had arrived. This alone would increase the power of the plant to 180 arc lights and New Whatcom was poised to have 54 lights glowing on the streets; plus, a mast light on the corner of Maple Street and Railroad Avenue. Two more mast lights on the wharf and three more on Mill wharf.

David Long was well aware that eventually all of the city would be lighted from businesses to private residences. Long had the forethought to realize not only would the city require persons to sting wire and assemble generators, but someone will have to repair the system when it failed. Long contacted several places in Seattle to learn the trade and was awaiting replies. He would tell Susan once he achieved the proper training they would be in the money. But she was enamored with Humes, and it was too late for her husband.

By September the situation escalated to a point where Susan Long may have attempted to end the life of her husband. One morning, Long took a few gulps of coffee his wife brewed finding it tasting bitter. He told her it was horrible and soon developed a stomachache. She claimed, "It was settlings from Lemm's poor coffee" (William Lemm was the closest grocer at 2512 Eldridge Ave). Long laid in bed most of the day. His muscles ached, he said.

Susan Long claimed it was settlings from Lemm's poor coffee and his bread that made her husband sick. William Lemm standing at the entrance of his store at 2512 Eldridge Avenue. Courtesy of Laura Jacoby's, Galen Biery collection

About two weeks later Long was eating supper. Susan had gone out to Lemm's Grocery for bread. When she returned, Susan removed the bread from a brown paper wrapper and handed her husband the first cut of the loaf. Long ate it and drank some coffee finding both to be bitter. About thirty minutes later he got up and staggered out of the house becoming violently ill. Long stated later his neck became stiff and his muscles began to twitch and spasm, losing control. When he got back inside he crawled into bed, laying in agony all night. His legs and whole body were cramping with such severity he thought he would die. He felt pain in all his muscles with no relief. It took a few days for him to fully regain his strength and be able to resume normal duties. All the while, Susan made no comment, nor did she aid her husband.

David Long took the loaf to Lemm's for examination. He told the German grocer the bread and coffee made him gravely ill. William Lemm was alarmed. He may have suggested his illness could have come from a variety of other reasons and not items from his store, but he knew Long as a good customer.

So Lemm examined the loaf and immediately noticed something queer. Looking into the cut of the bread Lemm noted some white particles. Placing a grain of the substance to his tongue he received the foulest bitter taste. He was quick to point out, of course, that John Burke baked the bread. Lemm, fearing all the loaves could be contaminated, told Long he would show Burke the half loaf. A horrified John Burke claimed rival bakers were known to sabotage the competition.

He had about 150 loaves from the batch. Burke and Lemm went to H. A. White, a local druggist, who analyzed the particles from the bread. White, on examination quickly concluded the substance crystallized strychnine. No other loaf from the batch was returned, nor were any of the loaves still in Lemm's grocery store contaminated.

A few days later, Long ran into Edward Gaar, a co-worker of Norman Humes. Gaar took Long aside, saying he had something confidential to tell him. "I caught a man and young woman in a compromising position near the Columbia school. The woman had on a red petticoat and the man worked on a pile driver." Gaar didn't mention names, hoping Long would get the hint he had troubles to contend with. Long held his head low, knowing that it was his little girl they were talking about. In a soft voice he asked if the man had red hair. "It made me feel bad," Long said later, "I called Ida in and asked her about it and she said 'no,' and began crying."

After the incident David Long's sister, Ella Hatler,[13] stopped to overnight before returning home to Lummi Island. Ella let herself in and sat down not seeing anyone but her brother. Long, looking rather grim, was pacing about the house. Ella asked where Susan and Ida were, to which Long replied they put on their good clothes and went into town. She had been going off most

---

[13] Ella (sometimes Ellen) Long married J. H. Hatler of Kansas and came to Lummi Island in 1891, purchasing ten acres.

every night now. They were with Norman Humes most likely and Long said he was at his wits-end with what to do about it. Long asked his sister if she had heard the news about Ida being caught in a compromising position, to which Ella answered with a sarcastic "You will not believe anything." Ella told her brother he was blind to what has been happening around him and not willing to hear the rumors. She then told her brother Humes was coming to see Susan, not Ida. Susan hung out a signal flag for him when David was gone indicating it was safe for Humes to stop in.

David Long, in a state of shock, jumped up and left the house to find his family. Flustered, he told Ella to lock the door and not let them into the house if they returned. A few hours later Susan and Ida did return, only to be turned away. Susan left Ida with a neighbor and sought after Humes. About nine o'clock the two checked into the Paragon Hotel in Fairhaven. Hotel manager Philip H. Blankenship gave the pair a judgmental glare.

Fearing he lost his wife, Long searched for her all night. The following morning he saw his nemesis Norman Humes on the street and begged him to help bring her home. Humes did, and Susan returned, but Humes also resumed his house visits. The next crisis occurred in early October. Susan thought Ida was pregnant and took her to a doctor in Sehome. The pregnancy enraged Long, but it was soon determined not the case. Susan then demanded that Ida marry Humes. Long was mortified. Arguments ensued, lasting days before Long capitulated. The couple were married on October 15 by Judge L. P. Palmer at the Long home.

The family lived a short time under the same roof, where the atmosphere must have been oppressive. So unpleasant was the relationship between father-in-law and son-in-law that on November 14, Humes called at the *Bellingham Bay Reveille* office determined to air his domestic affairs in print. The following article, published on the 15th of November, was the result of his interview:

"A very romantic story comes from the Great Northern railroad. A father-in-law meets his son-in-law on the track near Squalicum and asks him where the mother-in-law is. The inquiry is made with two No.10 shotgun tunnels staring the son-in-law in the face. The son-in-law professes ignorance of the whereabouts of his wife's mother, and all is again serene. It seems that the father-in-law locked out the mother-in-law from her home, while she was at church, whereupon the latter temporarily found shelter elsewhere. The son-in-law and daughter find themselves in a very precarious situation. It is an unpleasant thing to have harmonious family relations rendered inharmonious, and also very unpleasant to have one's head shot off. (*The Reveille* recommends all parties to take a tumble to themselves and prevent the washing of the family linen in public.)"

After the narrative broke, which wasn't very scandalous as most knew of the affair, Long's jealousy and anger rose to new heights. He cut a trap door in the floor of his closet to hide and eavesdrop on his family's conversations in his presumed absence. He made a clatter once and was embarrassingly caught by his wife. Humes and Ida moved to a double-cottage on 1015 Forest Street in Sehome, between Maple and Laurel Streets. Long continued to make threats to his wife about Humes, until Susan too left her husband about November 18, moving in with the newlyweds. Susan giving the reason she wished to escape the cruelty of her husband, but those who knew the circumstances, openly said she wished to be with her paramour. Long visited her daily for nearly two weeks, offering every inducement in his power to get her to return home, but she refused all his overtures.

On the second to last of these visits, Long watched from outside a window for a time. It was a new moon making it especially dark. He crawled beneath the cottage, working his way along the dirt ground until he reached underneath the kitchen to listen to the conversation above. What he claimed to have heard put ice into his veins. Susan and Norman were discussing forging a deed to his house and property, and gaining access to his bank accounts. But, before any of that was possible David Long would have to go. Long's first thought was his near-death strychnine poisoning several months earlier.

The following day, Wednesday December 2, Long went to Humes' house wishing to make up with his wife. The effort failed. He asked two friends to visit his wife in the afternoon to effect reconciliation. Former City Marshal Lewis Stimson, empathetic toward his friend said he would visit her on his behalf. Long next visited County Treasurer Ellery Rogers, talking excitedly about his domestic difficulties. He told Rogers he had a house and a quarter acre of land in Keeslingville, and an additional lot in Lynden needing protection. He also told Rogers to beware of forged documents coming into the office from Susan. He did the same at the banks and at city hall. Long then stated to various parties in the city he had three affidavits in his possession proving Humes and Susan lodged in a Fairhaven hotel overnight before his marriage to his daughter. He claimed to have written several places mentioned by Humes as locations he had resided to learn Humes' history; but no one knew him. Long repeated he could stand the infidelity of his wife, but the loss of his daughter broke him.

Long sounded like a madman as he ran all over town dispensing the news of his domestic problems like a town crier. Most knew about the drama, but on that last day it should have been obvious David Long was headed toward a meltdown, and calamity couldn't be far off. No thought was entertained at the time that he would carry his desperate threat of killing Humes and Susan into execution, as he had often made such threats.

The Deadly Deed

"The last act of a bloody tragedy was enacted at the home of Mrs. Ida Humes last night," reported the *Bellingham Bay Reveille* (Daily) on December 3.

About 7:30 Wednesday evening, David Long stood once again outside the window of his daughter's kitchen peering in. He saw Ida sitting on one side of the kitchen table and his wife up against her son-in-law with arms around one another. Long shook his head in disgust then crawled once more under the house to listen in on the conversation above. He held his cool until the dialogue took on an appalling twist. Humes had decided he wanted to bed both mother and daughter. Susan was all for a threesome, but Ida wouldn't play along and refused. Susan in turn threatened to whip her daughter if she didn't comply and give her husband what he wanted.

Meanwhile, below the floorboards Long was raging, and expedited himself from beneath the house. As he ran around to the back of the cottage he found Ida in tears, barefoot on the porch. She was shocked to see her father standing there with soiled clothes. He was steaming mad, stating, "So that's the way it is." Pulling his Colt .45 from his holster he stormed into the house.

According to John Hart of the *Bellingham Bay Reveille,* events occurred like this:

"Mrs. Long and Mr. and Mrs. Humes were sitting at the table talking and laughing, having had a late dinner. When the murderer entered, all arose. Mrs. Humes was the first who saw that her father had a revolver in his hand, and when he pointed the weapon at her mother she stepped to his side, took hold of his arm and said, 'Father don't harm mamma,' her only answer being the report of the revolver, the discharge of which entered Mrs. Long's breast one-half inch above her left nipple coursing between five and eight degrees downward and passing out at the lower part of the right scapula. Like an insatiate brute maddened by the sight of blood already shed, and while his son-in-law was trying to rise from the blood-stained floor, where lay the lifeless form of his mother-in-law, he fired at Humes, the ball entering at the right of the center of the right frontal bone entering the head and coming out two inches above, causing death instantly. He would have trebled his crime had Mrs. Humes not stopped him at her command. The tones of his daughter's voice as she pled for her own life returned his mind to her childish innocence and suffering by the sin he had already done, and he lowered his weapon saying: 'Ida, for God's sake do not tell what I have done,' and then fled from the house leaving his young daughter with the two victims."

David Long ran off into the night all right, but what really transpired that December night would have to wait to be revealed.

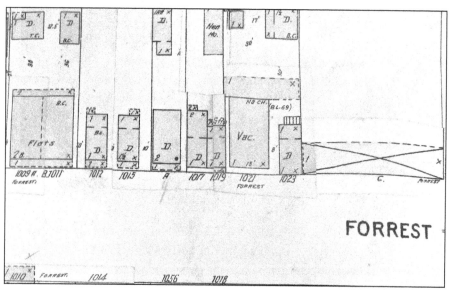

Norman Humes rented a double-cottage at 1015 Forest Street on Sehome Hill, between Maple and Laurel Streets, where the double-murder was committed.
From Sanborn Fire Insurance Map

Residents in the vicinity of Forest Street were startled by the crack of five shots fired in rapid succession. As Ida recovered from her shock, she ran barefoot into the street and raised the alarm. Patrolman Frank M. Sevier, just a minute away when he heard the first shot, was the first to arrive on the scene in time to hear the last shot fired. Giving Ida his wool coat he told her to remain there until he had a look inside. Sevier tried to force open the front door, but finding it locked he ran around to the rear of the house. Sevier heard someone beat a hasty retreat through the yard, but was unable to locate the intruder in the darkness.

The kitchen where the shooting occurred "looked like a slaughter pen,"

Sevier would note later. The home was a mere three-room cottage scantily furnished. The front room containing only a bed, two chairs, a trunk and a sewing machine; the second another but larger bed, a wardrobe, trunk and a small table, while the kitchen only a stove, a table and four chairs.

In short order, Deputy Sheriffs Newton Laswell and Barney Estabrooke, followed by Dr. William Cross, arrived on the scene. They were about to raise the lifeless bodies from the floor to a bed when policeman George Charlot and Chief of Police A. J. Lawrence arrived.

When Whatcom County Sheriff Felix W. "Jack" De Lorimer received word that David Long was suspected in the double-homicide, he placed men covering all exit roads leading to Skagit County and Canada. He sent several more men to observe boat traffic leaving the waterfront.

Fairhaven Coroner John M. Warinner arrived at the crime scene at eleven o'clock that night. By this time the bodies were moved from the floor and placed on a bed together side by side. Warinner couldn't remove the bodies to his morgue in Fairhaven until morning. He placed a man in charge of the bodies overnight. Sheriff De Lorimer, not wanting the cottage overrun by curiosity seekers, also placed men on the property.

Warinner examined the bodies verifying five distinct bullet wounds. Susan Long received one leaded shot entering at the left breast, passing through the heart and exiting below the right shoulder blade, causing instant death. Another bullet struck her in the right breast, which blew a hole out her back, while a third creased off her center forehead. Humes took a bullet straight through his skull tearing through his brain and another ball was fired into his neck, plunging downward smashing his right clavicle before exiting at the neck, slightly to the right of center. Neither felt much pain thought Warinner.

Witnesses claimed Ida appeared but slightly affected by the terrible tragedy. She told the story of the shooting with an entire lack of emotion, then went away with patrolman Sevier, who volunteered to find her a place to sleep. Some thought she was in shock, but others on the scene supposed that the marriage was a sham of Mrs. Long's to allow her continuing intimacy with Humes, not caring what exploitation Ida may have suffered.

Search and Surrender

The only clue left by David Long was in Keeslingville. It appeared after the shooting he walked down Holly and Thirteenth Street to his home, changed his clothes, wrote a note, which he left on the table and disappeared. The note was a "sprawling scrawl," which might from its appearance have been written in the dark and read: "There is $30 coming from the city. Pay Ida. I'm going to die myself. Goodbye."

On December 4, both *Reveille* and *Herald* reported Long was either a maniac or a desperate coward for the slayings. Sheriff De Lorimer was in the second day of his manhunt, sealing off all avenues of escape. He deputized a score of men, placing them on roads leading from the city, and along the wharves. He informed neighboring towns by wire of the tragedy, providing a description of the slayer. "It was only a matter of time," stated the sheriff, "before Long was apprehended."

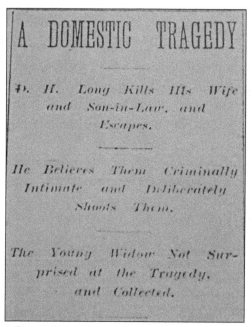

A Domestic Tragedy
Bellingham Bay Reveille, December 4, 1891

Also on the fourth, Ella Hatler, with her daughter, Lewis Stimson, Mrs. Lemm and Mrs. Haller went to Ida's home to retrieve her property from the house. Ella did not want her niece returning to the crime scene. They hurriedly bundled up what they found to be brought to Mrs. Haller's house to be sorted and repacked before forwarded to Lummi Island. Ella picked up Susan Long's cloak from the bed, and as she exited the room the fabric brushed the doorframe making a clunking sound. On examination Ella found something hard sewed into the lapel. Cutting the stitches she was shocked to discover a halfbottle of strychnine.

Saturday, December 5 there was still no sign of Long. The murderer had dropped out of sight, but rumors were rife. M. J. Clark reported having just seen David Long that morning on the beach near Fort Bellingham. He had a satchel, a Winchester, and was sitting on a log by a fire. He looked mean and ready for business. Sheriff De Lorimer descended on the individual with deputies coming from all sides, their guns drawn. Trigger-happy men nearly fired their weapons only to discover the man was a hunter. Later that day another definitive sighting was made in the woods just north of town. Again, Sheriff De Lorimer and deputies drew a firing line and walked into the forest. It was however discovered that it was the same hunter who had been previously mistaken for Long. De Lorimer suggested the hunter go home before he was shot.

Bellingham Bay Reveille reporter, John Hart interviewed Ida Humes shortly after the murders. His unprofessional reporting style would be ridiculed in court as he was a reserve police officer studying for the bar at the time, and a reporter profiting from the tragedy. Hart would continue to air the family's dirty laundry, feeding the frenzy for further gory details. Ida told Hart her mother knew Humes was not after me, but her. "One day father told me that he had a notion to kill all three of us, but he had made such threats many times before. Since I was a little girl I have learned to take them as a matter of course."

Hart's story continued: "About two months ago…father cut a hole in the floor of the closet, and told us that he had to go over to Sehome…but instead of going to that place he let himself down through the trap door. There is a carpet on the floor and everything was concealed. I heard a noise at my feet. I think it was my father's head striking against the floor, and when I called mother's attention to it she began to look for the cause of the noise. She lighted a lantern and looked through the closet, and while in the closet she discovered the door by stepping on the hinge. She raised the door and went under the house. Father had his revolver in his hand and threatened to shoot my mother while they were under the house."

"Mother left him before about two years ago and went to California. Father went after her and she came back with him. He often abused mother and she would show me marks of his cruelty. He accused her of being intimate with my Uncle Charley Long, and with two or three others here in town. He accused her of being intimate with a man in Texas where we lived before coming here. He has drawn his revolver several times before, but we did not think he would shoot. I think he would have shot mother long ago had I not interfered. He loved me and treated me only as fathers can a daughter."

On Saturday, December 19, David Long delivered himself up to Sheriff De Lorimer at his sister's home on Lummi Island. The hand over was planned with the help of his brother-in-law, J. H. Hatler, who had been secretly taking food to Long. Hatler sent word to Lewis Stimson to be at his home the day before to support his friend during the arrest. Hatler then invited Sheriff De Lorimer for dinner with his wife Ella and Ida, who by now was staying with her aunt. De Lorimer, looking at this as an opportunity to ascertain new information to Long's whereabouts, obliged the invite and arrived at noon on the island aboard the steamer *Brick*. Mr. Hatler was not present at dinner, which the sheriff thought rather queer. De Lorimer was on the verge of asking why he was there when looking out the window he saw Hatler, Stimson and Long coming in.

Long, showing deep emotion, broke down and cried. He claimed to have been living in a hollowed cedar stump, and subsisting on what he could forage. He had run out of food, and was half starved. Long told the sheriff he wrote the letter in his house that night before walking up the railroad track and stole a canoe above Squalicum Creek. He paddled to the reservation where he obtained food from an Indian and then paddled over to Lummi Island. "I was tired of the life I had been leading since I committed the murder and driven to madness by remorse, resolved to put myself into the hands of the authorities," he told De Lorimer.

Long then made a statement to De Lorimer. "On the evening of the murder...I could hear Ida and her mother quarreling. Humes and Susan were planning to sleep together, and Ida was opposed to that way of doing. Think of such a way to treat her child! I stepped in and Humes and Susan were sitting together. Susan sat next to the table and Humes had his arms around her shoulder. I said, "What a fine state of affairs!" And I turned to my daughter to bid her goodnight, when my faithless wife jumped at me and tried to get my revolver, which I always carried on my hip. My son-in-law, Humes, aided my wife in trying to overpower me, and I was demented. The shooting of my wife was accidental."

Sheriff De Lorimer shook his head looking at Long stating, "Accidental? You shot her three times, once in the head and twice in the chest. How was that accidental?" Long said nothing and the men returned to the mainland.

On Trial

On Tuesday, March 22, 1892, David H. Long was placed on trial for the first-degree murder of his wife, Susan.[14] When he appeared in the courtroom, Long was said to be in "good health, although pale and nervous," claimed the *Bellingham Bay Reveille*.

With the entry of the honorable Judge John R. Winn presiding, Superior Court was convened at niine o'clock. Born in Missouri in 1862, Winn pre-

[14] The two homicides would go to trial separately.

sided over Whatcom and San Juan Counties. He was admitted to the bar and practiced law in Grafton, North Dakota for four years before relocating to Snohomish to practice law. Later, he was elected Superior Court Judge of Snohomish, Skagit and Whatcom Counties on the Democratic ticket.

It was the day for jurors to be impaneled, and in consequence a larger selection than usual was present as jury selection was also underway in the George Swiloos trial, a Lummi Indian charged with the murder of Moses Younkin. In the State of Washington v. David H. Long, the case came up on motion to quash the information by Long's attorney, Thomas G. Newman of Fairhaven. The motion was overruled, exceptions allowed and Saturday set for the assignment of the case. The defendant pled not guilty.

Sheriff Felix De Lorimer returned a special venire of twenty-five jurors, most summoned from Fairhaven. Newman again moved that the venire be squashed on the grounds the defendant had not been served with the names as provided by statute, but the motion was overruled by the court and the work of impaneling the jury proceeded.[15] The *Fairhaven Herald* declared the "jury selected was considerably above intelligence due to the fact that nine were the residence of Fairhaven." Owing to the heinous nature of the killings, and coming on the heels of the Swiloos trial, it was decided jurors would be sequestered throughout the trial and not allowed to separate until a verdict was returned. The jury was sworn in and court adjourned until 9:30 a.m. Friday, March 25.

Friday morning the defendant was escorted into the courtroom by a deputy sheriff, and given a seat beside his attorneys, Thomas Newman, and J. W. Ivey, of New Whatcom. Miraculously, Newman was able to retain the assistance of Colonel James Hamilton Lewis of Seattle, considered one of the best and most successful criminal lawyers in the state.

Col. Lewis' reputation alone was expected to fill the courtroom to capacity. He was a phenomenon of his time, propelled to stardom by exotic wild stories and legendary tales. *Ainslee's Magazine,* a noted humor publication, often depicted Col. Lewis in artistic caricature. He had eccentric manners, wore outmoded dress and was renowned for his oratory skills. His trademark bushy Van Dyke whiskers were worn long out of style. Those attending the Long trial may have hoped to see Lewis wearing the "wavy pink toupee" he was noted for.

Col. Lewis came to Washington in 1885, stating to a Seattle reporter on

---

[15] The jury composed: G. W. Francis, L. B. Bagley, C. H. Allerton, J. T. Coffman, A. S. Balch, George. B. Dorr, L. W. Nestelle, John Cissna, A. M. Chapman, L. M. Bardo, W. H. Hill, and S. J. Knight.

Seattle's Col. James Hamilton
Lewis was on David Long's defense
team. A noted grandstander, Lewis
attracted great crowds to witness his
courtroom theatrics.
Ainslee's Magazine, May 1900

arrival: "I have come to this territory to go to Congress when it becomes a state...I don't care what you write about me so long as you give me a send-off."[16] Comical in appearance, no one took him seriously. As an attorney, he had only one client in the first months after hanging his shingle. The offender stole a box of cigars. Lewis secured an acquittal on the pretext that his client took the cigars for safekeeping.[17] As a criminal lawyer, Lewis defended thirty-two murderers and lost only one verdict, but secured a reversal in the case.

Conducting the prosecution for the state were Whatcom County Attorneys Major Albert S. Cole (1840-1902), a northern officer in the Civil War, who relocated to Whatcom in 1887 to practice law,[18] and Harry A. Fairchild.

Before proceeding on Friday, Major Cole asked the court for a rule excluding other witnesses from the courtroom except the one on the stand, while testimony was being taken. The defense made no objection and the request was granted with the mutual exception of the coroner, a deputy sheriff and former Marshal Stimson. Major Cole then proceeded to open his case for the state.

---

[16] *Ainslee's Magazine*, May 1900.
[17] Territorial appointee Governor Semple appointed Lewis a lieutenant colonel of staff of Washington State, a fictitious title. Lewis would serve a lengthy term in the US Senate.
[18] Albert S. Cole served as captain in the 22 Regt., Wisconsin Inf., Co. H. mustering out brevet major June 27, 1865.

Lewis in his most impassioned stump

A caricature from *Ainslee's Magazine* illustrates Col. James Hamilton Lewis' impassioned dramatics. Col. Lewis was known to wear a "wavy pink toupee" in the courtroom to mesmerize the jury. *Ainslee's Magazine,* May 1900

He read the information, charging the defendant with the murder of his wife, Susan A. Long on the night of December 2, 1891. Cole stated the defendant and his wife had been married nearly twenty years. All of which must have been unbearable, as there were threats of death, beatings, and frequent separations. Another separation had followed as the poor unfortunate woman sought refuge from the wrath of her husband in the home of her married daughter. "On the 2d of last December the defendant entered his daughter's home and with malice and premeditation shot down the wife," said Cole, "firing three bullets into her body."[19]

[19] A separate charge was filed against Long in the murder of Norman Humes.

Col. Lewis rose from his chair, his Van Dyke jutted straight upward as he tilted his head back. He stated to the court he had two objections. The first, the employment of private counsel to assist the state. The second, proceeding under the information on the grounds there had been no prior proceedings against the defendant, no preliminary examination and no investigation by a grand jury. Judge Winn overruled both of Lewis' objections and Major Cole's examination continued.

The state's first witness was former police officer, Frank Sevier, first on the scene after the shooting, now a member of the bar. Sevier testified:

"I was out on Maple Street about eight o'clock in the evening of the 2nd of last December, when I heard a shot. I then heard some screaming, and afterward four shots fired in rapid succession. I started for the place...It was in a double house on Forest Street. I tried to get in the front door, but it was locked. I then went to the rear and went up the steps. Just as I did, I saw someone disappearing in the darkness on the opposite side of the house. The rear door was open. I saw two persons lying on the floor. The man was lying with his head on the doorsill and Mrs. Long was lying about a foot or two away. The floor about each body was covered in blood. I rolled over the body of the woman and saw that she was dead. There was a lighted lamp on the table. I telephoned Dr. H. J. Birney and for police. I saw a bullet hole in the floor near where the head of Susan Long lay. The next morning, I found the bullet under the house directly under the hole. (The witness then produced the bullet.) There was grease and blood on it when I found it. There was a wound in each breast of the woman and one in the top of her head."

Col. Lewis approached the witness for cross-examination asking only a single question. In what direction was the bullet traveling toward Susan Long's head when fired? Sevier could not say positively if the bullet entered from the front or back.

Deputy Sheriff George Charlot, one of the first on the scene, described what he had witnessed. Following Charlot came Coroner John Warinner, who gave a history of the crime scene. He said a man was placed in charge of the bodies for the night until they were removed the following morning to his morgue in Fairhaven.

During cross, Col. Lewis asked why that was the case. Warinner claimed he had no transportation ready and the hour was late for proper examination. Col. Lewis then asked for a pause in the trial, asking the court why the jury were taking notes. The court decided it wasn't proper procedure and notes were to be handed over to Judge Winn. It was two o'clock, and Winn decided a recess was in order.

As expected, seating capacity was exceeded, with standing room only in the aisles when court reconvened. *The Fairhaven Herald* reported, "When the bailiff unlocked the doors the crowd rushed in like a flood and filled the room to overflowing."

Dr. Streeter of Fairhaven was the first witness called during the afternoon session. He testified examining the bodies on the morning of December 3, and recorded three gunshot wounds in Susan Long's body. One of the bullets entered her right breast above the nipple causing massive lung damage from close range. A second bullet entered her left breast below the nipple piercing the heart, exiting from her back. Both were deep penetrating mortal gunshot wounds. He claimed the wound at the top of the head was a glancing blow, gouging the scalp into a three-inch furrow and bruising the bone. Dr. William Cross of New Whatcom, testified, describing the same.

Deputy Sheriff Barney Estabrooke took the stand next. The officer testified he returned to the crime scene the following morning to search the kitchen in better light. He found a second .45 caliber bullet on the floor, producing the slug as evidence. He then entered into evidence the "frontier revolver" belonging to David Long.

On cross-examination, Col. Lewis took the weapon and examined it; whirling the cylinder looking at each chamber to be sure it was not loaded. Comically, perhaps for the jury, he played with the sidearm, taking aim and moving the Colt in a rapid manner. He hefted it up and down in his hand, feeling the weight. He then walked over and laid it on the reporter's table with the barrel pointed toward Major Cole. The rather perturbed councel disgustedly stood and walked over to the table and wheeled the gun around, pointing it away from him before retaking his seat. The performance got a rise from spectators.

Estabrooke then related to Lewis a conversation he had with the accused a day after his arrest. Long stated the shooting of his wife was accidental, just as he had told Sheriff De Lorimer. "I said to him, how can that be? She was shot three times." Long replied, "God only knows; but that is the way of it."

Newton Laswell was sworn in and gave similar testimony. According to Friday, March 25th's *Fairhaven Herald,* his cross-examination by Col. Lewis proved to be the most exciting event of the day. The witness had been a police officer when the affair occurred.

"Almost a month before," he said, "I went to the residence of Mrs. Byers on Thirteenth Street with Long. Mrs. Long was then staying there, and she had asked me to bring her husband. When we went in she told me that she was afraid to be left alone with him and asked me not to leave. Long began to plead with her to come home. He told her that he was sorry for what he had done, and promised to be better. She told him that he made those promises before, and she refused to go. When we left he asked me to go back and try to persuade her to return. I told him he ought to be ashamed of himself for what he said about her he knew wasn't true. She had accused him of threatening her life…, which he did not deny. He said he did it in a passion."

Now it was Col. Lewis' turn to cross-examine the witness.

"What have you been doing for the past sixty days?" asked Lewis.

"I have been a deputy sheriff part of the time."

"You have spent a good deal of the time hunting testimony for the prosecution, haven't you?"

"I have served some subpoenas."

"Were you a deputy sheriff March 17 last?"

"No."

"Did you serve any papers then?"

"Yes."

"You served them in your private capacity?"

"I suppose so."

Col. Lewis then produced a copy of the subpoena summoning Ida Humes to appear forthwith before the prosecuting attorney at the law office of H. A. Fairchild, on March 17, in a "cause then and there pending," entitled the *State of Washington v. David H. Long*. Col. Lewis waved the subpoena in Laswell's face.

"Did you serve this subpoena?"

"I did."

The witness then admitted he went to the home of Lewis Stimson and took the girl to Fairchild's office where she was examined while a stenographer took testimony. Stimson put up resistance, as he knew something was not right with the subpoena. But Laswell started threatening the former marshal with obstruction, that he could take Ida to the jail for interrogation. Ida was too scared to decline.

"Didn't you threaten Mr. Stimson when he protested against the proceeding?"

"He told the girl not to go, and I told him that he would get himself in trouble."

"Didn't you threaten to get a bench warrant?"

"Yes."

"Who did you think would issue this warrant?"

"That was a bluff on my part."

"O, you were bluffing? Do you expect that the taxpayers will pay you for those bluffs?"

"I don't know."

Laswell was then asked why he was visiting the jail so much over the past several months. The witness claimed he had a curiosity to see the prisoners, so he would recognize them when released. Col. Lewis burst out laughing in the courtroom, saying Laswell had a dull life to have to find friends at the jail. Lewis' jolly laughter ended abruptly when he told the jury Long was the only prisoner Laswell talked with and after took those conversations back to Mr. Fairchild.

Col. Lewis then demanded the original subpoena to be produced and entered into evidence.

Next, Prosecutor Major Cole asked Mrs. Paulina Byers to be called to the stand. Her testimony was as follows. She claimed to have known Mrs. Long for three years. "Mrs. Long came to my house four or five months ago and stayed three nights. Mr. Long came to see her twice, once with Laswell and once with Norman Humes. I heard Long say to his wife the last time he came that he wished she would come home. She said she was afraid that if she did that Long might shoot Humes."

Fourteen-year-old Emma Byers repeated her mother's story, but added that Susan Long said she would not go home unless he would let Ida marry Norman Humes. Long said that Ida was but a child and must stay with them.

Court adjourned for the day.

The following morning, March 26, court opened with Major Cole calling witnesses for the state. First to take the stand was Mrs. Anna E. Hallin, residing at G and Thirteenth Streets. She was a good friend of Susan Long, whom months earlier had to seek refuge at her home for a few days with Ida. Hallin said Long showed up one evening and urged his wife to come home. He would forgive everything she had done, if she had done anything wrong. She raised her arm to him showing black marks where he had struck her.

On cross-examination Hallin said Long was very agitated and anxious to have her home.

Mrs. W. R. Brennan of Keeslingville said, "I think Long had a cause for his jealousy. Long's sister, Mrs. Ella Hatler…was the cause of the whole affair, for Dave often told me different things which his sister had said concerning his wife's chastity. I know he accused his own brother (Charley), of illicit relations with her and he has even said to me that he had seen them at different times in compromising positions. He said my sister has told me often of my wife's infidelity."

Three years before, Susan ran away to San Diego. Mrs. Brennan helped Long write a letter asking her to come home. Brennan asked him why he treated her so bad that she left. She said Long "had a jealous fit and the devil was in him."

Major Cole then requested an examination of the crime scene, to which the defense concurred, and a recess was taken until 2 o'clock. Court spectators were not permitted to the house on Forest Street, but the trip was privy to a few choice reporters. So fast was the decision to visit the scene, that no one bothered to notify the current occupant, a dressmaker, who was taken by surprise at the unexpected intrusion. The jury was taken through the kitchen and told how the bodies were arranged when found.

At 2 o'clock Allan Shewey gave evidence. Shewey, a carpenter, testified as follows:

"I have known Long three years. I saw him on the day of the killing. I met him at the city hall and walked down the street with him. He talked about his domestic troubles. I told him I thought that was settled. He said: No, she has left me for good…He asked me what I would do if a man would break up my family in this way. I told him I believe I would kill him. He said: Then they would hang you. I replied that I would not care in that case."

Major Cole called several character witnesses, before announcing the state rested.

The Defense

Col. Lewis leapt from his seat and demanded before the state rested, they produce the other witnesses endorsed on the information, particularly Ida Humes, but the demand was denied.

Col. Lewis then proceeded to deliver his opening statement for the defense, which occupied more than an hour. He traced the life of the defendant from birth; their only child, a daughter, dwarfed in stature and of feeble mind; his brother in an insane asylum. On the night of January 1, 1891, he went with his family to a Salvation Army meeting:

"A young man of serpent-like eyes, reddish hair and a dare-devil demeanor sat behind them. It was Norman Humes. He became intimate with the family and seduced the weak-minded daughter. Long came to distrust him and learned that his wife had become infatuated with him. They carried on for months a criminal intrigue. They had a code of signals, by which the guilty woman would summon her paramour to her house when her husband went out to earn her bread. The mother was anxious that Humes should become the husband of her daughter. The father objected saying that she was but a child and should be in school. Humes and his wife insisted on a marriage. One night he was taken deathly sick. An examination of the loaf of bread of which he had eaten showed that it had been poisoned with strychnine. Last November his wife left him and went to Humes' house in Sehome. He became almost mad with a sense of shame. He went about the streets enquiring of everybody, friends and strangers alike, for his wife. He went under Humes' house to listen and there heard his wife and Humes plotting to forge a deed to his property. On the night of the tragedy he went to the house. He had the revolver which he brought from Texas and which he had always carried of late. While he was listening under the house he heard his daughter sobbing. She was remonstrating with her mother and husband against their proposal that the three of them occupy the same bed for the night. The mother threatened to whip the daughter if she did not submit. He could not stand it any longer and went up the rear steps and entered the room. Humes and Mrs. Long both sprang on him as he entered. He drew his revolver. Both assailants grabbed it. In the scuffle he fired five times."

As his opening statement reached its zealous climax, so did Lewis' voice elevate into a feverish pitch. Observers noted the attorney's faired nostrils from around his Van Dyke, and some even claimed seeing Lewis' spit spew into the jury box as he waved his arms with excitement, shouting out in the courtroom.

"Having shown all this, as we will do," concluded Col. Lewis to the jurors, "we will come to you as citizens to citizens; as we will go to the throne of God, asking for—justice." At which point Lewis looked to the heavens shaking his fist. The dramatics had their effect, gripping the courtroom, as a wave of murmuring rose as the judge struck his gavel. As the colonel took his seat, Judge Winn adjourned court until Monday, March 29. It was expected to be an exciting day, as Lewis intended to put Ida Humes on the stand. Seen as "dimwitted" it was believed it would require all the skill and tact of the counsel to draw from her the details of the horrible scene of which she was witnessed.

On Monday morning, a timid, yet surprisingly coherent adolescent took the oath and seated herself before a full courtroom anxious to hear her story.

"I am sixteen years of age," Ida gave a brief history then told of meeting Humes at a Salvation Army meeting. "When the meeting was over he went home with us. He was at the house quite often. He and mother were very friendly. I thought he came to see me, but found it was mother. Momma would put a white rag out the window when papa was away. Norman came whenever papa was away. Father did not want him to come see me. I was too young..."

Col. Lewis: "Do you remember...something your father ate that made him sick?"

"The first time he was poisoned was by the coffee. He drank it and it made him sick. The other time he was poisoned I cut some bread and put it on the plate. Papa ate some of it and it made him sick. I gave some to the dog and he acted like he was dying..."

Col. Lewis asked: "Did your mother eat any of the bread?" To which Ida said "No."

Col. Lewis: "Do you remember an occasion about coming home to the house when your father went out looking for you and your mother?"

"We came home and found the door locked. We then went to Norman's boarding house. The landlady came to the door, and mother told her that she wanted Norman to go to the drug store with her. They took me to Mrs. Byers and ma and Norman went off together. I stayed at Mrs. Byer's that night. The next morning I went home. Father was there, but mother was not. Father went out after her. He then came back and went after her again with Humes. I next saw mamma at Mrs. Byers. Father came and cried and begged of mother to come home. Then Humes went to her and asked her to come home and she came. I was in bed. Mother said to me that I was going to be married the next day. I did not know anything about it."

"I remember seeing Humes and mother at Mrs. Morris' home. They went up stairs into a bedroom. I went up but the door was locked. I looked under the door and saw mamma's hand on the floor. I cried about it because I thought they were doing wrong. I told Mrs. Morris about it. Norman and I were married by the justice of the peace at our house. We lived at my father's house in Keeslingville for a while. I saw mother and Humes on a sofa together. He had his arms around her. I threatened to tell father about the way mother and Norman acted and she whipped me with a switch and beat my head on the floor."

"On the night papa shot them, mamma and Norman were sitting together at the table. Norman had his arms around her. I tried to take his arm away from her. I did not like it and bit her on the arm. They were talking about all three of us sleeping in the same bed. I told them that was not the way to do. I was crying. They were both sitting on the same chair. Mother said she would whip me. I got up and went out the door onto the porch. I found papa there. He looked in and said, "Is this the way you do?" Both of them started for him. I went on the porch when the shooting was done. After the shooting I went back in the house."

Cross-examination by Attorney Harry Fairchild occupied three hours. The *Fairhaven Herald* citing it was "evidently directed not with a view to muddling the witness, but for the purpose of impeaching the testimony in the rebuttal." Fairchild read from "voluminous typewritten notes, evidently the result of pre-examination of the state's witnesses, propounding to the witness hypothetical questions" as follows:

"And did not your mother find out in some manner that you had done wrong and took you to the doctors?"

"Yes, she told me I ought to get married." Ida continued, "Father was good to mamma. I knew all the time she was doing things she ought not to do."

Fairchild rapidly bombarded Ida with questions, barely giving her time to answer.

"You say you did not see your father shoot. If people say that you said you did they say what is not true, do they not?" [*sic*]

Ida was totally confused but allowed a "Yes, sir." The questions came unrelenting with Ida applying the appropriate yes or no to each and not allowed time for anything more.

"Didn't you originally think your father said when he came in, 'I'll settle this,' and then, 'this is the way you do it?'"

"Didn't you tell Mrs. Hallin that your father had always been mean to your mother?"

"Did you ever tell Mrs. Hallin, if you ever met your father and have anything to kill him with, you'd kill him?"

And the badgering continued with Ida holding her own, until the cross-examination was interrupted by a noon recess. When court reconvened the courtroom was flooded with spectators. The recess cooled Fairchild's temperament as he closed out his cross-examination with questions relating to whether Ida told her schoolmates about her marriage.

On redirect, Col. Lewis asked his witness if Humes ever threatened to kill her father. Ida recalled the time Norman, her mother, herself and other kids went blackberry picking. Norman and Susan disappeared into the bushes and the children wanted to tag along, but were refused. As the children were waiting by the road Ida thought she saw her father coming and called out to him.

Humes and Susan leaped out of the patch in anger. The man wasn't Long. Humes, in a fury, said if it had been David he would have shot him.

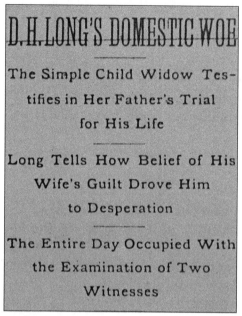

D. H. Long's Domestic Woe.
Fairhaven Herald, March 29, 1892

Ida's examination weighed heavilyy on David Long. Ida stepped down and Col. Lewis called on Long. Newspapers claim, "Long controlled himself, however, as well as a nervous man on trial for his life could have done while relating the revolting and horrible incidents of the ruin of his home." Long gave his testimony calmly, in a low, weak voice, with the exception of describing the killings. Twice he broke down on the stand.

Col. Lewis asked Long to give a history of himself, which he did:

Long talked of Humes stating, "I thought something was wrong with him and did not want him to see Ida. I told my wife I was suspicious of him, and that he frequented saloons and gambling dens. One day as I was going home I passed him. He stopped me and said: Dave, why do you object to my coming to your house? I told him I did not want Ida to think of marrying. She was too young and giddy. He said he would marry her in two years...I did not approve...she was too young to know the consequences."

"One Sunday he came and I told my wife I did not want him to come any more, and he stopped coming. I noticed my wife got negligent about her household duties. She was frequently away from home. It looked like I couldn't please her anymore. She opposed me in everything."

Long then recounted the poisoning incident: "I was soon taken sick. I went out doors. I saw Mr. Reidenheimer (neighbor) and tried to go to him. It seemed as though I could not get my legs under me. My muscles seemed to be cramping and there was writhing in my stomach. I went into the house and went to bed. I could not lie there and crawled out and went outdoors again."

Long continued histestimony:

"Well, I tried to get Susan to see as I did for the good of our daughter, but it did no good, for the more I was opposed the stronger she was in favor of Humes coming to see Ida. I told Susan I did not want him over anymore. Then they began to meet out. Then the trouble began. If only they had succeeded in poisoning me when they tried it twice... I always will believe she put the poison in the coffee and bread to kill me."

[The witness then related how Mr. Gaar told him about seeing Ida compromised by Humes. Then the night Susan and Humes went to a Fairhaven hotel.]

"I didn't sleep any that night. The next morning I went out to look for my wife. About 11 o'clock Ida came home. She said she had stayed at the Byer's all night. I immediately went out again to look for Susan. I saw Humes on Holly Street and asked him where Susan was. He said he didn't know. I told him if he could find where she was, for God's sake to let me know. I was in a terrible state. I went to Fairhaven and looked everywhere for her. I met (Fairhaven City) Marshal (W. S.) Parker and asked him if he knew where she was. He told me that she was at the Paragon Hotel. I went to the hotel but did not find her. Mr. Blankenship said a woman and man came there looking for a room to get away from her husband, but he told her that she could not have a room if there was going to be any trouble."

"I then came back to (New) Whatcom. On the way over I saw Humes and Ida. He came running to me and said he had found my wife. I told him that Parker told me they had stayed together at the hotel. He denied it at first but then admitted it, but said they left the light burning all night and the door open, and that she slept on the bed and he sat up in a chair. I believed him."

"The next day I started to go to Byers. I found Susan upstairs. I said to her, "Why did you go away?" She said, "Why did you lock me out?" I told her I did not mean to lock her out. I begged of her to come home and told her I would forgive her if she had done anything wrong. She told me she stayed at the Paragon Hotel. She complained I had been cruel to her. I pleaded with her but she would not come. The next Monday night I went again and pleaded with her. She said the only thing that would bring her back was to let Humes marry Ida. I told her Ida was but a child. About nine o'clock at night Humes came to my house. He said he was going to marry Ida. I told him I could not bear the idea of Ida getting married. I wanted to send her to the convent. He asked me if I would let them marry if Susan came home. I told him I would do anything to get her back."

71

"The next day they went down and got a certificate, and in the evening they were married. They afterwards moved to Sehome, and Susan went with them. It seems as if everything was lost. I could not persuade my wife to return. I went there one evening and listened under the house. I heard them plotting to forge a deed to my property and skip the country. I went to the county auditor the next day and told him not to file any deed to my property. The next evening I went there again. I heard them trying to make Ida consent to their sleeping in a large bed. I could stand it no longer. I met Ida on the back porch. I looked in and saw Humes with his arm around my wife. It seemed as if my brain was on fire. I said, "Is this the way you do." They both sprang at me. I commenced shooting and I shot and I shot and I shot; but I did not intend to kill my wife. I went out and placed my pistol against my head, but it would not go off it; was empty. It seemed to me the whole world was black. I then tried to get away from the horrible place."

"Now, just to think of a mother treating her only child in that way was awful; now, to think of her committing adultery with her son-in-law and made her only child marry the man to hide her own guilt. Besides Humes threatened to kill me, and Susan and Ida both knew of this threat and not tell me one word about it, my own wife and child! It was a thousand wonders I was not killed long ago with the only woman I ever loved at the bottom of it makes my heart stand still to think of it. I am not a murderer at heart, nor can I think that I am. I did not kill them on purpose, but people will think I did through madness and jealousy, but I had to save myself."

While relating this tearful testimony, the witness stood up before the jury and gestured wildly with his hands. When he concluded he sank down apparently exhausted. Cross-examination began but was interrupted by adjournment.

The following day cross-examination resumed with Major Cole standing before the jurors, facing the defendant. Cole ran through the testimony to date throwing out questions to Long to the effect of how naïve could he be not to know what was happening under his own roof. Cole asked, "You had never before been suspicious of your wife?" Long answering very confidently, "No sir; I never had a reason to be."

Cole then asked about Long's six-shooter and how many times he fired the handgun. Long couldn't remember. "You say you put the revolver to your head and it would not go off? Long agreed that he remembered that much. At which point the major put his questions to Long in a forceful, and more aggressive tone.

"Didn't you know there was one cartridge left in the revolver?"

"No; I do not."

"You testified that at the time of the shooting you fired and fired—then put the pistol to your own head and it was empty?" Major Cole paused, then changing direction, asked a series of unrelated questions as to occurrences after the shooting—then excused Long.

Ella Hatler, the defendant's sister, was called next and examined by Thomas Newman:

"Susan and David were very happy up until the time that Mr. Humes made his appearance. In August I went to the house and apparently, there was no one home, so I waited inside. After a little while Susan (came out of Ida's bedroom) and looked embarrassed. I said, 'You look a little warm.' We sat down and talked awhile [*sic*] and then I got up and went into Ida's room. I opened the door quick and it hit Humes' forehead, and he swore an awful oath. I asked Susan about it and she said he had hid from me. She then said it was nobody's business."

"The next time I saw David was in December on Lummi Island. He looked like a wild man. He was very pale and thin and his mind was all tattered and torn. He would at first talk about one thing, then another. It took an hour before he told me he killed them..."

The witness was cross-examined by Harry Fairchild:

"You had never seen David Long from the time you saw him on the third of December until he came in with the sheriff. What difference was there in his appearance? Had he made any attempt to disguise himself?"

Ella told Fairchild her brother appeared much calmer, but thinner. As far as being in disguise, only his moustache was shaved off. Fairchild's discourteous response was delivered in a sharp tone: "What's the barber's name in the woods?" Indicating her brother spent his time hiding out at her home and shaved there. "There is none," she shot back without hesitation, getting a roar of laughter from spectators.

On re-direct the witness related that on one occasion she heard Humes say that if Long took Ida to the convent he would kill him, and Susan spoke up and said she hoped to God he would. Asked about insanity in her family the witness said her brother Charley was found insane back home in Kansas in 1881 and taken to an institution in Topeka.

Court was adjourned until two p.m.

A significant number of witnesses were called and disposed throughout the afternoon session. Testimony was brief.

Mrs. J. M. Mullins, a neighbor testified: "One day last summer I went to Long's house to get Mrs. Long to go bathing with me. She said at first that she could not go, but finally she and Long came with us. When we got down to the beach she called me aside and said she must go back for Norman was coming to see her. She blushed and I thought something was wrong. She went away and in about an hour she returned. Soon afterward Humes came also."

Mrs. Payne: "Last August I went to their house and went in without knocking. Mrs. Long excused herself, saying that Ida's fellow was in the front room. I listened and heard her go upstairs. She came down with Norman Humes and he went out the front door. One Sunday we stopped at the Long's to get them to go bathing. When we got to the bank over the beach she said she should go back to lock the door. I saw Humes nearby and noticed him go back to the house with her. She stayed about three-quarters of an hour."

Andy Brand: "I have worked in the Cornwall mill since last June. I knew Norman Humes and had a conversation with him about Mrs. Long and Ida. He invited me to come to his house in Sehome to stay over. He said, "You can sleep with the girl or the old lady." …He said he was laying for Long and would kill him. He had a revolver."

J. P. Smalley: "Humes rode with me from Keeslingville to downtown in the express wagon November last. After we started he said, "Drive up, there comes Long." I asked what difference it made, he replied, "He is raising hell with me and his wife, and if he does it again I'll kill the son of a bitch."

Mrs. Ella Hatler was called to identify the cloak:

"Mr. Stimson, my daughter, Mrs. Lemm and myself, went to Long's house last December to take care of the goods in the house. [The cloak was passed to the witness.] I found this cloak on the bed. I picked it up to put it on the line to air. Something hard in the lapel struck the door. I examined it and found something was sewed up in it. I cut the stitches and found a bottle in it."

"Is this the bottle" asked Newman.

"Yes sir."

Lewis Stimson was called next: "I was present," he said, "when the cloak was found. I saw it laying on the bed in the house."

Cross-examination by Fairchild:

"Mr. Stimson, are you the same Lewis Stimson who was indicted for murder and convicted of manslaughter?"

Col. Lewis leaped to the floor and opposed a strenuous objection to this line of cross-examination on the grounds it was "upon a matter entirely foreign to anything touched upon in the direct examination." Fairchild insisted upon the state's right to impeach the witness. The court sustained the objection.

"I am."

"That is all," said Fairchild.

"Mr. Stimson," asked Col. Lewis, "who was your attorney when you were convicted?"

"Major Cole."

"You were pardoned by the governor before you served a day, were you not?"

"Yes sir."

This closed the proceedings for the day.

On March 31, 1892, the defense rested its case. Further interest in the trial was waived by the public, as testimony introduced was that of experts, physicians, etc, relating to emotional insanity and its causes. Spectators found the line of questioning dull.

Druggist, H. A. White was called: "Mr. Burke gave me some particles which he said came out of the bread, to analyze, and I did so. I found it to be crystallized strychnine." White explained the effect of heat and moisture on strychnine and how the baking process would affect it. Newman presented the bottle of strychnine found in Mrs. Long's cloak to White who recognized it as the same one brought to him some weeks ago. He explained to the jury that the bottle was a one drachm strychnine vial, informing the jury the size of bottle was the customary packaging for the poison.

Cross-examination of Mr. White by Col. Lewis:

"When, in your judgment was the drug placed in the loaf?"

"My belief is that it was put there after baking."

"Did you have any conversation with Mr. Burke?"

"Yes. We talked about it and he told me that the loaf fit the molds and that he believed some of the other bakers had done this in order to injure his business" (a bottle was then shown to the witness). White continued: "This is a drachm strychnine vial. The drug in the loaf was in large quantities. There was about three grains of strychnine in the one-half loaf I saw, and I should judge there had been fully six grains in the entire loaf. It was in a pocket of less a cubic inch. I think there was about one-half drachm in the bottle when I saw it."

In other words, White concluded one drachm or sixty grains when the bottle was full.

Chemist W. H. Hardy explained the effect of strychnine on the human system and the manner in which symptoms of poisoning were first made evident.

Analyzing the contents, Hardy concluded it to contain alkaloid of strychnine.

William Brown: "I know the defendant. I saw him during the month of November last. He told me of his family troubles and asked me to go see his wife and get her to return to him. I told him 'No' for I did not desire to go into a strange man's house under such circumstances. I met him the next day. He had the appearance of an insane man. I do not by any means think he would have been considered rational. He was frantic with his grief and not in his right mind."

Court adjourned until two o'clock. At the afternoon session:

T. E. Mason testified to Long's wild and worried appearance and frequent errors in his work performance at the time of his family difficulties. "He worked for me last October, and I saw that something was wrong with him and his work was bad. I had to discharge him. Before that he was all right. He looked wild and bad, and I thought he was deranged."

William D. Jenkins: "I saw the defendant on the day of the shooting walking down the street with a gentleman friend of mine. Passing my friend remarked, 'That damn fool will be in the asylum within thirty days.'

The next testimony introduced was that of physicians and experts upon the subject of emotional insanity. Doctors Henderson, Street, Cross and Jameson all testified that "intense nervous excitement, domestic troubles and a taint of insanity in the family were most likely to produce what is known by physicians and the profession as emotional or moral insanity, nevertheless it was a very difficult matter to distinguish between moral insanity and moral depravity." The ground was thoroughly gone over and diagnosed in all its details.

Then testimony closed for the defense and the case rested. As the hour for adjournment was near, the state announced it did not care to go into the rebuttal testimony at such a late hour. Court was adjourned until 9:30 the next morning.

The state commenced its rebuttal testimony, which was directed toward the evidence of Ida Humes. And an attempt was made by the state to introduce testimony as to the mental condition of Susan Long prior to the killing, but the court ruled out the testimony. Numerous witnesses were called and a vigorous effort was made to impeach the testimony offered by the defense, said the *Fairhaven Herald* on Friday, April 1. Frequent objections to the questions offered by Attorney Fairchild were made by Colonel Lewis, and in most instances sustained by the court. Testimony recycled what was previously told throughout the trial, continuing well into the night.

The most heated rebuttal of the day came when John Hart was asked to take the stand. Col. Lewis raised violent objection to his being allowed to testify, as Hart had been present as an officer of the court and heard preceding testimony. The objective was overruled and Hart told of his presence at the house on the night of the murder and his subsequent interview with Ida Humes acting as a reporter for the *Reveille*.

"At the time of the killing I was a reporter for the *Bellingham Bay Reveille*. I had a conversation with Ida Humes. Deputy Sheriff Estabrooke and George Charlot were present. Mrs. Humes was in the closet in the corner of the room. I asked her some questions and wrote down some portions of her answers. She said her father struck her mother a few days before, and had often done so, and that they had frequently had trouble. She said that her father had threatened to kill them both. I was standing near the foot of the bed, where the dead people laid, when she pointed at the bruise on her mother's arm, and said, 'This is where father pinched mother.' She further said that she never saw anything wrong with her mother, and that never at any time had she seen anything wrong between her mother and her husband."

Hart was the last witness examined during rebuttal and the court adjourned until 9:30 the following morning

On April 1, evidence in the Long trial was in and the opening of closing arguments began. A larger audience was assembled to hear the lengthy statements, making it exceeding difficult to enter or leave the courtroom. Spectators were expecting an eloquent oratory by Col. James Hamilton Lewis in his closing argument.

Major Cole opened and spoke two and a half hours, followed by Thomas Newman. Cole did not attempt a comprehensive review of the evidence, but confined his remarks to the points of the state's case. Newman followed, speaking with what the *Fairhaven Herald* referred to as an "impressive deliberation and force, reviewing the defendant's career and the circumstances leading to the homicide." He made a strong appeal to the sentiment of the "sanctity of the home and touched with feeling eloquence upon the circumstance offered by the defense in palliation of the fatal deed."

Col. Lewis delivered his own elaborate and polished argument for the defense, followed by Harry Fairchild for the prosecution. The *Bellingham Bay Reveille* noting spectators were enchanted by the colonel's charm of oratory. "His graceful flowing rhetoric, dramatic delivery and wealth of historical and literary allusion gave his address in behalf of his client..." Fairchild spoke for several hours, informing the jury a man's life was at stake, but they must do their duty.

In closing, Col. James Hamilton Lewis faced the jury, extending one arm above his head for dramatic flair, bellowed "This," and he paused, building a feverish pitch of anticipation in the courtroom, "is the Law. If a man be found lying with a woman married to a husband, then they shall both of them die—both the man that lay with the woman and the woman; so shalt thou put away evil from Israel, and the twelve, (jury) sworn to true deliverance…return a verdict in accordance this law and the evidence."

Judge John Winn delivered his "very impartial" instructions to the jury at 7:30 p.m., and the jurors retired to deliberate. Shortly after nine p.m. a call for the bailiff came from the door, a verdict had been reached. At 10:15 p.m. the jury filed in and rendered a verdict of "not guilty." David Long, acquitted, shook hands with his attorneys and with each juror. Several days later, Long was excused of all charges in the murder of Norman Humes. Little is recorded as to what happened to the family after the trial. It is claimed that David Long continued living in New Whatcom for a period. Ida moved in with her Aunt Ella on Lummi Island, and the trail ends there.

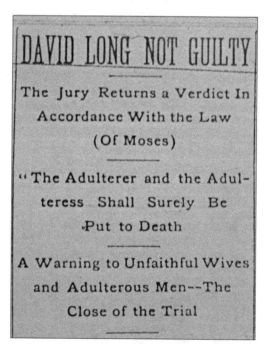

David Long Not Guilty.
Fairhaven Herald, April 5, 1892

Chapter 3
"Terrible" Jake Terry and the Siege of Sumas

By the turn of the twentieth century, the golden age of the wild west outlaw was over. Gone, were the likes of Jesse James' Hole-in-the-Wall gang. Long dead were Billy the Kid, Sam Bass, Zip Wyatt and many other legendary desperados whom once terrorized the American frontier. The era came to a close in 1908, when newspapers informed readers Butch Cassidy, leader of the notorious Wild Bunch, and his partner Harry Alonzo Longabaugh "Sundance" were gunned down in Bolivia. Yes, the curtains were drawing on the old west.

Sumas, Washington, about 1912. Courtesy of Jim Doidge

But a few holdouts persisted. Bill Miner "The Grey Fox" now in his fifties, was still robbing trains. Other outlaws were too old to change professions and would rather continue in the only thing they knew – robbing and stealing. No doubt they knew they were a dying breed. Some, were lingerers, remnants from busted gangs. A few upstarts attempted continuing in the tradition of the American outlaw, but were unable to obtain the glamour or status of a living legend.

Much can be said about the notorious, "Cowboy" or "Terrible" Jake E. Terry and his reign of terror. It can be equally acknowledged that for all his criminal activities, he wasn't a very accomplished outlaw; occupying prison cells most of the time. He was well known in Seattle jails and at the federal facilities of McNeil Island and San Quentin, to name a few.

Jake Terry, (lower left) inmate record at San Quentin State Penitentiary California, 1896.

San Quentin State Penitentiary prison records

Terry tried his hand at every criminal activity known, before finding his calling as a smuggler. He committed murder, assault, stagecoach holdups, robbery, train robbery, larceny, counterfeiting, opium smuggling and trafficking of illegal Chinese across the Canadian border.

Much of what we know of Terry comes from his own mouth. While most criminals were shy of the law and public exposure, Terry was quite the opposite. He was a braggart, relishing in talking with authorities and newspaper reporters of his exploits. And all indications attest they enjoyed hearing of them. Newspapers gave lengthy columns describing Terry sitting in police stations, legs up, smoking cigars with inquisitive officers huddled around; all ears tuned on the villain.

On one occasion, Terry provided a detailed account of Canada's first train robbery near Kamloops in 1904 by the Bill Miner gang. Amongst the loot taken were $250,000 in Australian negotiable bonds and securities. They were considered worthless by Miner, being too hot and difficult to interchange. Possibly, with Miner's prodding, Jake agreed to act as mediator in making a deal with authorities. Although Terry was certainly a participant, the law had no proof to pin on him. The outlaw was in his glory telling of the robbery. He claimed many details from a reliable source. Terry wanted to know what the railroad was willing to pay for the bonds, if by chance he was able to produce them.

"Cowboy" Jake Terry

A detailed account of Jake Terry's criminal career is beyond the scope of this story. But a short history of Terry's activities is essential in telling how the outlaw came to Sumas, Washington.

Little of Jake Terry's early life is known. For an individual intent on talking about himself, he leaves no trace of his early history. Was he hiding his past? Jake Terry claimed his birthplace as Missouri, August 1849.[20] According to his 1890s-criminal record, Terry stood five-foot and ten inches, and weighed one hundred-eighty pounds. He had a smooth complexion, with brown hair and brown eyes. In later years, Terry shaved his head.

It's rumored after Terry arrived in Washington Territory, locals gave him the title "Cowboy" because he worked a Texas cattle ranch. There is scanty mention in Texas newspapers of a Jake E. Terry arrested for stagecoach robbery. Others claim the title was bestowed upon him for his untamed wild nature.

---

[20] Terry claimed in the 1900 census his father born in Ohio and mother in Kentucky. Some sources claim he was born 1853.

Historians, crime authors and reporters claim once Terry arrived in the Pacific Northwest he assumed the name John H. Terry. In a dispute over payment for drinks in Seattle's Fashion Saloon on July 19, 1873, Terry drew his Colt .45 and shot owner Delbert Wright in the chest. Wright recovers, and Terry goes on trial charged with assault with intent to kill. Guilty of the charge, Terry is sentenced to five years at the territorial prison at Steilacoom.[21] On release, he leaves the region, returning in early 1883. During his absence, Terry becomes a train engineer running an engine out of Canada to Minot and Mandan, North Dakota. Not interested in an honest career riding the rails, Terry used his position to smuggle opium across the Canadian border. He was caught and served jail time.

In October, 1888, the weirdest occurrence in the Terry saga transpires. "Cowboy" Jake Terry joins the Seattle Police Department. Chief of Police J. C. Mitchell was ordered by Mayor Robert Moran to combat the growing crime epidemic in the city. The *Seattle Post-Intelligencer* must have been equally surprised, writing, "Chief Mitchell has appointed ten extra police authorized by the city council including J. E. Terry…"

Terry's first assignment was to enforce and clear the city streets of livestock. The October 21, *Seattle Post-Intelligencer* eagerly reported his progress:

"Officer J. E. Terry has been delegated by chief of police Mitchell to see that the ordinance prohibiting stock from running at large is strictly enforced within certain prescribed limits. Terry is mounted on horseback and most thoroughly does he do his work. He spares neither age nor sex, name nor condition, but lights onto everything with hoof or horn, and drags it off to the pound."

Becoming a crime fighter was not in Terry's blood. Instead of upholding the law he used his new position to ally himself with local criminals and abusing his power. He was fired within six months.

In October 1889, Terry was arrested and on trial for embezzlement. He is sentenced to a year in the King County Jail. Using charm and persuasion, Terry is made a Trusty. The position allows him special privileges, including the freedom to leave the jail to make official errands throughout the city. These opportunities permit Terry in warning unlicensed gambling establishments of potential raids he overhears being discussed. "Cowboy" Jake Terry is released on June 3, 1890 and made his way to Montana.

By August he is about to be arrested in Missoula, claiming to be a Seattle deputy sheriff who had managed to lose his money. Duped law enforcement

---

[21] Case file #993 Territory of Washington vs John Terry.

were eager to help a fellow brother, but Terry's actions soon aroused suspicion. In reply to a telegram sent to the Seattle sheriff's office, word was received that Terry was an ex-con, and an ex-law officer. He was about to skip town by train when apprehended. In his usual flamboyant manner, Terry was able to talk himself out of arrest. Instead, he amused Missoula's finest with "stories about his important arrests at Seattle and Spokane Falls, and played the officers here in elegant style" said local papers.[22]

Sumas

Returning to Washington, Jake Terry set up operations on the British Columbia boundary line at Sumas around 1890-91. When the heat was on, he would simply waltz across the line into Huntingdon where the law could not touch him. In this setting, Terry learned all the backcountry trails that would provide safe passage for counterfeiting, opium smuggling and running illegal Chinese across the Canadian border. No record exists of how many successful passages were made, but Terry was caught on multiple occasions in his illicit endeavors, serving time in several federal prisons. Terry must have found the risks *financially* rewarding, and may have accomplished dozens of crossings.

Lars Barbo, editor of the *Sumas News*, remembered of Terry's arrival: "Into this place of repose last spring blew Jake Terry, with his picturesque record and long .45 Colt's. He lived about as he pleased and did as he liked in the gambling halls and saloons, as by all accounts he has most of that section of the population 'buffaloed.' The town at large paid very little attention to him. On one or two occasions he went in and owned a saloon by the aid of his horse-pistol, and once or twice did some promiscuous shooting in the streets."

Terry's smuggling days nearly came to an end one Sunday night, on July 26, 1891. A mile and a half from Woolley in Skagit County a gunfight nearly cost him his life. The desperate battle took the life of one man, leaving another badly wounded.

Seattle U.S. Customs Inspector, James C. Baird was telegraphed by Sumas Customs Collector Reilly that a large party of Chinese had been smuggled across the border. Reilly asked the inspector to meet him at Sedro where the group was headed. Whatcom Customs Inspector James Buchanan was also ordered to join Baird in Sedro. Sunday afternoon they found the suspected trail

---

[22] *Seattle Post-Intelligencer*, "Deputy Sheriff Terry: Swindler in the Guise of Seattle Officer Dupes Montana Police." August 23, 1890.

over which the smugglers were to be traveling and built a blind. After dark the lawmen waited along the trail in ambush.

About ten o'clock they heard a band of men stumbling along in the darkness. As they approached opposite of the men in hiding, Baird stepped out to confront about fifteen Chinese, accompanied by two or three white men. At his command for the men to halt, the lead smuggler, probably Terry's partner, replied that he was a U. S. deputy marshal, and was taking the "Chinamen" to Seattle as prisoners. He also displayed his badge as proof of his assertion.

Baird considered this a ruse, then ordered the man to raise his hands. Who shot first is a disputed question, but both groups fired on each other in the dark. Baird's bullet struck the smuggler in the body, killing him instantly. About this time the second smuggler brought his revolver into action. Buchanan, meanwhile appeared on the scene and opened fire toward all the movement. A leaded round from the second smuggler's revolver creased Baird's scalp opening a bloody head-wound. Baird fell to his knees. In the dark, he felt the warm blood trickling down his face. He had no idea if his wound was lethal. The gun battle continued for a lengthy period. Suddenly, a shot rang out followed by a deep groan. Jake Terry fell to the ground with a bullet to the groin. Meanwhile, the Chinese had scattered through the woods causing all sorts of crashing sounds.

The dead man and a gravely wounded Terry were taken into Woolley. There it was discovered the dead man's name was George W. Poor, a King County deputy sheriff and a deputy United States marshal of Seattle. Poor was a 32-year old immigrant Englishman. The wounded man taken to a hotel room proved to be "Cowboy" Jake Terry. He was not expected to live the night. Lawmen crowding the smuggler's bed told Terry he had not long to live and may as well give up what he knew. Terry claimed to have had inside knowledge of a large Chinese group being smuggled across the border. Knowing the route taken, and moving slowly at night, he claimed to have telegraphed Sheriff James H. Wollery, of King County, if he had assistance he could capture them. He talked of a reward. Terry claimed Wollery commended him on his plan and sent Poor and another man, U.S. Customs Inspector Z. Taylor Holden to assist in the apprehension. Terry said the three of them had captured the Chinese on the trail at gunpoint. Nothing was mentioned who the original smugglers were, or where they went. Now that the Chinese were in Terry's custody, they were being taken to Wooley when they were jumped on the trail. Terry said he had no idea these were lawmen, but possibly criminals attempting to recapture the Chinese. When asked what he had intended to do with the illegals, Terry claimed they were to be loaded into a boxcar and taken under guard to Seattle.

The lawmen were uncertain what to think of Terry's story. Terry was a no-good desperado who would say anything. Then again, he was a showboat of a villain, and it would be just like him to take a train car full of Chinese to Seattle hoping for some reward. Poor had the reputation as a straight lawman, and deemed incorruptible. Was it possible that Terry was telling the truth? After all, why would he lie on his deathbed?

A coroner's inquest was held on the body of George Poor, and after the evidence was evaluated, a verdict of manslaughter was returned against Buchanan and Baird, who were at once taken into custody.

The *Bellingham Bay Express* reported whatever happened in the woods that morning the "men must all have iron nerves, as the shooting was started at such close quarters that the guns were almost touching each other, and the shot that killed Poor went right through his body and was found in the back of his coat. People who afterwards visited the scene of the shooting say that the fusillade must have been terrible, as the surroundings are full of the flying bullets."[23]

U. S. Customs Inspector Z. Taylor Holden, the third man in the group, yet to be determined a smuggler or lawman, was also taken into custody. He claimed he was making arrangements with railway officials for a car to transport the illegals when the shootout occurred. But witnesses claim Holden was in a saloon drinking beer at the time of the shooting. Sheriff Wollery was telegraphed of Poor's death. Wollery took the next train north to identify his deputy's body.

After the viewing, Sheriff Wollery claimed Poor had asked for a leave of absence, but he did not know where he was going. Holden, Wollery said, was indeed an inspector of customs, but left Seattle without authority. He knew nothing of receiving a telegram from Jake Terry.

Wollery said Inspector Baird was formerly a Blaine police officer, where he worked in connection with Inspector Buchanan. Both are known as reliable and good officers. As for George Poor, Wollery sadly added he "lived, as a whole-souled genial, honest man…He has been a prominent figure in Seattle society… appointed customs inspector, but did not retain his position long." George Poor started a jewelry business the year before, and remained so until Wollery was elected sheriff, and appointed him deputy.

An editorial in the July 30, *Bellingham Bay Express* said of the gunfight that "traces of the old King county ring, which operated so successfully a few years

---

[23] *Bellingham Bay Express*, "Battle in the Woods" July 30, 1891.

ago, may yet be found… a great many of the custom house officers are implicated in smuggling, but so cleverly are their actions covered that it has been
impossible to prove anything."

As for "Cowboy" Jake Terry: "The presence of Cowboy Terry, too, casts a
glamour of suspicion over the whole transaction. If Terry really wanted to catch
the Chinamen, why did he not get some assistance and run them into the nearest goal, instead of keeping them corralled for two or three days while he sent to
Seattle for Holden?"

Terry of course recovered. Doctors in Woolley refused to operate, claiming
to do so would only cause needless pain were kicked out of the room by the
smuggler. Terry took a pocket knife and operated on himself, extracting the bullet. The courts saw through the thin veil of the smuggling enterprise and Terry
was whisked away to prison.

As soon as his sentence was up at the federal prison on McNeil Island, Terry
returned to Sumas, but in 1895 was captured smuggling Chinese again, receiving three more years on McNeil.

When released, he joined a gang of counterfeiters engaged in the making
of spurious five-cent pieces. Again, he was captured, but this time sentenced
to seven years at San Quentin, California. While incarcerated his health broke
down and the last fourteen months of his sentence were spent in the prison hospital. When released he returned to Sumas a mere shadow of his former self, it
was claimed.

Love Triangle

The unflattering story goes that Matthew S. Kenyon (47), co-owner of Kenyon
& Smith Grocers, was one day reading a "Lonely-Hearts" magazine. Kenyon,
a bachelor of modest means, prided himself for owning the first automobile in
Sumas. Unbeknownst to friends and neighbors, Kenyon was shopping for a wife
and found her in the section seeking potential marriages. After a few weeks of
letter exchanges, Kenyon traveled to Minneapolis and married Annie Walker
on March 21, 1893. Arm-in-arm, the newlyweds stepped off the train in
Sumas, where a proud Matthew Kenyon showed off his new bride to a surprised
populous. The newspapers called her an "attractive woman" and "luring," but
photographs taken at the time don't do her the justice claimed.

Annie was born about 1865 as Anna Sickles, in New York to parents John
and Sarah. She married Jacob Walker in Chittenango, on June 5, 1881. What

Photos of Annie. The newspapers called her an "attractive woman" and "luring." Laura Jacoby's, Galen Biery collection.

happened to the couple after marriage is unclear, although at one point Annie is listed in a census as "widowed." It is not clear whether the couple, or if Annie alone, relocated to Minneapolis, Minnesota after marriage. Another claim has Jacob arrested and imprisoned a few years after matrimony. From Minneapolis, Annie's movements are unknown, but that she eventually met Matthew Kenyon. Until then, a void exists in her history; a void potentially occupied by none other than "Cowboy" Jake Terry.

Jake Terry was a wanderer, spending time in Montana, and the Dakota's where he was known to have been jailed. He traveled in and out of Washington and had been rumored to have lived in Texas. How Jake and Annie met is unknown. Their true relationship is clouded in mystery. Some historians claim they lived together a short time in Port Townsend, Washington, before hurrying back to Montana. Another has Jake and Annie marrying in Montana before another arrest. Jake telling Annie to meet him in Sumas, where he had established a smuggling operation. If so, did Annie establish herself in Sumas through the unwitting Kenyon? After Terry's near fatal gunshot wound outside of Woolley in July of 1891, the *Bellingham Bay Express* wrote of the shooting, "He (Terry)...has been separated from his wife, who he treated so badly that news of his approaching death caused her to smile..."[24] Was this Annie? His prison record also records a wife.

All we know, is after March 21, 1893, Matthew Kenyon and Annie arrive together in Sumas. Kenyon, delighted with his new bride, showed her off at every opportunity. But the blissful union wasn't to last, as peace in the Kenyon household was short-lived.

Before long a Swede named Gust (Augustus) Lindey[25] had eyes for Annie Kenyon, and Annie did not discourage the advances. Lindey was a lineman for the telegraph company, riding a rail speeder along the line each day, cutting brush and making repairs. He was said to be a short, blue eyed and bushy blond of small stature. Born in his native country in November 1855, he immigrated with his parents in 1866. Settling in Sumas in about 1890, Gust had never married.

Newspaper image of Gust Lindey.
American Evening and Morning Reveille, July 6, 1907

[24] Terry claimed single in the 1900 census.
[25] The name Gust Lindey has appeared with countless spellings. I have chosen to use the spelling appearing in all legal documents.

How long their liaison lasted before Kenyon decided enough, wasn't recorded when he filed for divorce in March 1898, but Kenyon indicated, "years." Annie's infidelity was a blow to the grocer. The disgrace was such that the once humorous rotund man shrank in embarrassment before the public eye. The affair swiftly became common knowledge throughout the small community, and it humiliated Kenyon. Whenever he was away, Lindey was at his home. At night, as her husband slept, Annie crept from her bed and walked to Lindey's house. People watched in disbelief as the Swede's light went out soon after she entered. After a time, neither attempted further discretion.

The suit against Annie lasted nearly a year. At first, she didn't fight against it, but left Sumas for Minneapolis. It was with great difficulty that she was tracked down. On April 11, 1898, Minneapolis Deputy Sheriff Thomas Chapman served a complaint and summons to Annie. She was to comply within sixty days and appear in court; she ignored it.

Finally, on March 10, 1899, Kenyon appeared with his Arkansas attorney, Oliver P. Brown, before Judge Hiram E. Hadley. The defendant Annie L. Kenyon did not appear, nor was she represented by counsel. The court thereupon proceeded and evidence was presented from the "Findings of Fact and Conclusions of Law," by Brown.[26]

Brown concluded Annie had, "…continuously, for a long time past disregarded her duties as a wife by receiving marked and improper attentions from Gust Lindey, an unmarried man, and has on various and sundry occasions during the absence of plaintiff from his home received Lindey into the home, concealing the visits from plaintiff; that Mrs. Kenyon has during said time on various occasions left the home and secretly visited the residence of Lindey during the night…over repeated protests of plaintiff."

Brown told the court Mrs. Kenyon admitted her improper relations with Lindey and stated she would not desist. "Therefore, due to the conduct of Mrs. Kenyon," said Brown, "it was impossible for plaintiff to live any longer with Mrs. Kenyon as his wife."

When all seemed concluded, Annie returned. In a last-ditch effort to capitalize on the divorce, Annie, with her attorneys in tow, attempted to take possession of some of her husband's property. A motion was filed by the law firm of Dorr & Hadley, demanding Matthew Kenyon state "fully and specifically what

[26] M. S. Kenyon vs. Annie L. Kenyon, Findings of Fact and Conclusions of Law, Civil Case #5593, March 11, 1899.

property he has, nature and value of the same and how he acquired it." Plus, she wanted her attorney fees paid. Obviously, the Court would have none of this.

On March 28, 1898, Judge Hadley announced the court was releasing "M. S. Kenyon from ever having to give his wife anything, but $200.00." Annie walked away with no support, alimony, property or claim on her husband's business.

Free from the bonds of her marriage, Gust and Annie were themselves married in Seattle on October 6, 1898. Gust was 43 and Annie 33. Gust Lindey wasn't a man of great wealth, but Annie may have had her eye on her new husband's land and holdings in and around Sumas. Over the years, Lindey accumulated nine lots within the city. One lot was occupied by a two-story hotel on Boundary Street. Outside Sumas, he owned forty-acres of undeveloped land.

After their wedding, Gust and Annie moved into a wood framed building on one of his lots. The back of the building served as their new home, while the Front Street side became Annie's place of business, selling notions. The rooms in the rear consisted of a sitting room, bedroom, kitchen, dining room, storeroom and woodshed.

All was well with the couple, until the summer 1905 when "Cowboy" Jake Terry crossed the international line into Sumas. It's uncertain whether Jake knew Annie was in Sumas, or if he just happened into her notions store for cigars and saw her at the counter. Whichever the case, Jake was instantly lustfully on top of Annie with no resistance coming from her. A peeved Gust Lindey entered the store and caught the two in heated action. Terry was taller, of larger build, and certainly the stronger of the two. Regardless, Lindey showed no fear of the ex-con and the two went at it with fists flying. They battled in the small store leaving wrecked counters and merchandise in their wake. Terry, with wild eyes bulging from his head, became a madman. Raging out of control, he nearly beat Gust to death. Gust was finally thrown out into the street, landing in a heap. Getting to his feet, he stormed back inside only to be beaten, and bloodily tossed back into the street. Terry followed the smaller man out and preceded to viciously kick him in front of a growing crowd.

Thrashed and embarrassed in front of the gathering crowd of friends and townspeople, Gust staggered toward the U. S. Saloon to regain his nerve. After, he visited the Mount Baker Saloon, the Bodega and Stambaugh's Saloon. Most of Sumas' men kept their neutrality when Gust took Annie away from Kenyon. Others shunned the Swede for what they considered a despicable act against one of the city's finest and most respectable citizens. The intolerable

Jake Terry was another matter, and soon one of the saloon patrons piped up if whether all the women in Sumas were fair game for the likes of Jake Terry. Backed by an outraged mob, some fortified with liquor, Gust marched back to his home. The group was stopped cold in their tracks when Terry stepped out from the store with his Colt .45 firing overhead. Then Terry took aim at their feet, kicking up dust.

If not bad enough, a crazed Terry chased the men down Front Street shooting in all directions. It was said he had the face of a crazed demon, screeching out an evil laugh as he chased the men.

Marshal Claude Smith was approached by townsfolk asking what he intended to do about the desperado. Citizens complained Terry had for years did as he wished; all but owning Sumas. Smith held up his gun hand, missing three fingers, stating he was ill equipped to handle gunmen. He was paid little and had never signed up for such danger.

Lars Barbo would later say: "Finally the trouble came, and Marshal Smith resigned. Harvey Siles was appointed in his place, and so far, as I know he arrested Jake whenever necessary. In a little while, however, the situation passed beyond where the marshal could handle it. Jake could not be pinned down on any charge, for he had the men who could testify, so frightened that they did not dare to."

In the meantime, Terry had thrown Gust Lindey out of his own home and slept in Lindey's bed. He defied Gust to come take his wife back, and threatened to kill any man who interfered with him. Ashamed and beaten, Lindey checked into the U. S. Hotel until Terry re-crossed the line a few days later. This became routine for the rest of the year. Terry would occupy the Lindey household when he chose, and Gust would move into a hotel.

The Siege of Sumas

After the fight, Jake Terry decided to let things settle down in Sumas. He continued to cross the border intensifying his illicit affair with Gust Lindey's wife. Gust had taken to heavy drinking, becoming a demoralized shell of a man. When Terry showed, Lindey would wander over to the U. S. Hotel until the "Cowboy" departed.

By early winter, the routine oddly changed. Gust was allowed to remain at his home during Terry's visits, where the "Cowboy" humiliated and plied him with liquor. If Gust displayed any resistance, Terry would beat on him.

Of course, this allowance didn't include sleeping with his wife. Drunk and sick most of the time, Lindey became easily manipulated. Terry force-fed him rotgut whiskey by the bottle keeping Lindey inebriated most of the time. Why the sudden change in behavior by Jake Terry? Clearly, he was up to something.

No one knows what ran through Gust Lindey's mind before marrying his love, the former Annie L. Kenyon. Maybe he observed her greedy attempts in seizing a share of Matthew Kenyon's property and wealth during the divorce. She certainly had no remorse in carrying on an open affair with Gust, which deeply embarrassed her husband. Whatever his reasons, just prior to his own marriage, Lindey transferred to one Charles Waltham of Illinois, all of his property to be held in trust, consisting of numerous lots in Sumas and tracks of Whatcom County land, valued at $3,000.00. Waltham was a protector of sorts, possibly holding Lindey's assets until trusting his own wife. It was fortunate for Lindey.

No doubt Annie had informed Terry of her husband's modest wealth, and the two greedy villians plotted against poor Lindey. Efforts were soon in the works to recover the properties and assets before Annie left her husband.

Months of heavy drinking took a toll on Lindey's mind and body. Slender and underweight to begin with, he was a ghost of a man by early winter. Incapable of retaining any good sense during his binges, and witnessing the doings in his own home, Gust would become agitated and lash out. He attacked his wife and even challenged Jake Terry. But any rebellion by the Swede was met with extreme violence from Terry's fists.

The week before Christmas in 1905, Annie Lindey attempted to file for divorce, and obtain a restraining order against her husband from interfering in her business. Unfortunately, the courts were full due to the coming holidays and were unable to hear her case. It was postponed until December 26.

Meanwhile, the week leading up to Christmas was developing into a powder keg, as Gust was becoming more aggressive from whiskey. Then, on Saturday night, December 23, the keg exploded. While Jake Terry was taking his supper at one of the local saloons, an intoxicated Gust Lindey manhandled Annie, forcing her to flee in search of her lover. Terry would later insist, "she came to me and asked me to protect her from her husband, which, as her agent, I felt it my duty to do. I had to resort to force and the force was in the nature of a knockout blow from my fist, while he had a gun in his hand and was trying to kill me. As a result, I have a broken hand and that is about all there is to the story."

Rushing back to the house, with Annie in tow, Terry caught the drunken man off guard and beat him like a madman. Furniture was broken in the brawl, and during the one-sided battle Terry broke several bones in his right hand. The ordeal ended when Gust was flung through the store's glass picture window and onto the street. Terry would claim he had no choice but to defend Annie.

Terry knew some form of civic repercussion would follow the altercation. His gun hand useless, Terry ran over to the U. S. Saloon and demanded the use of Otis Eslinger's Winchester rifle. At first Eslinger refused, until Terry painfully waved his Colt in his face. Eslinger grudgingly complied. Later, Terry told Whatcom County Sheriff Andrew Williams, "I remained in charge of the store over Sunday and Monday, protecting it and Mrs. Lindey...On that basis I remained in charge until the court's order was issued."

Jake Terry was correct; soon an angry torch-carrying mob appeared in front of the store. The citizens of Sumas had had enough of the "Cowboy" and were poised to toss the ex-convict back across the Canadian line. It was an infuriated mob, calling for the tar and feather treatment, while others shouted for a necktie party. Fearful of Jake Terry in the past, the mob was now bolstered by many of Sumas' civic leaders. These included two city councilmen, Lloyd Smith and John T. Peterson. Prominent merchants Anton Schumacher, and Thomas C. Slaughter fired up the masses by yelling obscenities at Terry. And, Mount Baker Hotel manager M. G. Digman was heard shouting they should lynch Terry.

The mob wanted Jake Terry for themselves, and damn the law. They also demanded Annie Lindey close her store and get out of town. As the rowdiness escalated the terrible side of "Terrible" Jake Terry stepped through the door, his cowboy boots crunched against the broken glass from the window Gust recently flew through. Standing his ground on the porch, Terry's face reflected an eerie flickering orange glow from the men's torches. The "would be" vigilantes' numbers would give them a false sense of courage.

Terry, holding the Winchester's barrel against his shoulder, told the mob to get, if they wished to enjoy Christmas with loved ones. Terry was quick to comprehend, that with all their bravado and boasting of lynching him, and tar and feathering Annie, no one stepped forward to apprehend them. They were afraid! Terry, taking advantage of their cowardice made his move. Lowering the Winchester, he fired off several rounds overheads. Several more bullet heads hit the ground nipping at feet. As the mob scattered in various directions, an evil laughing Terry ran in pursuit firing off a few more rounds.

Roy Franklin Jones[27] remembers the event as follows:

"Then Jake placed a shot close over their heads, one shot above those who ran north toward the depot and one above those who ran south and close enough to the heads that the feathery whir of the slug was heard by each... He sauntered down Railroad Avenue...People were not flocking around. When he got down to Stambaugh's a couple of customers came out...Jake, from ten feet, shot between them. The swinging doors of Stambaugh's never flopped in any faster."

"Over on Cherry [Street], Jake took a turn in Schumacher's store...Schumacher, who had once helped to arrest Jake, wasn't there. When he got to the Mount Baker corner, he shot three times in the gravel, throwing small stones against the Baker [saloon]...Jake shot a couple of slugs down Cherry Street, then turned and blazed away toward Harrison Street in the direction of the town marshal's house. He walked into the Baker where George Hilliard was tending bar. He asked George if he wanted any trouble. The customers had backed up by the far end of the bar. Jake went back and looked them over... and then sauntered out without so much as a glance behind."

Newspapers now referred to the "Cowboy," as "Terrible" Jake Terry. And as "Terrible" Terry held sway in Sumas over Christmas, Marshal Siles watched from the shadows. The following week, Siles told a *Reveille* reporter: "He (Terry) is undoubtedly a bad man, but he isn't looking for trouble, and will not try to bluff a man he knows will not take it. He bulldozes the class that he thinks are afraid of him, but lets alone men he knows to have courage and fighting ability. I have arrested him twice, and was ready to shoot and shoot quick each time...I regard him as a dangerous man."

As the night progressed, some of the discouraged men went home, while others trod back to the saloons to find solace in drink. Fortified once again, they regrouped. A few actually went home for shotguns, others grabbed their sidearms. But in their hearts, they knew they were not killers, and failed to brandish them any further than as lowered barrels.

"Terrible" Terry sat on the store's porch wrapped in a heavy blanket protecting himself from the late December cold wind blowing south from the Fraser River. He mocked the men, calling them cowards. Even with weapons in hand, they were afraid to use them against him. In response, Terry would occasionally fire off a round into the night, and with each report from the Win-

---

[27] Author of *Boundary Town: Early Days in a Northwest Boundary Town*, 1958.

chester, men scrambled for cover. Discouraged, they eventually retreated to bed.

The following morning Sheriff Williams journeyed to Sumas to look into the affair. But no one he encountered was willing to file a complaint or testify in the matter, so no arrests were made. None of the residents of the town seemed anxious to make any statements to Williams regarding trouble with Terry, so the sheriff returned to Bellingham.

Days following the event, news of the Christmas standoff reached newspapers in Idaho, Montana, California, Utah and Nevada: "Jake Terry Keeps Up His Reputation in the Border Town, Licks a Man-Takes Possession of his Store." "Jake Terry is Mixed in the Affair," "Jacob in Role of Protector of Fair Sex." And, "Terrible Terry Comes to Town."

The *Bellingham Reveille* reported: "It appears that the good people of Sumas have heard some of Terry's past history...Terry has helped them to fully realize just how terrible he is by doing some shooting on the streets of the town lately. As a result the marshal...does not appear to be anxious to take the former convict to jail and Jacob was having things all his way at last report."

Whatcom County Sheriff Andrew Williams
made several trips to Sumas to keep the peace.
File photo: *Bellingham Herald*

Court

On December 26, 1905, Annie and Terry traveled to Bellingham to begin divorce proceedings against her husband. Terry was not in the best of humor as a result of the damaging stories that had grown out of his efforts to defend the property, and body of Annie from both Gust Lindey and a vigilante mob.

Appearing in Whatcom County Superior Court, Annie Lindey filed a complaint and affidavit claiming her husband had threatened to do her "great bodily harm and has threatened to kill her, and that if not restrained by the order of this court he will carry said threats into execution."[28]

Annie claimed her husband, "a man of jealous and violent disposition; that he has frequently threatened to kill her, and that he has become so violent and threatening in his attitude toward her that she is afraid he will carry his threats into execution unless he is retrained by an order of this court."[29]

She told Judge Jeremiah Neterer that Gust had struck her with his fists, causing her body to become black and blue. All awhile, he cursed and swore at her, "calling her vulgar names and applying vile epithets too vile to be written in this complaint; that six months ago he struck and beat her." Annie continued, stating recently he falsely insinuated she was having intimate relations with another man, this being of course Jake Terry. Annie told Neterer she was living in fear he will carry out his threats. She said she has only acted in a kind and affectionate manner toward him, and has never given him any cause or reason to treat her so cruelly.

Annie pleaded the court issue a restraining order against Lindey from interfering with her or her property until the marriage could be dissolved. Annie stated since their marriage they have accumulated property to the value of $6,600, and that she has a store purchased with money she had had before the marriage. She asked that the court grant her a divorce with a reasonable amount of alimony and a division of her husband's property.

Judge Neterer, and those attending the hearing, were well aware of the drama in the Lindey home. He gave a sneering glance over toward Terry as he addressed his decision. He would grant the request and sign a restraining order inhibiting Lindey from interfering with Annie's business, but waved his

---

[28] Superior Court of Whatcom County, State of Washington, A. L. Lindey vs. Gust Lindey Civil Case #7728 Order.

[29] Superior Court of Whatcom County, State of Washington, A. L. Lindey vs. Gust Lindey Civil Case #7728 Affidavit.Lindey Civil Case #7728 Order.

decision of divorce and division of assets for a later date.

Clarifying his role to the *Bellingham Herald* as they left the courthouse, Terry stated: "I am agent, or in an unofficial sense, receiver, for Mrs. Lindey's interest. Mrs. Lindey is suing for divorce and is represented by Crites & Romaine and I am her agent in the matter."

Forever putting on the airs of his importance before the press, Terry added: "Yesterday I was with the sheriff in Sumas and he could have arrested me if he had had any [arrest] papers, but no citizen there was willing to swear out a warrant…This evening the sheriff and Mr. (John R.) Crites will accompany me to Sumas, and the affairs of the Lindeys will be settled out of court."

In Sumas that evening, Sheriff Williams served papers to Gust Lindey restraining him from involvement in his wife's store, and personal affairs. The group met in the law office of Charles C. Crouch, Esq., Gust Lindey's Sumas attorney. Crites had papers drawn giving all title of the store to Annie, preventing Gust from any future legal attachment.

Eslinger's Winchester Rifle

After the officers departed, tactics changed within the Lindey household. The two schemers went to work on Gust, plying him heavily with whiskey in attempts to make him sign over all assets and properties to his wife. Terry prevented Gust from leaving the house, and for several days he remained inebriated. Events from this point on are well documented by Crouch: [30]

"On my return from Bellingham shortly after Christmas. Gus Lindey came to my office and said Mrs. Lindey was about to sue him for a divorce and asked me to act as his attorney. I agreed to do so. Shortly afterwards Attorney Crites came to Sumas and all parties, including Terry, came to my office. There a division of property was agreed upon and deeds were drawn from Lindey to his wife and from her to him.

"I supposed everything was settled. Lindey went to a hotel and Terry went to Mrs. Lindey's home where he ate and slept. There the two fixed up a scheme to secure Lindey's property. They got him to come back home and they kept him in a beastly state of intoxication. I notified all the saloons not to sell Lindey liquor and got an attendant for him. Terry got Lindey away from the attendant and filled him up on whiskey. When Lindey was sufficiently drunk they would gather in witnesses and try to get him to deed his property, but I watched them

[30] *Bellingham Herald*, January 12, 1906.

97

too closely and besides, I had the notaries in town pledged not to take Lindey's acknowledgement.

"Finally, Terry gave Lindey some dope in [his] whiskey, and Dr. [Eugene S.] Clark, who was attending Lindey for alcoholism, refused to have anything further to do with the case so long as Terry was around. When I found I could not do anything with Lindey I drew papers to have a guardian appointed for him, as an incompetent, but Judge Neterer has been to busy to hear the application. This application, Crites will resist.

"The city marshal came to me at noon one day and told me that a notary and witnesses had been secured and Lindey and Mrs. Lindey was going to do the same thing. At 7 o'clock that evening I called up the sheriff who telephoned the local officers to arrest Terry and put him in jail. When arrested he offered the officers $5 each to let him go to Mrs. Lindey's and stay...

"I went down to the Lindey place and there I found that the woman had got Lindey out of bed, had him dressed and he sat there with glassy eyes awaiting the notary. Right there I read the riot act to the woman and told her if she did not quit trying to get Lindey to deed over his property, until he got well and in a disposing frame of mind, I'd have her arrested...I saved Lindey's life and his property in the face of Terry's threats..."

It was this little-known endeavor between Crouch and Sheriff Williams that saved Lindey's property and him from certain death. When Williams received the telephone call from Crouch, he said his hands were tied. No laws had yet been broken. Crouch pleaded they had to do something. Then Williams happened to remember when he was in Sumas after Christmas, checking into Terry's shooting spree, he heard the outlaw liberated a Winchester from Otis Eslinger. Terry's demand for Eslinger's rifle was at first refused when Terry next produced a revolver, stating he was a dangerous man. The rifle was relinquished.

Sheriff Williams made nothing of it then, but realized he could have arrested Terry for theft of a firearm. Williams at once telephoned Marshal Siles in Sumas to arrest Terry and hold him until he could remove him to the county jail. By the evening of Monday, January 8, 1906, Terry was held in the small confines of a Sumas cell.

Arriving on the morning train to collect his prisoner, Williams was met at the depot by Dr. Clark. A very concerned Clark advised the sheriff he must take Gust Lindey back with him to a hospital in Bellingham. Lindey was gravely ill and could barely move. Clark believed this had been caused by "dope" force-fed to Gust in large amounts of whiskey. He had ordered Terry and Annie Lindey to stop giving him whiskey, as the man's life was in danger if he continued to drink. They refused his orders.

The sheriff went to the house and found the man collapsed in bed, unable to rise. Sure enough, empty bottles of a "very poor quality of whiske" littered the floor. Williams made the immediate decision to take Lindey and ordered his wife to dress him.

In the meantime, Jake Terry was cuffed and all met at the depot. Terry was brought to the Whatcom County Jail charged with the theft of Eslinger's Winchester rifle. Terry was highly indignant at the charge and declared he would prove his innocence without trouble.

Gust Lindey was placed in St. Luke's Hospital. In grave condition, it was thought the Swede was on death's door. With the greatest care, although weak, Lindey was released a week later.

During a preliminary hearing the following morning, Terry was loud and disruptive in the courtroom in his denunciations of those who were responsible for his arrest. He declared, "I am a persecuted rather than a prosecuted man." Stating, "Officers have for a long time been trying to find something to charge me with and at last hit upon this to bring me to trial."

Represented by Attorney John Crites, Jake Terry was bound over in the amount of $500 to appear before Superior Court. Terry feared a long stay in the county jail, as he knew no one in town who would post his bond. For reasons unclear, Sheriff Williams agreed to escort Terry under his guard to Sumas, where Terry claimed he could raise the $500.

When the two reached Sumas on Thursday, January 11, Terry discovered he had no friends willing to post bond, with the exception of Annie Lindey. Williams refused the offer, fearing instigating further violence. Terry's "gang" or rather those he had bullied and cowedd over the years, ignored him now that he was in custody. Terry gave darting evil stares toward his turncoat friends, warning them he would not be in custody long.

The prisoner was allowed to venture about the city attempting to secure bail in the company of Marshal Siles, while the sheriff attended to other business. It wasn't long before Williams noticed gatherings on the streets and discreet mutterings regarding Terry. The sheriff worried a plot was forming to take charge of his prisoner and initiate rough justice.

Williams wasn't pleased with his escape options. The train was hours away—the open road was potentially hazardous—the local jail could easily be pulled apart, and the sun was rapidly setting. The situation further deteriorated when Williams discovered that Siles had taken Terry over to the Lindey's. Surprisingly, this went unnoticed by the citizens of Sumas. No longer seeing the prisoner with the sheriff, rumor had circulated that Terry had slipped across the border.

Believing Terry had escaped, an angry mob formed at the Lindey home. Wild threats and insults were shouted outside Annie's store. The citizens of Sumas were weary of the way the two had been carrying on and treating Gust. The trouble, reaching a climax when it was discovered Gust was being induced to sign over his property, and that the entire estate was to be turned into cash and divided between the two deviants. Terry had these plans entirely perfected when his arrest came it was said.

Lars Barbo was in the mob with other civic leaders, backed by ordinary townsfolk. He told the *Reveille* later at the time they supposed Jake was across the line, but demanded to see him anyway. When Terry came to the door they were considerably stunned to see him. Terry asked what they wanted. Adopting themselves to the situation as they found it, the men demanded he leave town at once, warning Terry he would be killed if he returned. Again, threats of tar and feather, and a necktie party were shouted toward Terry. Barbo boasted to have been the spokesman of the mob, and in answer to his ultimatum, Terry sneered and beckoned Barbo to come forward. About this time, Sheriff Williams arrived and pulled Terry back through the door into the store.

Placed in a desperate position, Williams asked Terry for his word of honor, if forced to take refuge across the boundary line to protect him from the angry mob, would he comply with his orders. Terry realizing his life, and that of Annie's was at risk, made no effort to deny Williams' authority once in British Columbia. He felt, for the moment he needed all the protection the law could afford him.

Thinking what danger may come Annie's way after they crossed the line, Terry asked the sheriff to see to Annie's protection once across. Williams was impressed that Terry was more concerned for Annie than his own life. Williams promised once he deposited him at the Huntingdon Hotel he would return to make sure Annie wasn't mobbed. When it was time for the train he would come for him.

The sheriff stepped onto the porch and made the mob swear no violence would occur to Terry if he were escorted across the line. He would re-cross later, and return his prisoner to Bellingham once emotions subsided. No one having to lose face; the agreement was accepted. The mob escorted the two a few hundred feet to the line.

Before the train departed from Sumas, Sheriff Williams retrieved Terry and escorted him back across the line. Arriving at the border, Terry began to talk, and "threatened to do some straight shooting if followed." Two Sumas men secured shotguns, but there were no further threats. It was discovered Terry had a gun on him at the time, which someone had given him in Huntingdon. This was collected by Williams.

A *Herald* reporter asked the sheriff later if he had told Terry the mob was there to lynch him. Williams replied, "Terry believed that there was a mob forming to do him violence, and I might have said something of the sort in order to pacify the men (outside), but I believed at the time, and still believe that there was a demonstration of mob-law planned and that I had to get Terry across the line for the sake of his safety."

Williams added after this was done he returned to Sumas and did what he could to quiet the people and keep them from doing violence to the woman.

Jake Terry's excursion to Sumas may have had other intentions beside obtaining his bond, as Otis Eslinger quickly changed his statement. The saloonkeeper now claimed Terry had simply borrowed the rifle. Eslinger told Prosecuting Attorney Virgil Peringer that "Terry had access to the saloon and to everything in it at all times" and that it was not necessary for him to hold up the saloonkeeper in order to get the rifle. The robbery charge was changed to flourishing a weapon in public.[31]

After Jake Terry's arrest, Sumas did turn on Annie Lindey. She was told, in no uncertain terms, it was time for her to leave Sumas. Annie claimed she was being persecuted by merchants who wanted to seize her property. Declaring that some of the people of Sumas had threatened to mob her and force her to leave, On January 11, Annie appeared in Bellingham at the office of Sheriff Williams demanding protection from those threatening to force her out of business, and out of town.

In support of her assertion the mob meant to do her violence, Annie produced a message she had found on her door. Drawn on it was a skull, crossbones and a coffin, with the words: "You are hereby ordered to leave town." She couldn't sleep a wink at night, as she heard shouts outside her window

---

[31] *Bellingham Reveille*, February 3, 1906.

calling for a tar and feather party. She claimed a vigilante meeting had been held to promote violence against her. She had been so frightened she had hired two men to guard the house.

Attorney Crites, after hearing her story, was sent into a rage, inducing the sheriff to accompany Annie to Sumas and make an investigation of the affair. Crites, defended Annie in the newspapers stating:

"These men, were afraid to attack Terry as a gang, to say nothing of meeting him individually, and then, in real, heroic courage, held secret meetings and resorted to the brave plan adopted by the 'black hand highbinders' and other socialites for an onslaught against a defenseless woman, and just to show that they were giving her a 'square deal' and had no fear of her, posted the death mark, the symbol of their order on Mrs. Lindey's door, to warn her that unless she quit town she would be made the mark for the wrath of this powerful and humane society organized for the purpose of furthering the best interests of Sumas...it is also suggested that they might take her to the city limits and tell her to 'get' or they might even horsewhip her publicly."

Lars Barbo lashed out in reply in the *Sumas News* the following day. He said Sumas was enraged at Mrs. Lindey's statements calling them "preposterous and untruthful." Barbo went on to write that the citizens of Sumas, "... reached a strong feeling of resentment...found themselves characterized as 'drunken rowdies,' as 'cowards' or as persons who for 'business reasons' were persecuting a defenseless woman, their denunciations of such reckless statements were couched in the strongest language."

Rumors flew that Annie had succumbed. She would dispose of her stock and goods at once and take the first train for Minnesota.

After one of his countless trips to Sumas over the affair, Sheriff Williams claimed, "Annie's decision to leave Sumas has met universal approval...The woman admits that she has done things that are not altogether right and proper in the eyes of the world, and in view of the fact that she will probably find it impossible to continue her business there with profit has come to the conclusion that for the benefit of her business as well as for her good health it is well for her to depart."

But would Annie really go?

On February 2, Crites decided he would take pity on his client and put up the bond for his release. Crites drew up an application asking that Terry be allowed release on a $250 bond. Prosecutor Peringer, who lost his witness on the charge of robbery, allowed the bond offered. Terry was released until the next jury term in May.

On release, Terry told the *Herald* "he had doubts, but that he will get the worst of the matter when his case comes to trail." When asked if he would return to Sumas, "Terrible" Terry didn't answer, but indicated he would leave for Vancouver. Before leaving on the train north Terry said, "he will be on deck when his trail is called and that he will prove that he is right, even if he does not get a square deal at the hands of the jury..." When the court term came in May 1906, "Terrible" Jake Terry never showed his face. And, defense attorney John R. Crites, lost his bond.

The next thirteen months remained quiet. To the best of anyone's knowledge, Jake Terry remained on Canadian soil, taking up his residence at the Huntingdon Hotel, in view of Sumas.

Terry would often come to the border, but never ventured across, as the citizens of Sumas threatened Annie would receive harsh treatment if he did. Terry would hand off letters to the customs officer to give Annie. Annie, would often venture over and visit her lover.

During this quiet spell, Annie traveled to Minneapolis to visit relatives, and met Jake Terry there. After a short sojourn, she returned to Sumas, and with her came the notorious Jake as far as the boundary line.

As for her little notions store, Annie didn't close it, but kept her business running. Rumors circulated Annie was supporting Terry. Terry was slowing down, and claimed not the man he used to be. Another rumor had it Jake Terry laundered stolen money through the store. It was speculated he had loot from the Canadian train robbery, and other ventures hidden away. Any of the rumors wouldn't have been far-fetched. Terry had never been known to hold a job, so where did his money come from? It's hard to believe the little notions store could support anyone at this point.

Fifth of July, 1907. A Day of Reckoning

Sumas was a sleepy town the day after the Fourth of July. As it was a Friday, some folks took the extra day for a longer weekend; while others got up and went to work as usual. Visitors slept in as there was no rush taking the afternoon train. No doubt, many suffered from hangovers.

The border inspector saw Jake Terry coming down from the Huntingdon Hotel. Terry probably had some letters to hand over for Annie. But today the routine would be different, Terry would cross the line. About 10 o'clock that morning, the men greeted one another at the line. Terry inquired about the other's holiday. The inspector questioned if Terry thought it sensible to visit Sumas, he still had a warrant out for his arrest. Terry looked across the line toward Boundary Street and said he was up to no trouble. He thought he would see some of his old buddies down at the U. S. Saloon. Annie had given him a five-dollar gold piece on her last visit and thought he'd setup the bar.

Few people hung about the street. Terry actually moved about unnoticed. In the saloon, some of his "old gang" were sitting amongst the card tables, and were surprised to see the old man walk in.

"Terrible" Terry put the gold piece on the bar and told the boys to drink up. Bartender La Bounty was on duty and started setting up drinks. Once the money ran out, Terry ran a tab and continued to drink. Around noon he told the boys he'd go over to Annie's store and get more money. Standing to leave, Terry was told that Gust Lindey was at home, and he'd had better not go. He gave a chuckling grunt, and proceeded to the swinging doors stating, he would put Lindey across his knee and spank him until he cried, if he gave him trouble. Several of the saloon customers later stated how Terry bragged how easy it was for him to get money from Mrs. Lindey.

"Where you going, Jake?" Terry was asked on the street by a passerby. "You know damn well where I'm going," he replied. "Gust is home," he heard. "Then I'll take the little bastard across my knee and spank him."[32]

Just after the noon hour, Terry walked down Front Street and into the notions store to find Annie in front. He asked Annie for a cigar. Lindey was in the sitting room, the door slightly ajar from the store. Terry made a sarcastic remark in reference to her husband, perhaps about the spanking. He may have suspected Gust was listening.

Gust immediately stepped through the door confronting Terry. Instantly, the two adversaries commenced to quarrel. Gust informed Jake he had better get across the line or he would get the marshal. Terry laughed at him, and the two exchanged further angry words. Terry, with a big smile on his face, swore at the Swede, calling him a "square head" and a cowardly little man. Advancing toward Gust, he threatened to take him over his knee and spank his ass red. Gust backed off into the sitting room. This only emboldened, Terry now in pursuit of the little man. According to one story, Terry started to whip Lindey

---

[32] State of Washington v. Gust Lindey, Virgil Peringer #753 Affidavit, Oct 5, 1907.

and the latter ran into the rear of the building.

Annie, in an affidavit stated, "I could see that Terry had been drinking, and concluded from his appearance and actions that there would be some serious trouble, and I became very frightened, ran out of the store onto the street to procure help. I went into the barbershop immediately north of my store. When I got there (some forty or fifty feet distant) I heard a report of a pistol or gun in the direction of the store." [33]

Gust had a .38 caliber H&R revolver lying on top of the bedroom bureau, just inside the door. Terry must have known Gust was retrieving something, as the bedroom was a dead-end. Terry's last known words were, "Now I will fix you!"

Gust Lindey reached out and clutched the grip of the revolver, cocked the hammer back and spun around toward Terry, now in fast pursuit. The outlaw must have been nearly on top of him, as Lindey crossed the threshold of the bedroom. There was no opportunity for Gust to fully extend his arm before discharging the weapon.

The first bullet entered Terry's right upper jaw ranging upward into the brain, cutting an artery in its path. The powder burns on Terry's face indicate the muzzle of the revolver being very close, perhaps touching his face. Circumstances further indicate a second shot followed the first in rapid succession, and that Terry's head had turned slightly. The second bullet entered his left temple spouting blood onto the door of the bedroom, and across the floor of the sitting room. Terry fell lifelessly backward, his feet remaining inside the bedroom, as his head and shoulders extended into the sitting room.

William W. King, who was passing by, met Lindey a short distance from the door, as he came out of the store. "I fixed him. Don't you think I did about right," asked Lindey. King entered the store. He found Terry gasping in the throes of death. He spoke to Terry, but the latter made no response. La Bounty and Louis Wulf, the barber whom Annie ran to, came running.

Jess Corbin was inspecting the tracks at the depot, across the way. Customs Officer Fred Strickling was on his way for some lunch when he stopped to chat with Corbin. They stopped talking when they noticed "Terrible" Terry entering the store. The men expected a show, but received more than they expected. "Oh, here we go again," said Corbin when they heard shouts from inside. Then, all of a sudden two shots rang out. "I was sure surprised when I saw that it was

[33] State of Washington vs Gust Lindey, Mrs. Lindsey #753 Affidavit, Oct 5, 1907.

105

Gus who came out." said Strickling. "That told the story for me. I knew, without saying a word to Gus that Sumas had a good day." Strickling then walked into the store to see Lindey's handy work. "I stepped in and Terry was rolling in the dining room floor with blood spurting from both temples."[34] Shortly after, Annie slowly walked back into her store. She looked down at Jake and said, "Mr. Lindey shot Mr. Terry while I was over at the barber shop." Strickling just looked on the scene before him.

Roy Franklin Jones remembered seeing a great crowd of people forming. "Ted Thomas came running from the fringe of the crowd. "I see him, I see him," he yelled at us. "Go up to the front window, you can see his feet." Jones said the marshal allowed the boys to get a quick look of the outlaw.

William Sorensen was a little boy, whose family moved to Sumas from Clayburn, B. C. in 1905. He'd never seen such excitement as he had in that little border town. Sorensen saw the other boys run to the window. "I was one of the first to see Terry on the floor dead. Then my dad caught me and sent me home."[35]

Jake Terry, Train Robber and Smuggler, Killed.
American Evening and Morning Reveille, July 5, 1907

[34] Letter from Fred Strickling to Roy Jones, from Vancouver, Washington, September 10, 1956.
[35] Letter from William Sorensen to Roy Jones, from Everett, Washington, January 12, 1959.

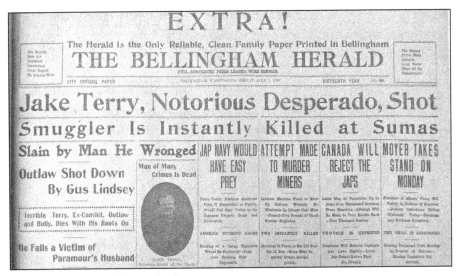

Jake Terry, Notorious Desperado, Shot.
Bellingham Herald, Extra edition, July 5, 1907

After the shooting, Gust left the house surrendering himself to Marshal Siles. He told the marshal he had shot Jake Terry. He had fired two shots, but thought only one had taken effect. Terry was not able to speak, but was grasping for breath, and within a few minutes died. Siles told Lindey to report to Justice of the Peace, John P. Knuehmann.

Marshal Siles entered the store by now filling with gawkers. Knuehmann soon arrived and took charge ordering the marshal to deputize Orange Hopkins. Hopkins was told to watch over the body until the sheriff and coroner arrived. No one was allowed to touch the body. Meanwhile, seeing an opportunity, Annie started selling her wares.

Dr. C. E. Martin, acting coroner, together with Whatcom County Attorney Virgil Peringer and Sheriff Williams, arrived a few hours later to open an investigation. When Williams entered the notions store he found a crowd around Terry's body. Disgusted by the scene, he ordered Annie to close her business until the corpse was removed. Williams then made arrangements for Terry's removal to Gillies' Hardware Store, where an autopsy was performed behind the front window in full view of the public. The procedure took a macabre turn when a borrowed handsaw was used to open Terry's skull to extract the bullets.

Peringer recalled their findings later in an affidavit before the court:

"The deceased when found by the coroner and myself a few hours after the shooting, was lying with his feet at the sofa near the bedroom door, and his body extending at right angles from the sofa... lying on his back. There was very little blood escaping from the wound in the left temple, but a great deal of blood flowed from the wound in the right jaw."

Peringer continued: "A post mortem was given by Dr. Martin, with assistance by Dr. Clark, which resulted in finding both bullets in the brain. The first bullet entered the outlaw's head and lodged in the brain, from the right side, a hole being found directly in front of the ear. The second bullet, went through the left temple, and also lodged in the brain. Either shot would have been fatal, as the examination showed both bullets were located in vital spots. Blood spouted from the wound, as gory spots were found on a pillow slip on a lounge in the room. Where he fell there was a great pool of red, as the outlaw bled profusely from his wounds and the room presented a stinking sight to the officers."

Upon Terry's person was found a dozen or so letters from Annie, which were addressed, "My Dear Darling," and were full of sentimental language. In one of these was a photograph of Annie. These were placed in Sheriff Williams' possession. Terry had only a few pieces of silver, a gold signet ring and a gold watch on him at the time of his death. The body was left in the charge of an undertaker in Sumas where Terry was placed on display. Later, Terry was transported to Bellingham where several hundred visitors lined the A. L. Maulsby morgue for glimpse.

Burning Love Letters Found on Outlaw.
American Evening and Morning Reveille, July 6, 1907

The *Bellingham Herald* and *Sumas News* had their own take regarding the body of the outlaw:

"To the phrenologist the corpse should be an object of great interest. The head is one of the most peculiar ever seen in the morgues of this city, with its low retreating forehead, bushy eyebrows and dropping mustache. That Terry was a degenerate can be seen by the shape of his skull. A close examination of the body of the dead man has revealed several scars, evidently left by bullet wounds, indicating that Terry has felt the sting of lead before. Another feature has come to light in the shooting of the outlaw that makes it apparent that Mrs. Lindey bore more than ordinary interest affection for Terry."

Gust Lindey was charged with murder in the first-degree having to answer at the next term of the Superior Court in September. He was expected to plea, self-defense and the "unwritten law"[36] for the killing of Jake Terry. Lindey was given a half-hearted preliminary hearing before Justice of the Peace John Knuehmann, at Sumas. The court was a circus with jubilation and celebration over the death of the outlaw. It was all Knuehmann could do to maintain order.

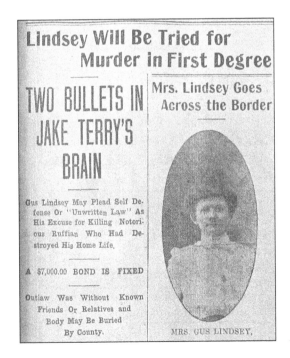

Lindsey Will Be Tried for Murder in First Degree

TWO BULLETS IN JAKE TERRY'S BRAIN

Mrs. Lindsey Goes Across the Border

Gus Lindsey May Plead Self De- fense Or "Unwritten Law" As His Excuse for Killing Notori- ous Ruffian Who Had De- stroyed His Home Life.

A $7,000.00 BOND IS FIXED

Outlaw Was Without Known Friends Or Relatives and Body May Be Buried By County.

MRS. GUS LINDSEY,

Gust Lindey must be tried for murder. But nothing would come of it.
Bellingham Herald, July 6, 1907

[36] The "unwritten law" being the right of an individual to avenge wrongs against personal or family honor.

Newspapers claimed, "Mrs. Lindsey appeared to be affected very little by the tragic affair." While the preliminary hearing of her husband was in progress Annie slipped across the border into Huntingdon. She stated she would return in time for the trial, but did not care to be subjected to the scrutiny of her neighbors in the meantime.

Virgil Peringer called only three witnesses at the hearing. Dr. Martin, testified as to the death of Terry and the nature of his wounds. He was followed by William King and the barber, Louis Wulf. And then the state rested.

Russ S. Lambert appeared for Lindey, but aside from making a few motions to perfect the record, he did and said nothing. Still a hefty $7,000 bond was placed on Lindey. Within the hour, Sumas merchants C. E. Moulton, George W. Bockling, Frank Hayworth, D. B. Lucas and William Gerstberger posted the bond and he was released at once.

The *Bellingham Herald* headlined, "Two Bullets In Jake's Terry's Brain" the following day. The *Morning Reveille*, "Notorious Jake Terry Bites the Dust." The story led most of the newspapers west of the Mississippi, and continued so as additional details were released on the wire. "Jake Terry, Notorious Desperado, Shot," "Smuggler is Instantly Killed at Sumas," "Outlaw Shot Down By Gus Lindsey Slain by Man He Wronged" and "Terrible Terry, Ex-Convict, Outlaw and Bully, Dies With His Boots On."

An editorial in the *Bellingham Herald* on July 6, 1907 summed up Terry's life best:

"He lived too long, and there is a certain grim justice in the manner of his death. Holding life cheaply, he had successfully played the role of bully...That, after having intimidated courageous men for years, he should meet death at the hands of an inoffensive, peace-loving, craven-spirited individual seems peculiarly fitting, not to say ironical. He is the last of the notorious gang that once engaged in smuggling and train robbery. He lived the life of an outlaw even after his pals had cashed in their checks or quit the business, and he died as he had lived. The death of Jake Terry brings to a close the career of a man who is the last one of the worst gangs that ever infested the country. He was an all-around bad man, a hard drinker; a man to whom laws meant nothing but something to be broken; a gambler, and one who cared nothing for human life."

On Monday, July 8, 1907 without mourners or even a crowd of morbid curiosity seekers in attendance, "Cowboy" the later "Terrible" Jake Terry, was buried in the Bellingham Bayview Cemetery's potter's field by Undertaker Maulsby. He wore the same suit of clothes and clad in the boots in which he died.

Lindey's Trial

On October 5, 1907, Gust Lindey sat in the Whatcom County courtroom charged with murder. A hearing was underway to determine if a trial was indeed warranted. Attorneys Russ S. Lambert and James B. Abrams representing Lindey, sat beside him. The men were prepared for a fight if needed, but worried little. It was obvious by all in the courtroom this was going to be a showcase of a hearing.

Several witnesses stated that prior to the death of Jake Terry, on more than one occasion he threatened to kill the defendant. All those taking the stand testified Terry was in the habit of carrying a revolver and known to be a dangerous man.

Finally, Virgil Peringer addressed the court:

"If called to trial the defense would be able to show conclusively that the deceased...was proceeding to make an attack upon the defendant. That he was a larger and stronger man.

"That the facts herein set forth...and from all the circumstances surrounding the killing of the deceased, affiant believes that it would be impossible for the State to sustain a conviction...therefore supports motion to dismiss."

With that, the case against Gust Lindey ended.

"Terry Slayer Sues for Divorce"

On Thursday, September 24, 1908, Gust Lindey started a suit for divorce from his wife on the grounds of desertion. Lindey stated that as of March 17, 1908, his wife no longer lived at home, but left for Minnesota to stay with relatives.

Attorneys Russ Lambert and Henry M. White worked the Lindey suit as they would any other, but in the process of discovery they unearthed some questionable inconsistencies, some provided by Annie herself. These were not shared with the public. Judge Edward E. Hardin, for the moment would delay the suit and refused to grant a motion declaring the marriage null and void. Instead, Hardin indicated that papers in the case had been sent east for verification, but believed they contained some highly sensational allegations. Being a highly-publicized suit, due to the Terry affair, reporters were mystified by the delay.

On Saturday, January 16, 1909, the Sumas saga took a shocking twist. It developed during the trial that Terry's true name was Jacob Walker. The same Jacob Walker who married Annie when she was just 16 years of age. When this was produced as evidence the judge signed the decree of divorce asked for by Lindey.

The *Bellingham Herald* morning edition:

"The developments in the case bring to light one of the most peculiar romances in the Northwest and clear the question of why Mrs. Lindey was on such friendly terms with Terry for several years prior to the killing of the border bandit by Gust Lindey, with whom she was living. Lindey himself did not know that the two had been married until some time after he had killed Terry."

A marriage certificate, placed on file at the courthouse, proved Jacob Walker and Miss Annie Sickles were wedded at Chittenango, New York, June 8, 1881. The license was produced by Annie after Lindey had shot Terry. She was in favor of a divorce and for that reason revealed the certificate, which she had kept from Lindey during Terry's escapades in Washington and British Columbia.

As Annie told it, Terry was a young man when he wooed her. They were wed just a short time, when Terry got into some trouble. He was tried and sent to the penitentiary for a number of years. Annie decided to go West, away from the humiliating circumstances she was thrown into.

After Terry's term expired she tried to find some trace of her husband, but could not. Annie was married again in Sumas, and found herself involved in domestic infelicities.

The Sumas saga takes a shocking twist during the Lindey divorce hearing, when Annie produced an 1881 certificate of marriage, claiming Terry her husband. Courtesy of the Northwest Regional Branch Washington State Archives

Annie Lindey did not participate at the divorce proceedings, nor did she hire counsel to represent her. Numerous summons were sent to Minneapolis, with no response. Finally, in October 1908, a response to the summons was answered by a notary public for the State of Nebraska. Annie would not come back to Washington, nor would she contest Lindey. She was apparently embarrassed enough. The fact the letter came from Nebraska, and not Minneapolis, suggests even Annie's relatives perhaps had had enough of her.

Judge Hardin might had sworn out a warrant on Annie Lindey for bigamy, but if Jacob Walker was actually the outlaw, "Terrible" Jake Terry, it made little difference now. The people of Sumas, and all of Whatcom County were tired of Jake Terry and the Lindeys and happy to be done with them. Judge Hardin declared the Lindey marriage null and void, whether it was valid or not to start.

If true, Jake Terry and Jacob Walker were one the same, then why did he claim Missouri as his home? Was he a cowboy in Texas, and was Terry in Washington Territory in 1873?

After 1909, Annie I. Lindey disappears from the written record. Perhaps she remarried and remade herself.

As for Gust Lindey, he remained in Sumas living alone in a two-story build-ing near the boundary line. On June 5, 1937, he failed to appear for his daily excursion on the streets of Sumas. His absence, noticed by members of the U. S. border patrol, who knew his daily routine, investigated and found the doors and windows of his house locked. Forcing open a window they entered the building and found the aged man dead in bed due to natural causes. He was 82 years old. Many years after the shooting Lindey was listed in a newspaper land transfer column. Beside his name in parentheses was written, Gust Lindey, "Hero of Sumas."

Chapter 4
All Night Wrangle

Frank T. Walker felt he had finally established himself when he built a crude farmhouse on the Everson-Goshen Road in September 1909. It was a small frame house, with a large open first floor, a side room and two bedrooms in the loft, but it had a strong roof for his 27-year-old wife Lottie and their ten-year-old son, Jesse to sleep under. Walker was born in Collinsville, Oklahoma in 1881 and was living there when he met and married his Indiana wife. They were still in Oklahoma in 1899 when Jesse was born.

The Deming Road, circa 1900s. Laura Jacoby's, Galen Biery collection

Walker may have decided to relocate to Whatcom County, as his 46-year-old mother, Mrs. Anna Belle Kerns had moved to Washington State several years prior. It would be good to have the family close again, and Anna Belle could see her grandson grow. Anna Belle's first husband was living in Collinsville, Oklahoma. She had remarried to Frank Kerns, 19 years her senior in 1901. They fought ever since due to his jealousy of her youth. The jealousy drove a wedge into their lives making it a miserable existence for both. Anna Belle might have considered a divorce, but didn't want a second ex-husband. From her first marriage, Anna had one daughter, Mrs. Amy Mount of Collinsville, Oklahoma, and three sons: James, residing in Texas; Walt of Long Mount;,Colorado; and Frank.

The Kerns' history is sketchy, but Anna Belle appears by all accounts a hardworking, levelheaded woman of intelligence. She undoubtedly possessed immeasurable fortitude for both harsh living, and against emotional mental strain, as evidenced by her second husband's cruel and demanding nature.

Between 1908 and 1909, Anna Belle worked as cook and laundress at the newly formed Lifesaving (Coast Guard) Station on Neah Bay. This isolated lifesaving facility was first established on Waaddah Island in 1908, consisting of a single "white keeper" George W. McAfee, and was comprised of an all Native-American crew. Disaster struck shortly after the station opened when on November 19, 1908 two "surfmen" drowned in a boating accident during a fierce storm. The incident closed the station for a short time. Then two years later the facility was moved to the mainland after large waves had destroyed its boat rails.

Frank Kerns would not join his wife in Neah Bay. Why the fiercely jealous man willingly let her go and not follow her is unknown, other than at the time he was employed in Bellingham and may have been too stubborn to relocate. Instead, he was furious she took the position and being excessively jealous, accused her of having numerous sexual affairs while at the station. When the station closed, Anna Belle returned to Bellingham on Thursday, November 25 and moved in with her son's family. Then on Saturday, December 11, the miserable sixty-five-year-old Kerns moved in as well, upsetting the harmony of the Walker household. Until a month prior he was unemployed and living in Everson.

Kerns needled his wife all awhile about her stay in Neah Bay. Frank Walker was accustomed to the couple's constant bickering, and tried to stay out of their arguing. Kerns accused Anna Belle of being intimate with another man. George McAfee, being the only "white man" at the station may have been the likely target of his jealousy. Anna Belle had been able to placate her husband

and ignore his tantrums, but everything turned dark and ominous when Kerns discovered Anna Belle was offered, and accepted, a cooking position at a logging camp east of Maple Falls. She was to depart on Tuesday morning. This did not sit well with Kerns, touching off serious hostilities in the Walker home.

All weekend Kerns became increasingly obsessed to the point of madness, fighting with Anna Belle, claiming she only wanted to be away from him so she could pursue illicit encounters with other men. Why Frank Walker put up with his miserable stepfather abusing his mother is unknown, but as the weekend continued toward a climactic tragedy we can only guess it was complacency, fear of the old man or his ignorance of the growing situation. In such a confined space one would think Lottie would have put her foot down for her son's sake.

Monday dawned with the couple arguing heavily. Anna Belle was to leave the next day and Kerns was making a fight of it. He threatened to kill his wife and took away a rusty old .38 caliber pocket revolver given to her by her son for protection while at the lifesaving station. The dispute continued throughout the day and well into Monday night. During the afternoon, the old man visited several of Walker's neighbors complaining his wife was deserting him to go whoring with the loggers. He said he knew of this, as why else would she live alone with the men of the lifesaving crew at Neah Bay. He declared this time around, he would not permit her to go to Maple Falls to work. Walker's neighbors, not knowing who this madman was, would later declare his "actions decidedly queer."

Monday evening Kerns started right in quarreling after supper. This time he accused his wife of being intimate with the native crewmembers of the lifesaving station. He egged her on regarding "bedding the Red-Man." Throughout the night the two quarreled relentlessly, allowing the Walkers very little sleep. Frank and Lottie failed to get involved. Possibly because the elder couple was staying for such a short time, and with Anna Belle leaving in the morning, Kerns would leave as well.

Early morning, Lottie was the first to rise while Frank continued to sleep in. She left her warm bed about five o'clock and came down the rough stairway, built a fire, and proceeded to make breakfast. A short time before six, Anna Belle, Frank Kerns and Jesse Walker arose and came down the ladder from the loft. The two soon took up their quarrel, which had kept them awake through the night. Anna Belle, worn down and exasperated, stepped out into the backyard trying to get away from her husband. Kerns, not letting her go, followed his wife outside. Moments later, an agonizing scream was heard, followed by a gunshot. "Only the surrounding trees heard what was said just before Kerns leveled a revolver at his wife's head and fired," said the *American Reveille* the following day. "The first shot fired outside the house cut the quarrel short. The woman fled to the house pursued by the infuriated man." The bullet apparently grazed her head.

Lottie heard the scream and started up the steps to the loft above, where her husband was just dressing. She was only half-way up the ladder when Anna Belle raced into the house screaming, blood running from her head. She managed to reach the bottom of the steps and hastily started to climb up as her daughter-in-law, reached the top. Lottie turned around, looking down and yelled for her to hurry. Kerns, at that moment, was directly behind his wife leveling the revolver. Unfazed by what he was doing, Kerns fired the last fatal shots. Jesse Walker was in the room at the time, standing directly behind the old man as he did the shooting. The boy shrieked grabbing the arm of his step-grandfather, seeking to prevent him from harming his grandmother.

Anna Belle's footing slipped from the ladder rung landing on the floor. She turned sharply facing her pursuer just as two bullets slammed into her right breast and another penetrating her left temple as her head turned. Perhaps she was avoiding the sight of her husband pulling the trigger at the last moment. Kerns was so close to his wife when he fired the shots that the right sleeve of her waistcoat burned off from the exploding powder, along with a scorched bit of waistcoat over her heart where two slugs entered. One leaden bullet passed through the middle of her back, spraying blood on the rungs to the ladder. Lottie, witnessing the slaughter from above, screamed at the top of her lungs as blood spewed from her mother-in-law's head. As his wife fell dead in a heap at the foot of the loft, Kerns paused for a moment, starring in sheer disbelief at what he had done. Lottie, from the loft, "shrieked and wailed." Jesse stood immobile inches from his grandmother's corpse, as blood flowed toward his bare feet. Before Walker could get out of the bedroom and reach Kerns the latter had fled out the door.

Chaos, had visited the quaint little home Frank Walker so proudly built with his own hands. As he looked down at the murder scene below, Walker was dismayed to see the bloodied corpse of his mother as life twitched out of it. The bullet to her head was merciful, as it left her skull and face intact. Jesse had backed away from his grandmother not taking his eyes from her. Walker didn't pursue the madman, instead racing to the nearest neighbor owning a telephone. He was gasping to breathe, asking them to place the call, as he couldn't speak.

Whatcom County Sheriff Spencer B. Van Zandt received the call, and went directly to the scene of the tragedy with Deputy Sheriff Wallace Coleman. Coroner N. Whitney Wear was notified by the lawmen before their departure, and was also in route. When the officers arrived at the little house, Kerns had not been seen again. Neighbors claimed a faint crack was heard from the nearby woods a half-hour after the killing. While it was believed Kerns possibly ended his life, it was also feared he fired a shot to discourage pursuit. When the sheriff, reinforced by deputies and a neighbor knowing the lay-of-the-land, ascertained the direction in which the shot had been heard, the pose followed a faint trail made by the old man along a rail fence. With their revolvers drawn they entered the underbrush.

The wet grasses and brush showed a trail where Kerns crept along, until

Whatcom County Sheriff Spencer B. Van Zandt. File photo: *Bellingham Herald*

he arrived at a thick clump of young trees. "This is dangerous," Van Zandt told his men. "Kerns could very well be hidden within the trees. He may be alive and had second thoughts about giving up." A few feet into the brush the old man was sighted sitting upright against a log. At a distance it seemed as though he had sat down for a rest. Van Zandt called out for Kerns to give himself up. The man by the log was motionless.

As the sheriff and his deputies closed in they could see Kerns was in fact dead. He evidently sat down on a partly burned log, bracing his back up against the timber, placed the barrel of the gun to a spot just below, and a little to the rear of his right ear, and pulled the trigger. The bullet was sent plowing through his brain and out through the neck. The rusty revolver lay at his feet. Van Zandt reached down and picked the weapon up to examine it. He opened the cylinder of the revolver to discover that the dead man had indeed reloaded, but it had failed twice in his efforts to end his life. Two shells had been struck by the pin, but failed to explode.

When Coroner Wear arrived moments later a small dog belonging to a neighboring family was jumping around in front of the lifeless corpse, seeking to draw attention by his antics. Wear looked over the killer's body and went back to the house. There he spoke to the family about the events of the morning.

Walker told the story of the vile weekend. Kerns had threatened to kill his mother and he also threatened to kill Walker if he got in the way. Walker declared his stepfather was of a jealous disposition and that the couple had quarreled ever since their wedding eight years before. The facts of the tragedy were so apparent that Coroner Wear decided an inquest was unnecessary. Wear, in a cynical tone told an *American Reveille* reporter: "The old man, half crazy and laboring under the belief that his wife was not faithful to him, had killed her and then saved a whole lot of trouble for the sheriff and other county officers by taking his own life." Coroner Whitney Wear, after looking more carefully into the evidence in the case concluded the old man was "cranky" and "became over-excited about some little trifle."

Taking statements, Sheriff Van Zandt asked Jesse what he saw. The eleven-

Suicide Follows Murder. *Bellingham Herald*, January 14, 1909

year old gave a rather incoherent account of the tragedy owing to his excited condition. He said when his grandparents came down from the loft, his grandfather was trying to kiss his grandmother, but she didn't like that and pushed him away. She refused and told him she intended never to kiss him again. The grandfather retorted, "this was better so, as she did not love me anymore anyway."

The sheriff visited Kerns' former employer to trace any mental condition, as his work record was very spotty. Years before Kerns worked as a "tinner" by profession for Munro & Haskell, in Bellingham. Henry L. Munro claimed those who were acquainted with Kerns agree that he was often unbalanced mentally. "Kerns never was just right when he worked for us," said Munro.[37] "We never could get any satisfaction out of him and never relied upon him in any work to any great extent. He told us that he used to be in the habit of drinking heavily and that during sprees he used to go home and temporarily break up housekeeping and everything else about his house."

"He talked that way often to the boys and we always credited his peculiarity to this habit. He always acted queerly. I never did think he was just right in the head. It's the first thing I thought of when I read the news of the murder and suicide."

Van Zandt closed the case citing, "Jealousy is declared to have been the cause of the murder and suicide. Insanity is ascribed to Frank Kerns whoseshot broke his own neck." The sheriff concluded, "the murderer became excited in an altercation with the woman, went mad, and in his mania committed the double deed."

The couple left no money or worldly possessions. Kerns had $40 in his pocket, a membership card of the Local Sheet Metal Workers International Alliance. Personal effects included one silver watch, one razor, and two guns all turned over to county treasurer. Kern's body was turned over to Mock & Hill Mortuary at 1055 Elk Street to be buried in the potter's field at Bellingham's Bayview Cemetery on Monday December 20.

The body of Anna Belle Kerns was also taken to Mock & Hill, where Frank Walker came into the city to purchase his mother's coffin and made arrangements for her burial. On Wednesday, December 15 the coffin carrying the dead woman was shipped from Noon Station on the Bellingham Bay & British Columbia railway to Everson for services at the Presbyterian Church, then buried at Nooksack Cemetery.

[37] *American Reveille*, Deed of Insane Man, Friday, October 16, 1916.

Chapter 5
Mrs. Pinkerton

Fisherman Sanford Shin died at three o'clock in the afternoon on Monday, October 16, 1916. He died of a self-inflicted bullet wound to the head bringing to a close the most gruesome tragedy in the City of Blaine since the 1907 slaying of Addie Roper. Sheriff Wilson Stewart was convinced almost to a certainty that Shin killed his housekeeper, Mrs. Emma Pinkerton a week earlier, packed her body into her own steamer trunk and dropped it into the harbor, but he couldn't prove it. If true, Stewart was absent a corpse and his only suspect was now dead.

Blaine, 1911. Courtesy of Bill Becht, Horseshoe Coins & Antiques, Blaine, WA.

Ten months earlier, Mrs. Emma Pinkerton, 70 years of age, came to Blaine from Seattle thinking it would be where she would spend the rest of her days. Stanford Shin, a single and potentially lonely man, having read and answered her advertisements for housekeeping work in a Seattle newspaper, made arrangements for her to work and board at his home. It was noted shortly thereafter that the two did not get along as well as hoped. Neighbors would overhear arguments emanating from the household. Mrs. Pinkerton told neighbors Shin had threatened her life on several occasions if she didn't leave. Shin clearly wanted her out of his house, but Mrs. Pinkerton refused to leave, stating they had an arrangement and she had sold all her belongings in Seattle to come to Blaine to work for Shin. He also owed her back wages, her sole income each month. She reminded Shin of her advanced age and that there was no alternative but to stay, as she had no relatives or a place to go. Besides, how would it look for Shin to toss an old woman onto the street?

The public perception of throwing an old woman out undoubtedly troubled Shin. Not knowing where to turn, Shin petitioned Whatcom County officials to provide financial support and a place for his housekeeper to live, whom he declared he was not responsible for. This was denied. Mrs. Pinkerton was interviewed by county officials and it was found she was indeed without finances, but desired to remain at the Shin home, until her wages were paid off for fear of losing them. She proved to officials she was keeping up with the cleaning and doing the cooking, earning her keep as agreed. Months prior, she also applied to county authorities for help and was told she could force Shin to pay her wages by court order. Why she did not follow through with the suggestion remains unknown.

Mrs. Pinkerton Takes a Trip

Over the following months neighbors heard the couple constantly engaged in verbal combat and bickering. It may not have helped that Shin was nearly deaf, making their arguments all the more intense. Loud banging resonated from inside and on multiple occasions Shin was witnessed by neighbors storming from the house presumably to cool down or drowned his anger at the local bar. Then, on Tuesday evening, October 10, Shin walked over to his neighbor, W. C. Cronister's home and asked to borrow a wheelbarrow stating he had a heavy object to move. Around 6 o'clock the following morning Shin was seen hunched over wheeling a steamer trunk wrapped in a quilt along the corner of Fourth and E Streets, leading directly toward the waterfront. He passed several walkers along the way offering a cheerful smile and a hardy "Hello, Good Morning," while strolling along his way. He was asked once or twice if he needed a hand, to which he declined stating he had not far to go.

Later it was thought, Shin placed rocks inside the trunk to help it sink before taking it to the dock. Witnesses would declare the trunk seemed unusually heavy. In fact, Shin staggered, hunched over under its weight and was forced to pause frequently for rest. Shin had his fishing boat at the end of a dock extension. The *Blaine Journal* printed later, "It should be remembered that there was a heavy fog these mornings" meaning he was soon out of sight after launching into the mist. Shin was seen loading the trunk aboard his little fishing boat, then rowing from the dock. He was gone for about two hours. On Saturday, he cheerfully appeared at a local second-hand store and sold three sacks of clothing for old rags. The sacks contained practically all of Mrs. Pinkerton's clothing.

Where is Mrs. Pinkerton?

No longer seeing Mrs. Pinkerton about the Shin home, nor any sounds of hostility emanating from the house, neighbors quickly became suspicious, and asked Shin about her absence. Shin would tell an incoherent story of Mrs. Pinkerton's son sending her money to join him in Victoria. Of all the prior communication with Mrs. Pinkerton, no one had ever heard her speak of a son. Not content, neighbors of Shin asked him repeatedly about the whereabouts of Mrs. Pinkerton without satisfaction. Concerned and getting eerie vibes from Shin, neighbors reported the matter to City Attorney George Montford. Montford in turn notified the sheriff's office in Bellingham, and Deputy Sheriff Ernest Nutamaker was sent to Blaine in response to the call. Whatcom County Sheriff Wilson Stewart, who would have responded, was working a recent store robbery case and would follow up on his man's investigation.

Montford and Nunamaker called at the Shin home on Sunday afternoon, October 15, and questioned the old fisherman regarding the woman's absence, and about the trunk he had taken to the dock. Little was known of Shin, who kept quietly to himself. He claimed to have formerly resided at Point Roberts, being a homesteader there. It was claimed he still had a brother at Point Roberts, but never confirmed. Shin came to Blaine about two years earlier and had little to do with anyone. He engaged in fishing to some extent. He was about 55 years of age, and nearly deaf. His weathered appearance made him look much older than his years. So far as known, he had no other relatives.

Sanford Shin repeated the story he had now become well versed in telling, Mrs. Pinkerton had gone to some town near Victoria, Canada to be with her son. As for the trunk, he explained he had taken it to the boat of a fisherman friend named "Jones." Nutamaker questioned Shin about this mysterious "Jones," but Shin was unable to describe his so-called friend. He didn't even know his first name. Montford, attempting to muddle-up Shin went back to asking questions about Mrs. Pinkerton. Shin could not say where his housekeeper was, or the name of her son. Suspicious, Nunamaker asked for and was denied entry to the house.

While the yarn did not sit well with the officials, they left Shin with the impression that his account of the matter was thoroughly satisfactory. Nutamaker told Montford he needed conclusive evidence before making an arrest. About this time Sheriff Stewart caught up with his deputy who reported his findings to his boss. Stewart and Nutamaker made a round of inquiries, including W. C. Cronister, the wheelbarrow owner, witnesses of Shin taking the trunk to his boat and the owner of the second-hand shop where Shin dropped off Mrs. Pinkerton's clothes.

After their investigation, the lawmen returned to Bellingham rather than follow up with Shin. Nutamaker did ask the Blaine night marshal, a man named Allen, to provide a special watch over the Shin residence. Allen said he would stand guard himself. Shin felt the officers were on to him, expecting their return at any moment. He grew anxious, becoming increasingly paranoid as the evening progressed. Wondering how the sheriff's office knew to question him he became suspicious his neighbors were spying on him. He particularly eyed his closest neighbor, Hans Thorasinson, who was always friendly with Emma Pinkerton. Shin suspected it was Thorasinson who brought the law to his door.

Shin knew Mrs. Pinkerton's disappearance would be fully investigated, and it preyed upon his mind, until he became nearly insane. His last acts demonstrate this. Shin continued to sweat it out though the night contemplating what to do. By four o'clock in the morning, Shin, in a panic, realized the jig was up—suspected of the crime, he set his home on fire. Half crazed, he ran out of the burning house into his neighbor's yard twenty-feet away with a .22-calibre rifle in hand and fired seven shots into Thorasinson's house. He then attempted to break into both the front and rear doors screaming out the owner's name.

Failing in his effort, he fired several more shots at the house, one going through a window, and then fled.

The flames engulfing Shin's house spread rapidly to the Thorasinson home, and both buildings were soon completely ablaze. Both would be completely destroyed. Night marshal Allen claimed later he had left his post, thinking all would be well the rest of the night. Thorasinson, before abandoning his home threw as much furniture into the yard as possible saving the bulk of it. Witnesses claim Shin actually threw a burning torch into his neighbor's home, but no evidence survives to prove this account.

Sanford Shin ran and hid in the basement of an abandoned house across the street from Odd Fellows Hall. Panic must have raced through Shin's mind as he sat alone in darkness for over three hours; he was as good as caught. At 7:30 a.m., he crawled out from his lair and started to advance toward the street. Standing for a time, Shin glimpsed his last look of the world. Then he promptly placed the muzzle of the .22-calibre rifle against his forehead. He fired the gun by placing the notched end of a wood shingle against the trigger. Willard Hall, aged 15 years, found Shin lying on the sidewalk in a pool of blood still breathing and called for help. The mortally wounded man was taken to the city jail rather than to a doctor, and was kept there in a cell. Coroner Henry Thompson arrived before Shin's death. Shin never regained consciousness from the bullet in his brain. Death came seven hours later.

Coroner Henry Thompson was all too familiar investigating the area's crime scenes.
File photo: *Bellingham Herald*

There was considerable criticism that Deputy Sheriff Nutamaker did not arrest Shin on Sunday, as the loss by fire would have been prevented, and perhaps the whole criminal affair could have been uncovered.

Sheriff Stewart spent Monday, October 16, sifting through the ashes hoping to find the remains of Mrs. Pinkerton. For the next week, Stewart searched for any clue as to the location of the trunk. The belief was advanced by Stewart, that Shin struck the woman during one of their frequent quarrels, with the blow being fatal. A letter and a notebook found in the basement of Odd Fellows Hall indicated Shin had hid there after setting the fire. The letter was addressed to him and the notebook contained his name on the flyleaf. To the sheriff's frustration, Shin made no entry of admission of guilt to clear his conscience.

Finally, it was agreed the trunk would never be found unless by chance it washed up on shore. Stewart believed Shin possibly burned his home to destroy evidence of the heinous crime on the upper floor.

The Catch That Didn't Get Away

July 31, 1917 was no ordinary day for C. E. Merle, a Blaine fisherman who untied from the city dock for a little dogfish catching in the bay. He worked at it for over an hour, when suddenly at around 3 o'clock in the afternoon off the old Blue Cannery, Merle's hook got fouled. Fighting the line with all his strength in getting it loose, Merle drew a heavy object to the surface. Just as something large floated up the hook broke loose and Merle saw that it was a rusted trunk. Merle must have thought he discovered lost treasure. In attempting to grapple the trunk and pull it towards his boat, its deteriorated lid popped open and a waxy-soapy white corpse of a woman floated out of the trunk. The sight horrified Merle. The trunk quickly sank, but the swollen featureless body hovered on the surf. With great presence of mind, Merle somehow managed to capture the body with a sail without damaging it. He secured in alongside the boat, not wanting to haul it aboard and excitingly rowed in.

The *American Reveille* on August 1, featured the banner headline: "Body of Woman Found in Trunk at Blaine Clears Up Old Mystery." Were these the remains of Emma Pinkerton who disappeared the previous fall?

The unrecognizable body was taken to the city dock where Coroner N. Whitney Wear was summoned to view the corpse. The remains were left untouched, for fear if removed from the water they would disintegrate. Dr.

Wear decided it was indeed Mrs. Pinkerton's body and ordered it buried at once. Offering up his morbid wit when asked how he knew it was the murdered Mrs. Pinkerton, he answered, "How many other women were in trunks at the bottom of Blaine's harbor?"

FISHERMAN AT BLAINE SOLVES LONG MYSTERY

Hook Cast for Dogfish Brings Up Trunk Containing Body of Woman Who Mysteriously Disappeared Last October.

EMPLOYER SUSPICIONED OF CRIME COMMITTED SUICIDE

Positive Identification Impossible But Little Doubt Exists As to It Being the Remains of Mrs. Pinkerton.

LEFT: Fisherman Solves Mystery
American Reveille, Evening edition,
August 10, 1917

BOTTOM: Body of Woman Found in Trunk.
American Reveille, Morning edition,
August 10, 1917

BODY OF WOMAN FOUND IN TRUNK AT BLAINE CLEARS UP OLD MYSTERY

GOVERNMENT CARPENTERS TO QUIT SAY LEADERS

Tides Today

THE AMERICAN-REVEILLE

WEATHER FORECAST

BELLINGHAM, WASHINGTON, FRIDAY MORNING, AUGUST 10, 1917.

Two Cents on Streets—Pay No More!

Chapter 6
Altercation on Point Roberts

Josephine Atkinson stepped outside their settler's home into the January air. Her father, John Harris, had left a little while before for his own home to retrieve some tobacco. She looked up the path in the direction of Charles Mitchell's house to see his progress. For a moment she stood thunderstruck, wanting to holler for help, but couldn't form the words. Then, all at once she found her voice and screamed to her husband James: "The Greek is killing the old man! For God's sake hurry up!" Josephine clasped her hand over her mouth as she watched Mitchell swing with all his might, breaking a muzzle-loading shotgun over her father's head.

Point Roberts

Point Roberts is an odd-looking neck of land. The "Point" was named during Captain George Vancouver's charting expedition in 1792 in honor of his predecessor, Captain Henry Roberts in command of the ship, HMS Discovery. The Point is tiny spot of land, a nearly five-square mile peninsula extending out below the 49th parallel. Today it's just a few miles below the huge ferry terminals at Tsawwassen, British Columbia. The peninsula was an unforeseen creation by the 1872-1876 International Boundary Survey, eventually creating the US-Canadian boundary. The survey ended between the international townships of Blaine, Washington Territory and White Rock, British Columbia, but no one seemed to take much interest in the jutting point hanging below the line between Boundary Bay and the Strait of Georgia. It would become a part of the Washington Territory's Whatcom County. Unfortunately, there was no practical way of entering the Point, except either by water or by entering through Canada. It made little difference, as there was nothing there anyway.

At the time of origin, the remote appendage was referred to as an exclave. Unpopulated, aside from being the Lummi Indians' seasonal fishing grounds when they encamped on its beaches, the land was eventually made a military reservation. Being an unoccupied restricted zone, the land was not open to settlement. The notion wouldn't last long.

John Harris

With all of today's resources available, John Harris is still a rather elusive individual. Even the location of his grave seems to be unknown.

Whatcom County historian, Lottie Roeder Roth[38] had written what she knew of John Harris, while recording the famous murder in her history. What Roth learned came from a February 1883 edition of the *La Conner Mail*. Roth noted the article worth citing as it presented a historical background on Harris:

"Harris had a curious history. He was raised among a tribe of Indians in New Mexico, having been taken captive when a boy. He subsequently served as a scout with General Scott's army in the Indian and Mexican wars, and had many adventures and hairbreadth escapes. Leading a most romantic life, he drifted up North about twenty-five years ago [about 1858] and settled at Semiahmoo, but soon after removed to Point Roberts, where he was engaged in raising stock. He had two daughters by an Indian wife, one of whom is married to James Atkinson...He was best known as 'Long-haired Harris.'

The sketch of Harris' life is brief and probably embellished by the *Mail* although under scrutiny there are some grains of truth, some lies, and of course—confusion. The *Mail* does offer one bit of subtle information, a minuscule description of Harris—that he had long hair.

Besides Roth, the leading authority on Point Roberts' history and the Mitchell-Harris murder comes from Professor Richard E. Clark, noted author of *Point Roberts, U.S.A.: The History of a Canadian Enclave*. Clark's history was published in 1980. Since that time some additional background of Harris has unfolded.

As near as anyone can tell, John Harris was born in Liberty, Texas in 1821 or 1824 to William and Ann Harris.[39] He was the second to seven brothers and a sister; by 1861 he had survived his whole family. In 1841-1842 his brother Enoch took part in the Texas-Santa Fe expedition to secure northern

---

[38] Author of *History of Whatcom County*.
[39] Other sources claim Louisiana, as the family lived there just prior.

New Mexico for Texas. As New Mexico was mentioned by the *La Conner Mail* it could be Harris followed his brother, but not as a captive boy of Indians. Harris is next found living in Calaveras, California in 1852 where another brother was.

The problem with a concise history is that various birth records, census data and land records from Louisiana, Texas, New Mexico and California verify family names, places, etc., but vary widely on dates and ages given. The 1870 Washington Territory census claims Harris to be sixty-nine years old - being born in 1801. This would make him much older than is likely by 1883.[40] Again, the elusive Mr. Harris.

It is a fact, by 1870 Harris had married a Native-American woman by the name of Biddy, born in Washington Territory about 1832. Biddy was Coast Salish, perhaps Lummi or Nooksack. The couple had three children: George, born about 1858, Emily, 1861 and Josephine, 1866. Josephine would marry James Atkinson and reside at Point Roberts.[41] The census also indicated no one in the household could read or write. Harris' real estate was valued at $600 and personal estate at $200.

Harris lived in Whatcom County prior to 1857, as he was employed by the Northwest Boundary Survey of 1857-1861 (not to be confused with the 1872-1876 International Boundary Survey) as reported in the *Blaine Journal*, "Among the boundary commission was John Harris who was a cook for Lieut. Park..."[42]

Historian Percival R. Jeffcott[43] added "John Harris, erstwhile squaw man and very early settler at Semiahmoo and Point Roberts, was engaged as a laborer, probably an axman or packer; contributed potatoes from his garden on the shore of the Bay, and sold the commission one Indian dugout canoe for $20..."

After Harris completed his stint with the commission in 1861 he moved his family into a small single-room cabin situated midway between California and Dakota Creeks, near Blaine. Here he established a fish-house and became involved in fisheries as his living.

Not satisfied, Harris gave up a fishing career and moved his family to Point Roberts. Accounts point to John Harris as the first permanent "white" settler to occupy Point Roberts.[44] Harris took no mind in the restrictions imposed

---

[40] Best guess is Harris was between 62 and 67 years old in 1883.
[41] This information was collected by Peyton Kane for "Native American-Early Settler Marriages, Image and Reality: Life in Whatcom County 1860-1890." Wagenweb.org
[42] *Blaine Journal*, December 12, 1889.
[43] *Nooksack Tales and Trails: Historical Stories of Whatcom County*, Washington. P. 279.

by the military not to settle on the reserve. Harris figured if the army didn't want him living on the Point they could send a force out to remove him. That wouldn't be likely.

Lottie Roth indicated the year of Harris' arrival at Point Roberts as 1873, as indicated by the *La Conner Mail*. Harris must have tired of the smelly fish-house and decide to try the cattle business instead. The openness of uninhabited Point Roberts must have appealed to the Texan. In defiance of the Federal Government, he built a farm and homesteaded the peninsula. Soon he had forty head grazing on the Point.

Alone with his family, Harris began taking on the role of an English Lord watching over his estate. It was said Harris patrolled the Point on horseback watching over the herd with his reliable gun at the ready.

Harris grumbled one day to the *Bellingham Bay Mail* while in Whatcom "of the threatening attitude of certain Indians from beyond the British line who came to the…point and ordered him off their fishing ground, stating that they were sent there by the agent and representing themselves as belonging to the United States Reservation. Mr. Harris was too sharp for them, however, and told them they had no rights there that he was bound to respect and refused to leave; that they didn't belong to the Reservation, and even if they did the place was outside the limits. This made the Indians very insolent, and nothing but the coolness of Mr. Harris, and the close proximity of his trusty rifles, prevented a collision with serious results."[45]

With no threat of government intervention others soon joined Harris' secluded exclave. John and Kate Waller being the second to arrive engaged in the fishing business. Another was Charles "the Greek" Mitchell, who would be of foremost interest. Mitchell's background is as elusive as Harris'. The June 15, 1883 *Whatcom Reveille* writes, "Mitchell is a powerfully built man, standing about six feet high. He has always been considered a Greek by birth, but his appearance - his light hair and blue eyes - would appear to denote that he is either a Swede or a native of Poland."

Mitchell and his "Indian woman"[46] built a cabin, sheds and small barn about 2,500 to 3,000 yards north of James Atkinson's (Harris' son-in-law) place. The

---

[44] Some sources insist the first being John and Kate Waller in 1877.

[45] *Bellingham Bay Mail*, July 12, 1873.

[46] In court transcripts, she was referred to as, Mary or Charlie's wife. In other cases, it was Susan. Mitchell called her "My Woman." Whether the two were married is unknown. Mary was illiterate, signed her name with an X on documents. She was very shy on the witness stand, answering questions with few words.

homesteads were said to have been well in sight of one another. The ground separating the two was mostly level sandy prairie and tule (bulrush) marsh. Court notes called it tule laurel.

The relationship between Harris and Mitchell is unclear, but that Mitchell was owed money and Atkinson was somehow involved. On January 10, 1883, Harris was forced to appear in Semiahmoo for a lawsuit brought against him. Court was held in Muriner's mercantile establishment with Justice of the Peace John E. Freese presiding over the argument.

Henry Henspeter Jr., son of emigrant German farmers in Semiahmoo, was at the mercantile courtroom:

"Yes, I was in Mr. Muriner's store after he (Harris) had paid costs of the lawsuit. He made a remark close to me, saying I am not broke yet. He then sat down upon a box behind the store and said there was no use in him coming to Semiahmoo with any more lawsuits, he could not get justice there anymore, and I will get even with Charley before a week."

Money was a sore subject with John Harris who owed countless debts throughout the region. Paying people back was just against his principles. One example comes from Semiahmoo store merchant John Elwood, who describes his attempt to pursue payment of $116.97 for goods owed him. After mounting a debut, Harris stopped coming into the store.

Elwood relates:

"Some two or three years ago or more I took a bill to Harris for collection. It was for goods sold to him on a running account. I presented it to him at Point Roberts. He took the bill and said, "I don't owe you anything," at the same time asking me if I came to collect that bill I told him yes. He then took a gun that was lying alongside of him and told me to get off the Point or he would shoot the damned heart or liver – I don't recall which – out of me. I told him I would not go. He then advanced with the gun pointed at me and told me if I did not leave he would shoot, saying that there was no damned son of a bitch living could collect that bill. I was afraid of him and walked towards the beach and got into my boat. He followed me to within a hundred yards of my boat..."[47]

Showdown

---

[47] *Bellingham Bay Mail*, July 12, 1873.

It was a rather windy January thaw day on Thursday, the eleventh of 1883. The day all hell broke out on the Point. John Harris had been visiting his seventeen-year old daughter, Josephine all morning. It was a day of visitation, as John Peterson (26) and Fred and John Williams (22) were over at the house. It was comfortable enough outside that Josephine's husband, James Atkinson[48] decided it was a good enough day to repair the front room door. Harris had run out of tobacco and decided he'd go home and fetch some. He asked Atkinson where he had laid his gun. Atkinson pointed to a wall corner where it rested. The gun in question was an old style, double-barrel muzzleloader with external hammers. When the trigger was pulled, the hammers ignited little caps sitting on nipples, thus discharging the gun.

It was between three and four o'clock in the afternoon. Harris had a long walk, about three miles if he traveled around the beach to his house. Or, he could cut the distance by half if he traveled through the tules, an area of marsh—wetlands. Harris could have taken either direction, but would have had to pass Mitchell's house, who he had been feuding with over money he owed. He had not seen Mitchell since the lawsuit in Semiahmoo the day before, and likely held resentment against him.

Charles Mitchell and Susan were seated at their cabin table eating dinner. The dogs started acting up, barking as they would when someone was around. Charles looked out the window. "Harris was down the beach and crawling in the direction of my shed," he said to Susan. That is a bad sign he thought.

Mitchell would later claim that he went outside seeing Harris going into his shed. "I stopped a while there to see what he was going to do. At the same time I left my door and started to walk to the beach..."[49] Harris, by this time was inside Mitchell's shed. He watched through the seams of where the wallboards came together as Mitchell walked down a path. Mitchell could also see the man behind the cracks spying on him. His cover blown, the old man emerged from his hiding spot. "He pointed the gun at me as soon as he came out of the shed and said, "You're my beef now!"[50]

Mitchell's trial testimony of their exchange of dialogue:

"I told him, me and you are good friends—all the trouble is between me and Ross and Atkinson. And I edged up closer and closer to him."

"I said. Don't now, Harris! Look out! The gun might go off and kill me!"

---

[48] Andrew was Atkinson's true first name.
[49] Washington Territory v. Mitchell, 1883.
[50] Ibid. Mitchell's testimony. In the Semiahmoo inquiry Mitchell states: "You're my meat now!"

"That is what I came over to do. Kill you on purpose!"

"I said, Don't Harris, wait a while. I want to speak to you. You know what a gentleman is?"

"Yes," he said, "I am one of them."

"And you call yourself a gentleman," I said, "and all gentlemen give a man a chance to speak before he dies."

Mitchell then moved toward his house. He told Harris he wanted to speak to his wife and child. "I wanted to talk to them if I die."

Harris said, "Damn short time I'll give you. You're my beef."

"I looked back toward my wife."

"I don't know Harris what is the reason you're down on me like that. I never harmed you…I don't know what is the reason you are down on me like that."

He said, "You robbed me the other day in Semiahmoo at the lawsuit!"

"I said, Well, Harris, it was not my fault I ask you to pay me and you said, No, I don't owe you nothing…if you had no money and told me so I would have waited awhile for you."

At that moment, Mitchell looked into Harris' face watching it change before him. At first it changed color from a winter's pale to a glowing red that made his veins puff and turn purple in color. His eyes were "dropping drops" said Mitchell. The gun commenced trembling. Mitchell thought it was the last of him.

"I kept my body in a crooked position as Harris was pointing the gun at my breast. I was afraid he would shoot." In a desperate act, Mitchell sprang to one side, at the same time seizing the gun by the barrel. At that moment one of the two barrels discharged, sending a stream of shot through Mitchell's open wavy coat, not touching him. The incident surprised both men.

Mitchell forced the muzzleloader from Harris' hands, and as he did so, struck Harris across the head. Dazed, Harris ran; Mitchell in pursuit struck him again on the arms. Another blow knocked him down to his knees close to the shed.

Susan stayed in the house until she heard the gunshot. Fearing the worst, she ran out to see what was happening. Watching as the desperate fight ensued, Susan said in court later, "I got afraid and ran in the house and began to cry."[51]

About this time, Harris' daughter Josephine looked up seeing her father being beaten down, sound an alarm. "The Greek is killing the old man! For God's sake hurry up!" In the distance, she could see her neighbor, Charles

[51] Susan's testimony.

Mitchell, swinging what appeared to be a long-gun over her father's head, clubbing and smashing it down on the crouched the old man.

Alerted by his wife's cries, James Atkinson, with John Peterson, Fred and John Williams immediately headed up the path to see what was happening.

After the Beating

Left alone by his neighbors, Mitchell took his gun and left for John Waller's, leaving Susan behind. "I told Mr. Waller what had happened. And asked him to come over and stop awhile with me as I was afraid to stop alone for I might get shot. Mr. Waller said to me, "I'm afraid to stop alone for I might get shot myself; but the best thing for you to do is to take my boat and go over to Semiahmoo and tell Mr. [John E.] Freese all about it and get Harris arrested."

Waller asked Mitchell if his gun was loaded or not. Mitchell affirmed it was. Waller put the ramrod in the gun to see for himself and found there was a heavy load in the gun. He pulled the charge out and found buckshot, but no powder in the gun.

John Harris died on Sunday, January 14, after suffering greatly from his wounds.[52] A coroner's inquest was held in Point Roberts the following day. Farmers F. M. Cain (47) and S. P. Hughes (43) examined the body during the inquest. They described the wounds recorded in the coroner's report:

"Wounds over right eye 1.5 inches long cut to skull—another above about 2 inches long cut to skull—concluded skull broke—bruise 2.5-inch diameter on top of head—three cuts in that place to skull—wound above left ear like right—two wounds in back of head—three bruises on breast and in middle of it two small holes that look as if made by nipples of gun about 1.5 inch apart—was bruised from shoulders to knees, except a patch about 3 inches in diameter in small of back."

Three days later, Mitchell was arrested and had a preliminary hearing before Justice of the Peace Freese at Semiahmoo, and was discharged on the grounds of justifiable homicide. "I certify," stated Freese, "that the enclosed depositions were taken in my court at Semiahmoo on the examination of Charles Mitchell accused of the murder of John Harris on 11th day of Jan 1883." Depositions were taken on the January 20, 1883. Mitchell remained a free man.

Mitchell never denied the fact he struck and killed the deceased with his own

---

[52] *Northwest Enterprise,* January 27, 1883 reported Harris died at the age of 68, making him born 1815 according to that newspaper's reporting.

gun, but alleges what he did was done in self-defense. Harris had shot at him and showed his coat as evidence where buckshot had passed through the material. It was determined he had no choice but to act out of self-defense. Mitchell remained in the vicinity for two weeks after the trial going about his daily routine. He never made any attempt to elude the law or escape with the intent of evading justice. As far as he was concerned, he had done nothing wrong.

Mitchell crossed the boundary into British Columbia and went to Canoe Pass on the Fraser River to fish. Soon after, he returned briefly to Semiahmoo to fish, but no fish were running and decided to return to Canoe Pass where fishing was more profitable. No attempt was made to stop Mitchell from crossing the border. That would change.

Charles M. Bradshaw (42), Prosecuting Attorney of the Third Judicial District[53] pleaded before Roger S. Greene, Chief Justice of Washington Territory, on April 18, 1883 that it wasn't the duty of the justice of the peace of Semiahmoo to make such a decision to free Mitchell, but the law of the Territory. Bradshaw, in his plea to Greene, stated:

"Being first duly sworn upon his oath says that he is informed and believes that…Charles Mitchell…did purposely and of deliberate and premeditated malice make an assault upon one John Harris and did then and there with a certain iron gun barrel in the hands of him…purposely and with deliberate and premeditated malice did beat, strike, and wound the said John Harris and give to said John Harris three mortal wounds on the head and other two of said wounds on the breast of said Harris of which…John Harris then and there did languish…until the 14th day of January AD 1883."

Bradshaw informed Greene that Charles Mitchell was now at or near Canoe Pass near the mouth of the Frazier River in British Columbia and needed to be arrested immediately. Greene agreed and reversed the preliminary hearing decision by the justice of the peace at Semiahmoo. Greene ordered Bradshaw to have an arrest sworn and to approach authorities in Victoria.[54]

On April 19th, the law firm of Davie & Wilson, of Victoria, acting for the authorities of Washington Territory, was contacted and instructed by Whatcom County Prosecuting Attorney Bradshaw to arrest Charles Mitchell. Bradshaw applied to Justice McCreight for a warrant for Mitchell's arrest under the extradition law. The warrant was issued and given to Sergeant Bloomfield of the

---

[53] Territorial Prosecuting Attorney of the Third Judicial District, Jefferson County 1869, 1871 and 1882. Attorney 1858-1889. Born in New York.
[54] Washington Territory v. Mitchell. 1883: Affidavit for Warrant.

Victoria police, who proceeded to the mainland, and tracked Mitchell down to a shanty he built at Canoe Pass. On reaching Ladner's Landing, Sergeant Bloomfield had to secure the assistance of local Indians, and traveling by canoe in the darkness of the night, under sheets of drenching rain Mitchell's shanty was reached. He was taken by surprise, and at first did not like the idea of being arrested for a crime he been tried and acquitted.

Taken into custody under Bloomfield's authority his prisoner was brought to Victoria to be held. Sheriff James O'Loughlin left during the second week of June for Victoria to secure and bring Mitchell back to Whatcom County. Mitchell was forwarded to the Port Townsend, Jefferson County Jail on November 21, 1883. He was held for 121 days before a decision was made what to do with him, costing the taxpayers one dollar per day.

Trial

On December 19, 1883, Bradshaw's indictment was read to Charles Mitchell, who pleaded not guilty to murder. Mitchell still couldn't understand why he was being charged. Furthermore, he was confused when the court ordered

Subpoena to report as a witness in the Territory of Washington v. Charles Mitchell trial. Courtesy of the Northwest Regional Branch Washington State Archives a change of venue from Jefferson County back to La Conner in Whatcom County. No reason was given; perhaps Jefferson didn't want to foot the bill.

Charles Mitchell retained legal representation through Attorneys Thomas Burke (29, NY) and Orange Jacobs (53, NY).[55] Burke criticized the indictment citing more than one crime was on the information and was "fatally defective in other essentials." Then the most outrageous offense took place when five women were called to serve on the jury.[56] It was more than the defense could stand.

Burke and Jacobs contested the impaneled "petit jurors," filing on March 8, 1884 to have the women removed, claiming women were not qualified under the law to sit as jurors. The filing was "Overruled." Then, just to rub salt into the wound, juror Mary Brown was made foreman.

Highlights from the testimony:

James Atkinson was the first witness to take the stand. He described the events as he saw them unfold:

"My wife came out and hollered to me that the Greek was killing the old man, for God's sake. I went in company with rest of the men to his assistance." Atkinson continued his testimony regarding the encounter with Mitchell and the retrieval of his father-in-law.

"What position was Harris in when the Greek was pounding him?"

Ans. "He was taking shelter on the ground."

"What did Harris tell you about the row how it commenced?"

Ans. "After they dressed Harris' wounds I asked him how the row commenced, he told me he was going home on the trail past the Greek's house. The Greek came out and spoke to him. Told him he had something against him. That he and myself were the ones to blame, he then came up towards Harris and wanted him to go down to my place with him. Harris told him he was going home. He could go down and settle with me."

"Describe the wounds on Harris as near as you can."

Ans. "He had two cuts over his eye about two inches and a half long. One cut on the back of his hand, one on the left side of his head above his ear. His back was bruised between his shoulders, was also bruised on the right thigh and across the kidneys."

John Peterson:

[55] Jacobs was in 1869 a Washington Territory Supreme Court Associate Justice.
[56] Mary Beake, Mary Brown, (24) a married housekeeper from Penn., Anna Eckeldson, Caroline Hermandy and Margaret King.

"Harris said he was going to his place for tobacco…20 minutes later his daughter called to me, the Greek is killing my father. I took my hat and started towards the Greeks house. When I was the distance of about two hundred yards I see the Greek strike Harris about four times with the gun. The Greek went into his cabin, came out again and started to load his gun. He showed us Harris' gun broke in two pieces…The Greek told me that Harris wanted to shoot him with the gun. The Greek showed me how he shot past his right leg."

"Did you hear him say anything about how the trouble commenced between him and the Greek?"

Ans. "Yes, he said after I washed him and cut the hair from his head. Good God Peter — I will never get over this. I asked him how did you come to get in a row with the Greek. He said he went past the Greek's cabin; the Greek came out of his cabin and called to him. Harris tripped himself and fell. The Greek commenced pounding him with the gun."

"Do you know if the Greek was at Atkinson's house the evening before the row?"

Ans. "Yes, the Greek came to Atkinson's house and asked if Harris was home. I answered yes. Harris came to the door, the Greek, stayed outside the fence. They talked about the lawsuit they had at Semiahmoo. The Greek told Harris to come outside of the fence. The Greek took hold of a pistol in his pocket pulling it out. Harris said, 'I wont come out to you.' Mitchell asked four or five times. Harris went back in. Moments later we heard two shots from a revolver. It wasn't at the house, just nowhere."

John Williams:

"Mrs. Atkinson went outside and came in and said Charles Mitchell had her father down. I jumped on my horse and seen the Greek hit Harris four times while going down…I looked towards his house; he was loading a gun as I went by. I went up over the hill and found Harris at the edge of the tules. I got off my horse and got hold of Harris by the hand…I stayed up with him all night."

"As you passed the Greeks place did he say anything to you?"

Ans. "No, he did not say anything to me, but said to James Atkinson, 'so you want to shoot?'"

"After Harris was taken home did you hear him tell how the trouble commenced between him and the Greek?"

Ans. "Yes, The Greek came out and was making friends with him. He grabbed hold of the gun. He got his foot in a hole and let go of the gun and began the scuffling. The gun went off. He hollered for help and the Greek struck him over the head with the gun."

"Did you hear the Greek make any threats against Harris the day before the row took place, or on the same day?"

Ans. "I was riding along the beach. We saw the Greek cutting a piece of maple. My brother asked him what he was going to do with it. He said he was going to make a maul. They commenced to talk about Harris and the Greek said, the first time he got Harris out he would whale him until he could not stand. He would get them all one at a time." (Meaning Harris and Atkinson. This event took place in the morning as the brothers were riding to the Atkinson home.)

Fred Williams:

"After Harris got up which way did he go?"

Ans. "Towards the tules. I saw Harris try to get away from Mitchell. His hands were drooped down this way. (Demonstrated) Harris staggering—he went close to a marsh there alongside of some tules."

"Was he on the trail usually traveled from where he started to his own house?"

Ans. "There's not a trail, it is all prairie."

"Did you hear him say how this trouble commenced between him and the Greek?"

Ans. "Yes, he said he went down to settle a little affair with the Greek. The Greek made a grab for the gun and in the scuffle the gun went off. His foot fell in a hole. The Greek hit him with a gun."

"Did you or did you not hear the Greek make any threats against Harris that day or the day before?"

Ans. "Yes, I heard him say he would pound the old man and Jimmy until they could not stand. He would take them one by one. That was the same day the fight was."

Fred Williams added that on his deathbed Harris said, "When I die, I want to be buried over at Whatcom alongside of a man buried there named Col. D."

Charles Mitchell took the stand and related all the events that transpired from his recollection. He told about having dinner, the barking dogs and seeing Harris sneaking up toward the house, and confronting him.

"I stopped a while there to see what he was going to do. At some time I left my door and started to walk to the beach to see what Harris was doing in my shack… at which point Harris appeared through the door with his muzzleloader in hand."

Harris was steaming over losing a lawsuit to Mitchell over money owed to him.

"I told Harris, it was not my fault I ask you to pay me…I was so scared I dared not move; I was afraid I would get shot…The gun commenced trembling. I said to myself, Poor Charley, that is the last of you!"

"I kept my body in a crooked position as Harris was pointing the gun at my breast, his finger on the trigger."

Mitchell stood up and illustrated his stance and the distance between he and Harris.

"I suddenly sprang to one side; at the same time I caught the gun by the barrel. That moment the gun went off."

"That is when the beating commenced?"

Ans. "I got so mad and trembling. I beat him."

"Had you and Harris any quarrel before you served him for debt?"

Ans. "No, I was as good friends with Harris."

"What day was Mr. (John) Peterson in your house?"

Ans. "10 January 1883."

"What did he say at that time?"

"…He said look out for that old fellow, meaning Harris. He will shoot you in a minute…I said to him its not so easy to shoot men and he said now be quiet you know nothing about it. He said…Harris gave me (Peterson) powder and shot and caps to go down to Harris' house and get his big gun that is there and to load it up and go inside the fish house and if I see you (Mitchell) passing by… to shoot you. Peterson said don't be afraid, I am not going to shoot you."

John Waller:

"Charles Mitchell came to my house I think on Thursday 11th January 1883. He told me that there were 4 men after him. One was James Atkinson and the other John Peterson the other two were half-breeds. I asked him what they were after him for. He said J. Harris come to shoot him and fired one load at him. He then took the gun out of Harris' hands and beat him over the head and shoulders with it. I advised him to go and have Harris arrested."

The Jury is Out

The trial ended with little drama. The attorneys concluded their closing statements. On March 11, 1884, the judge laid out eleven instructions to the jury regarding the law and how it should be applied in determining their verdict. There seemed an inclination of sympathy and mercy in the case against Mitchell. Even the judge's instructions provided the jury with a wide margin towards leniency:

"…every presumption of law is in favor of his innocence; and, in order to convict him of the crime alleged in the indictment…every material fact necessary to constitute such crime must be proved beyond a reasonable doubt; and if you entertain upon any single fact…it is your duty to give the prisoner the benefit of such doubt, and acquit him.

"If any evidence, in this case, leaves upon your minds any reasonable doubt of the defendant's guilt, that makes it your duty to acquit him.

"If there were any other reason to account for the death of the deceased upon any reasonable hypotheses…it is your duty to account for it, and find the defendant not guilty.

"That when the evidence fails to show any motive to commit the crime charged, this is a circumstance in favor of his innocence.

"You are instructed that the killing of a human being is justifiable or acceptable, when done in the necessary defense of one's self…the defendant, so threatened is not required to retreat, but he had the right to stand and defend himself, and pursue his adversary until he had secured himself from danger if in so doing, it was necessary to kill his antagonist, the killing was justifiable upon the ground of self-defense.

"…the policy of our law, deems it better that many guilty persons should escape rather than that one innocent… be convicted."

The five women and seven men of the jury deliberated and immediately returned with a verdict. Jury foreman Mary Brown read it aloud—Not Guilty!

The *Port Townsend Argus* stated, "We believe this verdict meets the general approbation of the public. The general impression seems to favor acquittal, or manslaughter. Mitchell is undoubtedly a hard character, but the evidence showed Harris to have been a desperate man, to have threatened Mitchell's life, and that he went to Mitchell's house armed with a shotgun for the avowed purpose of settling their difficulties…Whatcom County will have a heavy bill of costs to pay…"[57]

Outside the folded handwritten verdict, *Territory of Washington v. Charles Mitchell* trial. Tried March 11, 1882.
Courtesy of the Northwest Regional Branch Washington State Archives

145

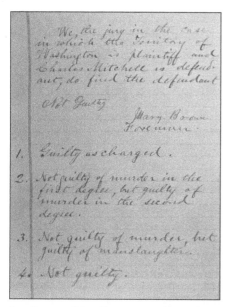

Jury foreman, Mary Brown wrote the verdict. The defense fought a losing battle to remove women from the jury. Courtesy of the Northwest Regional Branch Washington State Archives

Harris left behind more debts than wealth. What estate that existed was squabbled over by those he owed and family members. Claims and liens were filed on Harris' property with no happy endings. The estate was administered by James Atkinson, who put the appraisal into the hands of James Cain and S. P. Hughes. The estate evaluated at $928.75.

Josephine even became suspicious of her own husband. She sent Henry J. White, Judge of Probate Court, a letter stating, "I have heard from more than one that he [James Atkinson] is secretly disposing of the property belonging to the estate." White looked into the matter and immediately dismissed Atkinson as administrator, appointing M. H. Upson. Upson reported to White, "I think there was some chicanery now in regard to the ten cows that Josie (Josephine) claims were given to her by her father."

Professor Richard E. Clark, in his research discovers for the first time that, "it is by this record that we learn of Harris' other daughter, Emily Quinn, whose husband living on the British side of the line was attempting to move Harris' fishing seine across the border." Harris actually owned two fishing seines and a large skiff; possibly the unmentioned two had already slipped across the border.

Whatcom County "orders and decrees" records list property set aside for the "said widow of John Harris to wit: Two cows, with their calves named respectively 'Young Red Head' and 'Frosty' also one iron kettle of about 20 gallons measured. Done this fourth day of August, 1883." The wife being Mary Harris, the records state Mary is "John's Indian wife." This leaves the Harris story with the mystery of Mary Harris. Was "Biddy" a pet name of Harris or was this a second wife?

It was to be a quiet Sunday morning, April 20, 1941, and Whatcom County

---

[57] *Whatcom Reveille*, March 21, 1884.

Chapter 7
"I Held Her Too Long!"

Nora Gossett, circa 1900s.
Courtesy of Patterson Smith, Detective
Magazines Archives

Sheriff William T. Farmer[58] planned on raking his lawn now spring had arrived. Aside from daily routines and patrols, the winter months had passed with little criminal activity in the county. As usual, Farmer had the weekends off, while his deputy, Claude H. Carlson manned the desk at the Bellingham Sheriff's Office. But Sheriff Farmer's quiet spring morning would soon be interrupted when the telephone rang shortly after eight o'clock. Senah Farmer called her husband

---

[58] William Farmer was Whatcom County sheriff from 1935 to 1943. His wife Senah, remarried in 1948 after her husband's death. Her marriage certificate claimed she was a widow. She was fifty-six.

from the backyard. Duty calls.

Deputy Carlson (47), was on the other end of the line, and very excited. He informed his boss, in broken Swedish, he had just received a call from the Monroe Funeral Parlor at Ferndale. A woman's body had been found about an hour earlier. The body, belonging to Nora E. Gossett, had been discovered by her husband floating on the surface of a well at her Kickerville Road farm, west of Ferndale. Her body was untouched; waiting for the authorities to investigate the scene first.

Carlson said Nora's estranged husband, Berton Leander Gossett, upon discovering her, immediately went to his married daughter's home about a mile distant on the same road. The two were so grief-stricken, they decided it best to call the nearest undertaker and have them report the accident to the sheriff's office. No assumption was made of foul play, as it was quite possible the woman simply fell in while retrieving water.

Sheriff Farmer still had difficulties understanding Carlson's accent, but heard him loud and clear today. Sundays were normally quiet, so understandably the department was minimally staffed. Farmer told Carlson to contact Deputy Fred Turner, the night jailer, before he went off duty; and to notify Coroner Hulbush. The officers would gather at the sheriff's office, then drive out to the Kickerville Road to make an investigation. Hulbush, who was at church, would follow later.

William Farmer had become sheriff in 1935 and knew the ropes of his trade very well by now. Most crimes in the county were related to theft, drunkenness, domestic disputes and perhaps a bar room fight. The majority of crimes were the results of 'hard times' due to the Great Depression, but by 1941 things were looking up. That couldn't be said with the daily news coming out of Europe. The war was at its darkest hour. London was being bombed by the Luftwaffe. Rommel was continuing his drive on Tobruk. And, it seemed Greece was about to fall to the Nazis any day now. But for Farmer, Europe was a million miles away.

The Farmers had no children, although they had been married many years. They married in Virginia, where Farmer was born in 1882. He completed high school, and his history stops there, until the couple purchased a house in Marietta, Whatcom County. His sheriff's position paid $2,400 a year, more than he could hope for.

No one greeted the officers at Nora Gossett's small farm. The Gossetts had six daughters. Four were grown and married: Ada Marie Bishop, of Bellingham; Bernice Slater, lived on the Kickerville Road, Delia and Gladys

148

resided in Seattle; and Eunice and Rita, were living with their father. The officers assumed Berton was at his daughter Bernice's home further down the road.

Sheriff Farmer ordered his men to spread out, and look for the well. He knew several were somewhere on the property. He warned them to keep their eyes open. He didn't need one of his men breaking a leg, or worse. Having been told the approximate location where to search, the officers paid little attention to the farmhouse. They passed it, walking 50 feet toward the barn, and then another 150 feet beyond the structure.

Deputy Fred Turner (24) was the first to find the well, and hollered to the others. The well lay in a clearing of short grass practically flush with the ground. It was partially covered by heavy wood planks. When found, the body was floating in about nine feet of water. Deputy Sheriff Carlson noted the surface of the water being only 23 inches from the surface of the land. This immediately made Carlson suspicious. Unless the woman snapped her neck in the fall, she should have been able to easily crawl out.

Sheriff Farmer kneeled beside the well. He looked over the corpse, but

The well Nora Gossett was found floating in. There were three wells on the property; Sheriff Farmer had them all drained searching for evidence.
Courtesy of Patterson Smith, Detective Magazines Archives

didn't touch it. "Might be accident, suicide, or murder," he mused. "I've seen a lot of cases fished out of the water, and I'd say she's been dead four or five days." It was determined not to remove her until the coroner arrived.

The flesh around her bare arms was bloated and water-soaked, fingers yellowish white and crinkled. Her long grey hair, usually done-up in a bun, floated suspended on the top of the water. The light faded print dress she wore billowed grotesquely about her.

Coroner William A. Hulbush arrived soon after. Hulbush, (56) had been a doctor of medicine and surgery since 1908. On the coroner's orders, the men pulled the waterlogged body out of the well and laid it out in the sun. Hulbush and Farmer gave the body a quick examination. Carlson noted some bruises on the woman's arms.

"No wounds, no broken bones — just these few bruises," the coroner stated, pointing to slight discolorations on the arms and legs. Hulbush stated he could tell the sheriff more after a complete examination.

"But it's queer," Farmer said, "if she fell in there accidentally, why couldn't she climb out?" Farmer looked over at Deputy Carlson, who mentioned the same observation earlier. "It's barely six feet wide and seems to me she could have reached the edge..."

The Sheriff ruled out suicide stating, "There's no weight tied on her. It would take a lot of determination to keep from crawling out at the last minute."

Hulbush added, "The body's floating. I can't tell until the autopsy, but it's either floating because there's no water in the lungs, meaning that she was dead before she hit the water, or the lungs are full of water, meaning that death was from drowning, and decomposition and bloat brought the body to the surface."

Farmer ordered his men to search the property for clues. About this time, a stocky man in blue denim overalls trailed by a distressed girl in her early teens approached. It was Berton Gossett, and daughter Rita (15).

Gossett[59] was a man of about sixty, but admitted he wasn't sure of his age. He had little knowledge of his own history. Gossett was born in December 1886, in Granby, Newton County, Missouri. The date places him at 56 years old. He was second eldest to four brothers, and a sister; born to Thomas and Martha, both Kentuckians. He made it through the eighth grade, which was an accomplishment.

Gossett married Nora in Granby on April 7, 1909. Nora would later re-

---

[59] Four census years referred to Gossett as: Burton, Berton, Benjamin and Bert. And, being born in 1880, 1881 and 1882.

mark how they moved around a lot after their marriage, with no thoughts of settling down. By 1910, the couple was in Enterprise, Wallowa County, Oregon. Sometime later they were in Montana. Nora would relate while living in Montana, some eighty-five miles from the nearest doctor, she gave birth to one of her daughters. She had only Berton to rely on during the delivery. By 1920, they are in Boise, Idaho. And, in 1921, trailing children, the family arrived at Mountain View, Whatcom County. On the Kickerville Road, Gossett leased an unfinished shack from State School Lands they could have if they improved upon the house and property.

Gossett always claimed to be a poor farmer, raising chickens and some livestock. Nora however, said he was just a frugal miser, who kept every cent to himself. Divorce filings claimed, "Although able to furnish a comfortable home, (he) failed, or neglected to, except to a very cheap and run-down house, which is uncomfortable and incomplete." Nora's statement was true. A description in court documents claims the house entirely incomplete, and very meagerly furnished. Nora said she was used to these homes, as her husband, "neglected and refused to furnish any place of residence for his family other than an old dilapidated shack or hut...incomplete and which admits the elements..."

Berton Gossett stood five-foot, nine inches in height. He was of large build, with a paunchy belly and puffy face. His wavy, light brown hair worn short, and shaved above the ears. His face was friendly enough, with smiling sad grey eyes. Gossett walked up and introduced himself. Sheriff Farmer was quick to ask Gossett why he didn't report his wife missing sooner. It was obvious from her appearance she had been in the well for days.

Gossett was taken aback, then slowly explained he and Nora had separated. "We've never had the final divorce decree, but we filed for it in 1937. In July of 1938 we got the interlocutory decree[60] and our eighty acres was split in two. I got the forty undeveloped acres facing on the Aldergrove Road over there and the court gave her the property with the house on this side facing the Kickerville Road." Gossett then explained that the family continued to live together, until he built his own place. "We were happier that way. She's been living alone for the last eight months. Really, my wife was my best neighbor."

The Gossetts had been in Superior Court a number of times over the last four years, starting with the filing of a divorce action by the wife in

---

[60] Interlocutory decrees were commonly used in divorce cases in which the terms of the divorce were stated in the decree, which would be enforced until a final divorce decree could be granted after a period of time. The theory being to provide a period in which reconciliation might be possible.

1937. An interlocutory decree of divorce was entered on July 2, 1938, in which Nora was given the forty acres of land and the house. Berton did receive the other forty. The latter tract was unimproved, but he since built a small house on the Aldergrove Road.

Since the hearing of divorce action, Berton, had been brought into court several other times on show cause orders in connection with the provisions of the interlocutory decree. Some charges were made, and a restraining order imposed. The last hearing was in October of 1940. No final decree of divorce was entered in the case.

Sheriff Farmer obviously knew about the decree, having served subpoenas several times regarding contempt of court, and principally for Berton to vacate the premises. The sheriff continued with his questioning, asking why the marriage failed. Gossett didn't have a readied answer, and then shamefully said, "Just like a lot of couples I guess. Discovered there wasn't any real affection between us and stuck it out until the family was raised."

The sheriff asked about the younger children, and why they were not with their mother.

Gossett said they both agreed he was in a better position to support them. And it was easier for Nora to work if she didn't have care of them. "I just have the two youngest, Rita and Eunice," said Gossett, while stroking Rita's hair. "That's why I didn't notice. She goes away to work for days or weeks at a time and we don't think about it…"

Gossett told the sheriff he also works for the WPA, and overnights with a bedroll at times, if he knows in advance.[61]

Sheriff Farmer shifted the conversation. Using a tone reserved for interrogations, he demanded to know why he was there so early in the morning. And, how was it he just happen to discover his wife, so hidden from the casual eye.

Gossett momentarily gave a dull look, with his mouth slacked open. Farmer could hear the gears turning in the man's head, searching for an answer. Gossett snapped out of his trance and said, "Feeding my chickens. I don't have space enough cleared yet for them and we made the arrangement that I'd keep them here and she could use all the eggs she wanted. The path from my place runs along over there and I just happen to catch a flash of something white out of the corner of my eye this morning."

---

[61] Gossett had worked for the WPA since 1939, making $48.00 per month.

Gossett would later tell the *Bellingham Herald*, he had been going past the well twice a day for some time, to feed the chickens. He was performing this task Sunday morning when he noticed the barrel at the well had been moved and he stopped to reposition it. That is when he discovered the body of his dead wife in the water.

"I don't know. It must have been an accident. Nora was a very awkward woman — was always bumping into things. And she bruised so easily. Always had marks on her arms and legs."

When asked what the "flash of white" was catching his attention, Gossett just shrugged his shoulders.

Coroner Hulbush interrupted, indicating he was ready to leave and asked for help loading the body. "I'll have Mr. Gossett show me around the place," said the sheriff, "then I'll see you." Farmer called over his deputies to give Hulbush a hand. Gossett asked if he could continue with the sheriff later. He said he'd been so upset he forgot about the chickens.

The sheriff nodded, but told the man not to leave the property. In the meantime, Farmer decided to look inside the house. The door was unlocked as he entered the kitchen. There were no signs of a struggle. Remains of a meal were still on the table. She must have finished and was fetching water to wash dishes. Everything was neat and orderly.

A shack of a home Berton Gossett had his family living in.
Courtesy of Patterson Smith, Detective Magazines Archives

Carlson and Turner joined the Sheriff in the kitchen. Gossett soon entered. He asked if they were through with him. He had finished feeding the chickens and needed to return home.

Farmer looked over toward the sink with no water faucet. He asked Gossett if she got all her water from the well?

Gossett nodded, stating the wash water came from the well. "There's three wells on this place, but none of 'em are any good for drinking and we always had to get it from a neighbor about a half-mile away. Their well is on this end of their property and they let us have all we wanted…It's quite a ways from their house and there's trees between."

"What are your thoughts on suicide?" He quizzed Gossett.

"I'm positive it wasn't…Nora was always one to get ahead. That's one of the reasons for our separation. She wanted enough ahead for a comfortable old age, and she figured if I and the kids got out she could save more. She got all she could off the place and made extra by going out to work. She never banked any. Always kept it hidden somewhere."

Farmer ordered his men to toss the house and search everywhere. Nothing was found. Deputy Carlson noted that not only was there no money found, but nothing of value either. Farmer told his men he had three theories to go on — accident, suicide, and murder. It didn't look like an accident and suicide was pretty well out of the picture. That left murder. Farmer thought robbery was a pretty good motive. Then decided to see what Hulbush had found out.

The body of the woman was taken to the Monroe Funeral Parlor in Ferndale where an autopsy was performed by Dr. Earl I. Cilley (38). Cilley informed Farmer that he and Hulbush had, "…been thoroughly over that body from scalp to toenails and we didn't find a thing! There was no water in the lungs so she didn't drown. There weren't any wounds or the slightest suggestion of a fracture so she wasn't hit nor did she injure herself in the fall.

"…All the organs are in good shape so she didn't have a heart attack. The lungs were nice and pink which would suggest an exaggerated capillary action but that doesn't mean anything, as people living in the country have good pink lungs…"

Hulbush indicated she only had a few little bruises on her arms and legs. There was one bruise on her chin. "We cut in and found a clot about an inch long…there wasn't a mark to indicate strangulation." He ruled out poison, as all the organs were clean and healthy. Cilley added that she was dead about five to seven days.

Back in his office, Sheriff Farmer looked over some old reports, and noticed one of interest. Two months ago, Nora filed a complaint with one of his deputies stating some doors and windows, stacked along the barn were stolen. Nothing was found. She claimed someone had been prowling around her place, as she found other items missing. Another day she discovered the wire screen of her kitchen door torn.

Farmer thought about it. The screen was ripped downward when he entered the house. If she wasn't home, someone could have torn it, and lift the hook on the inside. Farmer thought it may be nothing more than simple theft, but it did prove the woman was vulnerable to people creeping about her property.

Days Following

The *Bellingham Herald*, on Tuesday, April 22, headlined, "Further Probe of Woman's Death Planned." The results of the autopsy provided little of value. The doctors and authorities were stumped. The sheriff announced to reporters that further investigation was considered justified in the case.

Wednesday the situation hadn't improved when the *Herald* reported, "Officers Conduct Fruitless Probe." Sheriff Farmer could offer no conclusive evidence as to the cause of death. In the meantime, a funeral was conducted that Wednesday at 2 p. m., with interment in Enterprise Cemetery. The Rev. Clifford C. Hovda officiated.

On the evening of April 20, Sheriff Farmer had called on Whatcom County Prosecutor Edward E. Johnson (35). Johnson was thought a bit young for a prosecutor, but he had a reputation of a crafty New York attorney. Being of Swedish descent, he fit in well with a community dominated by Scandinavians. The two met, and the Sheriff informed Johnson of the day's discoveries. Farmer told the prosecutor he was positive it was murder, but could offer no proof or motive. A plan was decided upon to grill family members, and see what shakes out.

Monday morning, Farmer and Deputy Turner made a call on Mrs. Ada Marie Bishop, in Bellingham. The interview gained nothing, but to confirm her father's statements and Ada could give no inkling of anyone who would harm her mother. She had last seen her at Easter services in Ferndale.

The officers next called on Bernice Slater, another married daughter, and the one Gossett ran to after discovering Nora's body. She too, had last seen her mother at Easter services.

Sheriff Farmer asked if another man or woman were involved in their separation?

"No, no! Neither Dad nor Mother were like that. They were just a lot happier to be by themselves."

Farmer asked if she knew of anyone who might perhaps been forcing unwanted attentions on her? He also mentioned the thief on her mother's property. Bernice knew nothing of such activities, but mentioned a neighbor her mother recently said she wasn't going to work for any more. And she was a bit perturbed. The name of this neighbor was never disclosed to the public. He is simply referred to as a "mystery man."

The sheriff reported the day's events to Prosecutor Johnson. He admitted to have learned little. "There are four angles that I can see. It may have been just any old tramp passing by, or someone fairly close who knew her frugal habits and the fact that she was alone, or it may be somebody who was mad because she wouldn't pay any attention to him. Or, it may have been the person who stole the doors and windows and prowled the property. Maybe she caught him at it and paid with her life."

He told Johnson about the mystery man, whom he knew the name of, and would check the lead.

The prosecutor indicated it came to his attention Gossett had been shooting his mouth off to his fellow WPA friends. Johnson said Gossett had been mocking the sheriff's department for not closing the case. That his wife's death was obviously an accident, nothing more. He claimed, if the well were drained there might be something at the bottom to prove it.

Farmer informed Johnson that he had already intended on contacting the Ferndale Fire Department. He wanted the well drained in the morning. In the meantime, it was still light outside — he'd visit the mystery man.

When Farmer arrived at the man's home, he discovered the owner was away on business in Tacoma. He left a week ago. The house sitter, a young man, claimed normally Mrs. Gossett would watch the place, but she was either unavailable or not at home. The young man only knew the owner had to leave right away.

Sheriff Farmer thought the kid had few wits in the head, and was confirmed when he boldly added, "They found her dead, you know."

On the way to his car, Farmer snooped around back of the house. There he discovered a stack of windows and doors. That was suspicious for sure. Farmer wondered about the reasoning behind the hurried business trip to Tacoma. He detailed Claude Carlson to make the trip to Tacoma and check for the missing man. Then, he made arrangements with the Ferndale Fire Department for draining the well early Tuesday morning.

The following day, pumping operations were underway at Nora Gossett's death site. Sheriff Farmer would remain at the well's side throughout, but ordered Deputies Fred Turner and Syd Stewart (47), to search the property of the mystery man, just up the Kickerville Road.

It took no time for the well to drain. Finally, the bottom was reached and a ladder lowered. One of the firemen climbed down and searched the mud with a strong light. The treasured yield was an old bucket and a few hairpins. Just in case, Farmer ordered the other two wells on the property drained. They too revealed no secrets.

After a rendezvous, Farmer discovered they had found nothing either.

Thursday night, Claude Carlson returned to Bellingham. He found no sign of the mystery man. Maybe he told the kid "Tacoma" in general, so Carlson covered the area of Puyallup, Auburn, Kent and Sumner. Nothing! Farmer told his man to go home and get some sleep. Tomorrow, he could take Fred Turner back out to Nora Gossett's place and search the grounds again.

Friday, April 25

Friday the two deputies prowled around the Gossett property. They paced off sections into grids and worked back and forth. About 2:30 in the afternoon, Carlson made a possible discovery, shouting across the field to Turner. In the bushes lay two doors and windows. The discovery became more interesting when the deputies realized they were on the husband's side of the property line. Looking further, the men found another door in Gossett's barn under the hay.

Sheriff Farmer wondered about Berton Gossett, but had little on him to warrant suspicion, other than a broken marriage, and plain weirdness. Now he could bring Gossett in for questioning about the find and his relationship with Nora. Farmer and two deputies drove out to pick him up, but warned his men, "we'll have to take it easy for now, this really doesn't mean much you know."

Returning home from work, Gossett was met by the law. The sheriff asked about the doors and windows. Mystified, he retorted to Farmer, "I don't know anything about those things! Somebody else must have put those things there." Farmer suggested it would be best to come on down to his office, where they could sort this all out. At the office, Farmer and his deputies put a crossfire barrage of questions on the man. Gossett broke down and sobbed hysterically. His grief was so genuine, that Farmer called the deputies off, and put the man in a cell to calm down.

Farmer suggested they go slow on Gossett. He had yet to ask for an attorney, and they had no motive. The couple were already separated, so there'd be no point in killing her. Nora Gossett gave him custody of the two young children. The four older daughters claimed no hostility between their parents. "That says a lot for a man's character," said Farmer. It was decided to sit on Gossett, and let him sweat. The deputies needed to find the mystery man.

The following morning, Farmer decided to interview Gossett's two youngest daughters. The most he was able to get from the girls were tears. Neither had anything negative to say of their parents. Each claiming never to have seen them argue in front of them.

Sunday, April 27

On Sunday morning, a man came roaring into the sheriff's office. He was red in the face and stomping about. He demanded to know why the cops were out after him. It was the mystery man. The sheriff calmed the man down, claiming he was only wanted for questioning, as his name came up in the investigation of Nora Gossett. Farmer assured him he was not under arrest. "Just give me an explanation for your whereabouts for the past two weeks?"

"I went to Tacoma on business," he explained. "I was staying with friends and that's why you couldn't find me." Obtaining a telephone number, the Sheriff confirmed his alibi.

The sheriff asked him to explain the old doors and windows on his property. The mystery man answered, "I bought those articles from a house-wrecker for a cabin I'm building up by the mountain." Farmer wrote down the approximate location of the cabin for routine checking, but he felt the alibi was sound and dismissed the man.

That evening, Berton Gossett had the jailer relay a message; he'd like to see the Sheriff. Prosecutor Johnson was immediately notified and came straight over. Gossett walked timidly into the office from his cell.

"I was scared to tell you before," he stated, "but I've been thinking it over and guess I'd better come clean. You see, I saw Nora die. It was a week ago Monday, about 4:30. I went to feed the chickens. Just as I got to the gate she was leaning over to get a pail of water and the creak of the hinges startled her. She just toppled in, I ran and pulled her up out of the water, but I could see that she was dead so I dropped her back in and ran. I thought it would be the easiest for me to discover her Sunday and let you know."

The sheriff thanked Gossett for fessing up, but wanted to hold him until he checked on the facts. Gossett hesitantly agreed, and was taken back to his cell.

Farmer turned to Johnson and said he felt something was wrong with his story. There was still a lack of evidence or motive to convict anyone. One item the sheriff picked up on was a prior conversation with Johnson. The prosecutor had said Gossett was telling his WPA buddies that the authorities needed to drain the well for evidence. The pail they found would indicate the woman was getting water at the time. Did she drop it in when she slipped? Or, might it have been thrown in after to make it appear as she was retrieving water at the time?

Monday, May 5

Forenoon, Carlson excitingly rushed into the sheriff's office, declaring he had a witness. A neighbor, Sadie Keller, saw the mystery man at Mrs. Gossett's around four o'clock the Monday she died. She had seen him ducking into the bushes. Keller had been afraid to come forward.

Moments later, Gossett, sitting in his cell asked to see the Sheriff. He admitted

Sadie Keller saw the mystery man at Nora Gossett's home the day she died. He was ducking into the bushes. Courtesy of Patterson Smith, Detective Magazines Archives

his account of the death of his wife was a fabrication, explaining he told it so he could get some rest from strenuous questioning.

"I heard what Mr. Carlson said…I guess it's no use trying to protect anybody any longer. I just made up that story I told you cause I wanted to get out of here. But it didn't work, so now I'm telling the truth."

Gossett reverted back to his first story, claiming he went to the edge of the well and found Nora there. He reached down and pulled her out, saw she was dead and dropped the body back into the water. He claimed he did not inform authorities at the time because he was afraid he would be accused.

Farmer found his story faulty on a number of points. Gossett was told flatly his story of the death of his wife was untrue. The sheriff called attention to the point that he was not being grilled at the time he told the story, but that Gossett himself called the jailer to his cell and said he wanted to tell what had happened.

Farmer informed Gossett the mystery surrounding the disappearance of doors and windows from Nora's house had been closed. A door was found under the hay in his barn, along with the windows, and other articles. Gossett said nothing of the discovery. He made no effort to be released or asked for a lawyer, even though no formal charges were filed against him. Gossett was obviously lying about something.

Exasperated, Sheriff Farmer said, "Take him back!"

An hour later, Farmer and deputies pounded on the mystery man's door.

The man was told, they knew he was at Mrs. Gossett's that Monday. "We have a witness he was told, so come clean." The man was caught in his lie. "I did go to Tacoma that Monday afternoon but I got there a lot later than they (his alibi, friends in Tacoma) told you. I had them back me up because I was scared to death. My calf got away that Monday afternoon. I chased it over to Nora's place and I saw her floating there! It was awful! Honest. I didn't have anything to do with it, and rushed off to Tacoma. When I saw in the papers that it'd been discovered I stayed another week and fixed up my story with those friends. You've got to believe me Sheriff that's the truth."

Sheriff Farmer next decided to go speak to Mrs. Keller, to see what else she knew.

May 17

Gossett was again brought from his cell for questioning. In the office was Deputy Sheriff Syd Stewart; John A. Gillis, of Nooksack (46) and Joe H. Dunn, a former deputy sheriff (63). Sheriff Farmer, in the presence of Prosecutor Johnson, went in for the attack.

"I've got the goods on you Gossett!"

Gossett countered, "You're right Sheriff. The first story I told you was the truth! I was scared."

"You're scared all right, and you should be. I couldn't get your family to talk, Gossett, and I don't know as I blame them, but dug up an old friend. Mrs. Keller, know her? She says she's known you and your wife for twenty years. She told me plenty! You've nursed a canker every since the separation, you wanted that all right, but you also wanted the cleared end of the property. Thought if you took the children you'd get it. Then when you didn't you swiped things off the place whenever you could!"

Gossett again related his first story, straining that it was the truth. When he finished, the Sheriff shook his head.

"You threw her in, after you smothered her! I checked with another doctor and he told me that a person can die by suffocation without a blood vessel bursting."

At that moment Gossett broke. "Yes, yes, you're right," he said in a low voice.

Farmer, not letting up, continued:

"You were on your way to feed the chickens and she came out and accused you of breaking into her house, stealing money, anything you could get your hands on. You clapped your hand over her mouth to shut her up and in your rage killed her...It might have worked if you hadn't made mistakes. You allowed rigor mortis to set in which caused the body to float in an unnatural position. And your biggest mistake was an overplay when you loudly suggested to your friends that we drain the well to find the bucket you'd so carefully thrown in to prove accidental death."

Gossett caved, agreeing he was caught. "That day," said Gossett, "she started hollering and calling me names, and that's what made me so mad I shut her up!"

Written Confession

Bellingham, Wash., May 17, 1941. Saturday, four p.m.

"One Monday, the 14th day of April, 1941, at about 4:45 p. m., I went to feed my chickens at Nora's place. When I got there I saw Mrs. Gossett at the well and tried to talk with her about renting the place; the well was approximately two hundred feet west of the barn. We got into an argument, which we always did. One thing led up to another. She called me a German son of a bitch, yelling at the top of her voice.

"I grabbed her from behind and held her with one hand around her waist and one hand on her mouth. I was going to hold her until she would behave herself and quit her yelling. Being mad, I guess I held her too long. The first thing I knew she was limp in my arms. When I let go of her I found her to be dead.

"I was so scared that I did not know what to do. The only thing I could think of was to put her in the well. She dropped the bucket in the well when I first grabbed her.

"I then went and fed the chickens and after that went home. I did my chores on her place daily, making two trips. On Tuesday, April 15, 1941, I went inside her house and looked around and came out and locked the screen door.

"I came down on Sunday morning and went near the well to get a barrel and looked in and Nora was floating. I went home and got the car and drove to Vic Slater's place and told them; then drove to Ferndale to the undertaker's.

This is my free and voluntary statement, made without fear or under duress.

- Berton L. Gossett."

Court

Prosecuting Attorney Edward Johnson filed charges against Gossett on Monday morning of the 19th, having him immediately brought into the court. The accused farmer, pale from five weeks spent in a jail cell, told the judge he had no funds to employ a lawyer. Attorney Joseph T. Pemberton (37) was thereupon appointed for the defense.

Seemingly reconciled to spending the remainder of his natural life behind prison walls, Gossett pleaded guilty. Johnson, in a press release, told the *Bellingham Herald*, "the last story told by Gossett coincided in nearly all points to the information that had been gathered by investigators."

A show trial commenced on June 2, 1941, before Judge Hobart S. Dawson (44) taking his seat at the bench. Sheriff Farmer made a statement outlining the history of the strange case of Nora Gossett.

Coroner Hulbush stated Dr. Earl Cilley made an autopsy on the body of Mrs. Gossett. His report revealing the woman had a bruised spot on her chin, another on her right arm and one shin was "barked." The lungs contained "very little water." Hulbush determined the examination indicated the woman suffocated, rather than drowned.

Attorney Pemberton addressed only a few words to the court on behalf of the defendant. He questioned some of the details of the story, as related by the officers. The only strategy open to the defense was a minimal sentence.

Judge Dawson asked Gossett the age of his wife. Gossett thought she was about 60, but the sheriff didn't agree with him. Sheriff Farmer told the court papers found in the house indicated Nora was 57 years of age, and Berton Gossett, 56 years. "My older brother (Alfred) told me I was born in 1879," Gossett said, which would make him 62 years of age. He was surprised to himself more youthful.

Both state and the defense rested their cases.

Judge Hobart Dawson held the crime to be second-degree-murder, explaining the slaying was intentional, although not premeditated. Gossett was sentenced to 15 years in the State Penitentiary at Walla Walla. As the accused walked from the courtroom, he paused for a moment to exchange a few words with one of his daughters and then went down the corridor, whistling.

Berton Gossett's mugshot. Washington State Archives, Olympia. Board of Prison Terms and Paroles files

Gossett was released on parole January 20, 1946. Breaking it, he returned into custody on February 20, a month later. He was again released June 2, 1951.[62] Gossett returned to Whatcom County, where he died at the age of 89 years on December 10, 1977.

[62] It's possible Gossett was released July 15, 1955. Dates on his prison release conflict.

Was Enough Done?

Did Sheriff Farmer and Prosecutor Johnson exhaust their investigation before implicating Berton Gossett in the death of his wife? Were there stones yet unturned in the case, that would have suggested Gossett earlier on, or at least used to leverage a confession? Farmer, knew of the interlocutory decree for divorce; having served subpoenas to Berton Gossett. Gossett himself told Sheriff Farmer the case had been in litigation for four years. At no point during the trial, or in the information submitted for trial or in newspapers a mention of authorities looking into the couple's interlocutory Decree civil court case file for motive or history.

The file, an inch in thickness, held many potential leads and witnesses who could have been interviewed. It would have offered investigators a history of escalating violence and documented the growing animosity existing between the couple. Information culled from these records might have solved the murder sooner. More tragic, if acted upon by the courts years earlier, and a divorce granted rather than the interlocutory decree for divorce, Nora Gossett may not have been killed.

If Sheriff Farmer had leafed through the file, it would have been discovered legal action had been in progress since 1930, and not 1937, as indicated. He would have read that in June 1926, Gossett left his family for Oregon and remained there until December, leaving the family penniless. That in 1929, Nora came home to discover a public sale in progress, designed by her husband to sell their belongings. He managed to make a thousand dollars, but refused to use any of it for maintenance of his family. It would have been found that Nora, and the children, at times dressed in rags, as Berton considered it a luxury to purchase new clothing. Nora claimed during their whole married life, and especially since 1931, she has been compelled to depend upon kindhearted neighbors and friends for clothing.

Documents and court records showed Berton Gossett deprived Nora of the benefits and comforts of life. On one occasion, the Washington Co-operative Egg & Poultry Association issued and mailed Gossett certificates of stock dividends in the value of about $15.00. Nora used it to buy necessary clothing for herself. When discovered, Gossett threw her out of the home and refused to let her return. A daughter ran out with a coat for her, as the temperature was freezing. Nora was forced to walk to Ferndale for shelter.

Court documents going back to 1930 indicated Gossett abused his wife, heaping indignities upon her, and referred to her as an "old heifer" and an "old bat." He started slapping her face during fits of rage. In recent years, it escalated into punching, knocking her down and kicking and beating her — leaving black and blue marks on her body. Nora would leave. Gossett would claim he would do better by her, and she would return to him, until he became so vile she could not tolerate him. She had lost all love and affection for her husband.

The decree documents went on to state, "the defendant has denied to the plaintiff the benefits and comforts of modern civilization...She is broken in health and is a nervous wreck." If this background were to have been acted upon earlier, Nora Gossett may have still had the opportunity of a joyful life.

Chapter 8
Dead Man Walking:
The Story of Alfred Hawkins, Scene II[63]

In the story of Alfred Hawkins, alias Alfred Hamilton,[64] (please see the footnote regarding the usage of Hawkins and Hamilton.) I have taken the liberty in dividing the following events into halves; scene II, below, takes place in Whatcom County, while the first half of the story begins in Skagit County. I have also chosen to forgo much of the first trial for reasons of repetition, and that the second trial provided better information of the two proceedings.

The murder of David M. Woodbury in Anacortes on September 7, 1899 and the subsequent trial of Alfred Hawkins spans a period of thirty-three months, involving trials in two different counties. The reader will find in the Skagit County section of this book a history of Woodbury's murder, the setting in which the crime takes place and Hawkins' first trial. It continues with a failed appeal by the defense for a new trial by the Skagit County Superior Court. But in November 1900 the state Supreme Court ruled in favor of the prisoner and Hawkins was granted a stay of execution. The chapter concludes with Alfred Hawkins' transfer to Whatcom County, where a second trial awaits him.

A Skagit Murder Trial Comes to Whatcom

The first time Bellingham residents heard about the shooting of Anacortes attorney David M. Woodbury came from a short blurb in the *Bellingham Daily Reveille*, September 8, 1899. In a single inch paragraph on the front page it was

[63] Scene I of this story will be found in the Skagit County section of this book.
[64] Alfred Hawkins had many aliases. At the time of his arrest he gave his name as Hamilton, which stuck with newspapers, and in court records. I have chosen to use Hawkins when referring to him, and "Hamilton" in quotes and other such places in the story to keep with sources of the time.

The Whatcom County Courthouse served both as a court of law and the county jail.
Laura Jacoby's, Galen Biery collection

claimed a drunk had dealt Woodbury a "probable" fatal wound. At the time of printing, it was only known that a bullet had entered the victim's chest, and was considered very dangerous. No name of the fiend was offered.

The following day a front-page column headline read: "Bad Man With A Gun Holds Up Every One In Sight." The story reported an eyewitness account from a Whatcom resident just returning from the city of Anacortes on Fidalgo Island. J. H. Sargent had spoken with Dr. George B. Smith, who was treating the mortally wounded David Woodbury, claiming there was no hope of his recovery.

Sargent was well acquainted with the accused murderer, Alfred Hawkins, having patrolled the fish-traps of the region capturing fishery pirates and smugglers. Sargent said Hawkins and his partner, a man named Burgess, owned a green sloop together. Sargent had boarded and searched it several times looking for smuggled goods, but claimed Hawkins was clever and he could never pin a thing on him. "Hawkins," Sargent stated, "was always pleasant about such matters, and was apparently a harmless sort, as far as hurting anyone was concerned. He was suspected of stealing fish from the traps and admits himself, that he smuggles."

Whatcom County residents interested in the trial taking place in Mount Vernon, could glean from local newspapers the daily proceedings during the month of November 1899. Alfred Hawkins of course was found guilty and sentenced to hang, which came as no surprise.

Hawkins' attorneys would of course appeal the verdict at the state Supreme Court level; demanding a new trial for their client. Amongst the arguments, a prejudiced jury and the court not allowing for a change of venue to obtain a fair trial and judgment. Secondly, as the state could prove no cause of premeditation due to intoxication, Hawkins should have received a lesser sentence.

Granted a retrial, the venue would be moved to Whatcom County. Now the people of Whatcom would listen to evidence and decide whether to uphold Skagit County's ruling, or apply a lesser verdict. Skagit County's own Prosecuting Attorney, Maynard P. Hurd, would prosecute the case once again, with Henry W. McBride, who sat second chair in the first trial. McBride was presently serving his fifth month as Washington State's fourth Lieutenant Governor under the Governorship of John Rankin Rogers. Prosecuting Attorney Albert E. Meade of Whatcom County would represent the state, being his jurisdiction.[65] Whatcom County Superior Court Judge Jeremiah Neterer would preside. Seattle Attorneys, Colonel Robert H. Lindsay and John B. Wright would reappear for the defense. The trial would see many of the same personages of the first.

Prosecuting attorney Henry W. McBride, who sat second chair in the first trial, returned for the second. Courtesy of Washington State Digital Archives

[65] McBride will succeed Rogers, who will die in office on December 26, 1901. Albert Mead will in turn succeed McBride in 1905.

Alfred Hawkins' Second Trial

On the 11th day of March 1901, Skagit Sheriff Edwin Wells handcuffed Alfred Hawkins, boarded a train in Mount Vernon and transported his prisoner to the Whatcom County Courthouse to stand trial. Sitting in his jail cell, Hawkins waited while his team of lawyers worked diligently to secure their client a better deal from the legal system. The second trial of Alfred Hawkins began Monday morning, May 20, 1901.

The first day was taken up securing an impartial jury.[66] Three jury viewings were required. Hawkins was present in the courtroom, but seemed by reporters to take no particular interest in the proceedings. The *Bellingham Daily Reveille* described Hawkins as:

"A striking feature…He is rather under the medium height, dark, smooth shaven, and slender and apparently quite young. He has dark piercing eyes, white even teeth, a large mouth, prominent nose, rather low forehead, and dark brown hair. He was dressed in a dark well fitting business suit and instead of looking like a murderer, he resembled more a rather spruced up-to-date clerk or businessman." Once the juror's box was complete the trial was set to be heard.

Skagit County Prosecutor Maynard Hurd gave opening statements to the jury. He retold the shooting of Woodbury by the defendant, which occurred in Anacortes at 3 o'clock, September 7, 1899; death resulting three days later.

Addressing the jury, Hurd said, "At the time of the murder the defendant, who then was known as Al Hamilton, but after being taken into custody gave his true name as Hawkins, had but recently arrived in Anacortes. On the afternoon of the day of the shooting he entered a barbershop, where 'Billy' Londerville was being shaved." Hurd went on describing the heated exchange of words within McHale's barbershop with Hawkins waving his revolver about until the city marshal arrived.

He described the marshal's efforts of being the peacemaker: "Charles Becker endeavored to quiet him. He (Hawkins) turned and threatened Becker, ordering him out of the building. The marshal went to the office of the city attorney, H. D. Allison, in the Platt Bank Building to consult him in reference to the matter…the city attorney was not in his office and Becker went to the office of Mr. Woodbury and asked for Allison. Leaving Woodbury's office he was confronted in the hallway by Hamilton and covered with his gun. Becker was unarmed."

---

[66] The jury: G. Slater, H. A. Smith, H. Oster, J. N. Selby, William Ream, Carr Bailey, C. Jorgenson, T. Delong, Jeff Steward, Charles Cissna, A. H. Dunlap and J. A. Markhart.

Hurd went on describing the events, portraying Hawkins as a madman, as he eventually would have three men covered with his revolver, with seemingly no plan to end the encounter. Hurd elevated his voice as he approached the climactic moment. "Attorney David Woodbury, attracted by the unusual noise came out of his office and was in turn covered by Hamilton (Hawkins) and was commanded to stand still. Not complying readily Hamilton said, 'Oh you won't stand still, damn you!' and fired. The bullet penetrated near the heart and lodged in the victim's spine, causing paralysis."

A groan of disapproval echoed in the courtroom, and Judge Neterer had to quell the spectators with his gavel.

Hurd ended his opening statement by relating Douglass Allmond's—editor for the *Anacortes American*—plea for help from the second-floor window. Below, City Attorney Allison, who was just returning, grocer Ernest Kasch and policeman Dan McDonald responded. Allison grappled with the murderer in a death struggle at the top of the stairs and was twice fired on, but in neither case, did the revolver discharge. Pushing past Allison, Hawkins continued downstairs until he met Kasch, who tripped the villain, throwing him headlong down the stairs. Before the desperado could recover his senses, he was captured and disarmed.

Seattle attorney, John Wright's opening statement for the defense admitted to the shooting of David Woodbury. Wright admitted Woodbury came to his death at the hands of the defendant. But he would prove the defendant was intoxicated and not in his right mind at the time of the shooting, and that he had been doped for the purpose of robbery.

Wright stated:

"Hamilton came to Anacortes on the 6th day of September, 1899; that he was drinking at McCracken's saloon all night, where he fell in with some gamblers among whom was John Wall, a desperate character, and 'Billy' Londerville; that he had a large sum of money, nearly $1,000 on his person and that these men were trying to rob him of it; that Wall stayed with him all night trying to accomplish that end and that they drank together; that Wall pretended to be his friend and told him that others were trying to rob him, all of which lead up to the gun play in the barber shop.

"The defense will undertake to show that after Hamilton was taken to the city jail," said Wright, "that he swooned and vomited, and that in the vomit was found strychnine. On this will be based the claim that the defendant had been doped and evidence will be introduced to show that there is a dope containing strychnine. It will also be shown by defense that Wall, after the shooting hastily left Anacortes, giving as a reason for his peculiar actions that he did not want to be a witness in the case..."

At 5:15 p. m., the first witness, sixty-one-year-old, James W. Bird, a contractor and builder, was called to the stand and testified regarding the layout of the Platt Building in which the shooting took place. After taking his testimony the court adjourned.

Day II

With the opening statements and other preliminaries out of the way, the second day of trial started with testimony fully underway. The *Bellingham Daily Reveille* reminded its readers on Tuesday morning, how Hawkins was already once tried for murder, found guilty and the death penalty stayed by the Supreme Court. He was again being tried before a tribunal of justice—Whatcom justice. The *Daily* updated potential spectators of the trial so far, stating, "… they had missed nothing as yet of the fight to save Hawkins from the gallows."

Tuesday, the prosecution put their key witnesses on the stand. William "Billy" Londerville was the state's first sworn in, who relived the day he was sitting in McHale's barbershop getting a shave when Alfred Hawkins entered and said:

"You __ __ __, I've got you where I want you now, and I am going to kill you." Londerville said he eventually succeeded in pacifying Hawkins when Becker entered. "The marshal asked Hamilton if he hadn't better put up his gun and go back to his sloop with him. Hamilton replied, "You __ __ __, do you want some of this?" Waving his revolver at him. Becker replied, "No, I guess not." Whereupon Hawkins said to him, "Get out of here, __ __ you or I will blow your head off." Becker went out and Hawkins said to Londerville: "He wants to get a warrant for my arrest, but I will kill him first." Hawkins then exited the shop, following Becker up the street.

McHale was next on the stand. He owned the barbershop where the trouble between Londerville and Hawkins occurred and corroborated the statement of Londerville.

The next two state witnesses were City Marshal Charles Becker and *Anacortes American* editor, Douglass Allmond, who both witnessed the killing.

Becker took the stand after being placed under oath. Once seated, Prosecutor Maynard Hurd, told the jury that Marshal Charles Becker, a man of undisputed reputation, was the state's key witness. He had observed the actions of Hawkins from his first encounter inside the barbershop, all the way through Woodbury's murder and capture. Hurd asked the marshal to recite from memory the events once he departed from the barbershop.

Becker testified how Hawkins pursued him up P Street toward the Platt Building with his revolver drawn and in hand. Becker said he called out over his shoulder to Hawkins several times, turning back to look at him, but Hawkins wasn't interested in conversation. As the men came closer to the Platt Building, Hawkins followed with his gun still drawn not caring as people along the street watched on. "He came up closer to me and said, "You __ __, can't get a warrant; __ you, you can't arrest me."

Becker told the court once inside and ascending to the second floor of the Platt Building he went direct to City Attorney Henry D. Allison's door, but found it locked. He next went to Attorney David Woodbury's office and asked the whereabouts of Allison. As Becker exited Woodbury's office, he found Hawkins standing behind him with his revolver pointed directly at him; hammer cocked. Hawkins said, "If you move another step I'll blow your brains out."

About that time, Douglass Allmond came up the stairs heading toward his office, and walked right into the two.[67] Hawkins promptly ordered the *Anacortes American* editor to throw up his hands. At this juncture, Woodbury, hearing the commotion came out from his own office only to be confronted with a drawn gun and the two men with hands raised.

Marshal Becker continued to describe the conversations and events that followed:

'What's the matter here?' Woodbury barely uttered the words when told to throw his hands up as well. 'This won't do, young man, you had better put up that pistol,' and Woodbury begun backing away. Hawkins ordered the man to do as he commanded. Not complying, Hawkins yelled, 'You wont throw up your hands, damn you,' and fired his gun."

Woodbury, with blank expression, fell backward toward his entry. He stood there stunned for a moment, then, his legs gave out from under him collapsing to the floor. Hawkins swung his gun back toward the other two men as a smoky haze filled the room, and the smell of cordite reached everyone's nostrils. It took a moment for Woodbury to gather his wits before crying out in surprise, "Boys, I am shot—I am killed—Why don't you summon

---

[67] There is a discrepancy in the testimony. During the first trial, it was claimed Allmond was in his office and came out to see what was happening when Hawkins put his gun on him.

aid?" The man's face twisted in pain.

Hawkins attention turned to the bleeding man, and said: "Lay still, you __ __ __."

As Hawkins diverted his gaze, Allmond darted into his office and hollered for help from the upper window down to the street below. In moments, yelling and footsteps were heard coming toward the Platt Building's entrance. Hawkins panicked and dashed for the stairs. Halfway down he was confronted by City Attorney Allison, just heading up. The two struggled. Twice the revolver's hammer snapped, but never fired. Hawkins threw the man aside and continued to leap down the stairway.

Becker told the court after a quick check on Woodbury, he heard the struggle at the stairs and ran to assist. At which point Ernest Kasch, a grocer on street level, was bounding upward. Hawkins nearly cleared the man, when Kasch stuck his foot out tripping Hawkins who tumbled to the bottom. Becker testified he immediately pounced on the murderer, pinning him in place just as policeman Daniel McDonald arrived on the scene and disarmed the fiend.

On cross-examination, Colonel Lindsay asked only a single question. "What, while walking to the Platt Building were you calling over your shoulder to the defendant?" Becker told Lindsay his reason for calling to Hawkins, was that Hawkins' sloop partner, Burgess, had asked if found he would would bring him back to the boat. Burgess claimed his partner carried a great deal of money and had not returned from his all-night bender of drinking. Burgess worried Hawkins maybe in a ditch somewhere.

Douglass Allmond was next called by the state, whose testimony was the same as Becker's, but within the confines of the second-floor Platt Building.

The defense made no effort to shake the testimony. Colonel Lindsay declined cross-examining Allmond even when asked by Judge Neterer. Next followed Daniel McDonald, the policeman who aided in the arrest. Henry Allison told of the stairway struggle, and Ernest Kasch was proud to give testimony of tripping Hawkins.

Drs. Lewis Butler and George Smith described the mortal wound Woodbury suffered and testified his death was caused by a single bullet. After medical testimony, the state closed its case. None of the witnesses of the state were cross-examined to any extent by the defense.

The morning session closed after a non-stop parade of testimony, with nearly no response from defense counsel. It would appear that after all the work done by Lindsay and Wright to gain a new trial, they now seemed content throwing their client under the horse-cart. After a recess the defense opened its case calling the defendant himself to the stand.

Alfred Hawkins Takes the Stand

A packed courtroom greeted the afternoon session as everyone wanted to hear what the accused had to say in his own defense. "Alfred Hamilton" (Hawkins), said Clerk of Court Olson J. Haier, and the accused man rose and stepped up to be sworn in.

The *Bellingham Daily Reveille* reported: "Not a tremble, not a quiver of the eyelid told the awful strain under which the man must have been laboring as he took the oath. Calmly he stepped into the witness stand and faced his accusers, the state's attorneys. No matter what the man may be, murderer or innocent, everyone in the courtroom admired his nerve as with a steady voice he faced the jury and told the story of his life."

Alfred Hawkins gave his history for the record, telling the court he was 29-years old, born 1872 in Bristol, England. At the age of 11 he was put into a naval training school and went to sea in the merchant marine service as a cabin boy. He followed the sea for several years. In his travels, he visited the Holy Lands, Africa, India, Australia, New Zealand, the Hawaiian Islands and South and North America. He came to Puget Sound in 1896 and had been here ever since. Hawkins claimed to have been fishing during the summer of 1899, and when he reached Anacortes on September 6, he had on his person $1,000 of honest money. He walked uptown on that night and spent some on drinking and gambling in McCracken's saloon. Here he met Jack Wall who was running a gambling game in the back room. They became friendly and before the night was over they took many drinks together. Wall discovered Hawkins carried considerable money on his person and warned him to be careful, and look out for Billy Londerville and another man named Steward for they would rob him. As a new morning dawned, he and Wall started out together for breakfast and afterwards had a few more drinks. Here Hawkins claimed, his senses left him and he remembers no more until he awakened in the city jail. He remarked to the jailer he didn't know what he was in for, and one of the officers said, "You'll know what you're here for when we hang you."

Hawkins said later, when taken to Mount Vernon, he became awfully sick and vomited continually, claiming to taste absinthe[68] in the vomit. He denied

---

[698] A potent distilled alcohol once considered an addictive psychoactive drug and hallucinogenic, it was banned in the United States in 1915.

all knowledge of the shooting or the circumstances leading up to the act. Hawkins swore to the jury he had no recollection of going down to the boat for his revolver. His first recollection of that day was being in McHale's barbershop for some reason he could not say. All other circumstances leading up to the shooting, he claimed no memory. He claimed, as would his attorneys that he had been "doped" and thereby rendered irresponsible for any acts he may have committed.

Cross-examination by Hurd brought out the fact the accused had been in jail several times on other charges and has used various names since living on the Sound. Hurd however could not shake the defendant's story of the shooting.

Witnesses for the Defense

The next witness for the defense was 58-year-old, F. H. Reid, who at the time of the murder worked as a steward aboard the steamer *State of Washington*. Reid testified Jack Wall, the gambler, boarded the boat the day after the shooting and paid for a stateroom. Wall stayed secluded in the stateroom for 18 hours. Later, in a conversation on deck he admitted to Reid he was afraid to return to Anacortes until the inquest was over.

Anacortes Police Judge Frank R. Bullack, who was also a bartender of that city, was subpoenaed as a witness. His story as reported in the *Bellingham Daily Reveille* is as follows:

"On the second day following the murder he was on the *State of Washington* on his way to Seattle. On the steamer he met, and recognized Jack Wall who he knew well in Anacortes. He had some conversation with Wall in the presence of Reid. Wall admitted he did not want to go back to Anacortes until the inquest had been held. When the boat reached Seattle, he and Wall went to a hotel together and Wall registered under an assumed name. Wall telegraphed McCracken's saloon for money to keep him until he could return to Anacortes. Bullack also testified that on the morning of the day of the shooting, he was tending bar in a certain saloon in Anacortes. Wall and Hamilton came and had a few drinks together. Hamilton said that he was going to kill Londerville and pulled his gun out of his pocket. He seemed to be pretty well filled up and dropped his cartridges from the gun all over the floor. 'Hamilton's eyes,' he said, 'looked as if he had been out all night, and he seemed dazed and not in his right mind.'

Dr. Emil Bories of Seattle was the next witness called. Bories, a 50-year-old physician from Austria, explained to the court the use and effect of "knockout drops." "Sometimes," said Dr. Bories in his Germanic accent, "the drops have just the opposite effect to what they are supposed to have, instead of putting the victim to sleep. It makes him wild, insane, and when in this condition, he is able to do great bodily harm to anyone within reach." The testimony of Dr. Bories, regarding the effect of knockout drops, was the whole fabric of the defense's case.

The last witness was Clyde Brown, a 25-year-old teamster, who testified to the intoxicated condition of Hawkins on the day of the murder. Brown claimed the defendant was a fallen down drunk, and couldn't possibly see how the man could think straight. He couldn't say he had been drugged, but was under the influence of something strong.

The defense rested.

Day III

Wednesday morning opened with Prosecutor Maynard Hurd introducing rebuttal testimony. The primary objective was the refutation of Clyde Brown's testimony that Hawkins was drunk on the afternoon of the murder. Hurd claimed Brown's reputation for "truth and veracity" was not good. Testimony from several character witnesses were taken stating Brown was a drunk and many had "swore they would not believe him under oath." It was imperative Hurd refute all allegations that Hawkins was neither drunk nor doped, but stone-sober when he knowingly shot and killed David Woodbury.

Hurd paraded a dozen witnesses who testified Hawkins was sober when waving his revolver along P Street, while following Marshal Becker. The testimony of many Anacortes saloonkeepers claimed Hawkins had probably no more than ten glasses of beer during the twenty hours prior to the murder, no drugs appeared administered to him, and at no time did he show signs of drunkenness.

City Marshal Becker, recalled to the stand, said during the time Hawkins was following him he gave no signs of being doped or intoxicated.

John Wall, who was with Hawkins all night prior to the shooting said Hawkins only drank beer and was sober when he left him.[69]

Skagit County Sheriff Edwin Wells testified while he was taking the prisoner to the Mount Vernon Jail he walked slowly. "I had asked him to hurry it

---

[69] John Wall appears a peculiar character in the Hawkins affair. Aside from this snippet of testimony nothing else appears in the court record regarding Wall who becomes a man of mystery. A John Walls does appear in the state penitentiary records convicted in King County for grand larceny in 1905, age 24. Would this be the same person?

up." Hawkins replied, "I hurt my ankle in the scuffle," then vomited. "That damn beer went back on me."

By two o'clock closing arguments were underway; running into the night.

Closing Arguments

Skagit Prosecutor Maynard Hurd made the closing for the state. It was in substance and condensed as follows:

"The evidence has shown that the witness without a doubt, Hamilton fired the shot that killed Woodbury. Witnesses have testified that he was not drunk or drugged. Let us not picture the murderer of modern times as a Moloch with awful, ugly face and form, but as Webster has said, let us picture him a smooth-faced, bloodless figure in action not in repose. This man Hamilton, foul fiend that he is, not content with having robbed a peace-loving community of one of its most loved and respected citizens, not content with having robbed a wife and children of a loving husband and father, this fiend I say not content with this must hurl at the prostrate and dying man, as he lay there on the floor of the hall a reflection on his birth and an insult to his mother, when he said: 'Lie there, you __ __.'

Hurd reviewed the testimony of Marshal Becker, Attorney Allison and All-mond in detail, and referred to the probability of the defense claiming that Hawkins was not in his right mind, he said:

"When Allmond succeeded in reaching his room and calling for help, Hamilton at once made a dash for the stairs and freedom, did not look like the action of a man who had been drugged? In the scuffle with Mr. Allison at the top of the stairs he tried twice to shoot Mr. Allison. Did that look like the action of a man who didn't know what he was doing?"

Hurd graphically followed the course and actions of Hawkins from the time he threatened Londerville, until he was placed on trial, and showed conclusively that all his actions were of a sane and conscious man. "These are not the actions of an imbecile or a 'doped' person." Hurd said, "When Hawkins was taken to jail at Mount Vernon he vomited, but never told his jailers that his vomit tasted of absinthe. He has never told anyone this, but his attorneys. He said only at the time 'the damned beer had gone back on him.'

"I am not looking for a compromise verdict," said Hurd. "It is either murder in the first-degree, or it is nothing. If he did not know what he was doing he has committed no crime under the law; on the other hand, if he was conscious of his actions, it is murder in the first-degree and he should suffer the consequences of his deed.'

"What is the defense?" Hurd asked the jury. "They have none. They attack the reputation of Londerville and Wall; they do not attempt to disprove the testimony of these men. They insinuate that Hamilton was drugged; they proved nothing. A defense that is not a defense is worse than no defense at all. There is no testimony in favor of the defendant except the testimony of the defendant himself, and his testimony is discredited… he is guilty of murder, the greatest offense in the criminal annals of our country. The defense is simply a subterfuge to escape the just judgment of the law."

After making his closing argument as to the sobriety of Hawkins at the time of the shooting, Hurd closed on these words:

"Now gentlemen, I don't want to tire you. I think I have covered this case. The only defense will be the eloquence of Colonel Lindsay, but you must judge by the evidence, not by the eloquence. You desire the protection of the law. I ask you to uphold it. I will await your verdict with confidence that the honor and laws of this state will be upheld."

Colonel Robert Lindsay, "the veteran pleader in many a hard fought murder trial" made the plea for the defense. The *Bellingham Daily Reveille* would declare "It was a most magnificent effort, considering the slight foundation on which it rested." Everyone in the courtroom had heard of the "eloquence" of Col. Lindsay and as he arose to face the jury a hush fell over the room. "Nor were they to be disappointed," said the *Bellingham Daily Reveille*, "for never before in this city has so eloquent and passionate an address been made."

Attorney Lindsay opened as follows:

"May it please your honor and gentlemen of the jury. For many years I have been in the habit of addressing juries in just such cases as this, but each time it becomes more difficult, and as I approach this stage of the trial I become nervous as I feel the delicate position in which I am placed. The life of this young man is in my hands, but a few minutes will elapse before his life will be in the hands of you twelve men. Mr. Hurd charges me the crime of eloquence. I plead not guilty and I think that you will have no trouble to find a reasonable doubt on which to acquit me. Had I the eloquence…I could make a temperance lecture in this case that would ring from one end of the state to the other"

Col. Lindsay took the opportunity to criticize Attorney Hurd and Lieutenant

Governor McBride for not enforcing the law by closing the gambling halls of Skagit County.

"Had these gentlemen," said Lindsay, "enforced the law and closed up these games, as they swore they would do when they took their offices this awful crime would not have occurred, and Alfred Hamilton, instead of being here charged with murder, would have been climbing up the ladder of fame. Would this crime have been committed had it not been for McCracken's den of infamy; Jack Wall the degenerate and Londerville the Gambler?"

"According to the prosecution, he (Hamilton) in a few hours is transformed from a law-abiding citizen, into a devil incarnate, the foulest fiend out of hell. There must have been some controlling influence that made that boy a fiend on that day. There must have been some motive for his actions...I believe that he was drugged. Of course these honorable gentlemen, Mr. Wall...and Mr. Londerville—who was driven out of every town on the Sound—would not drug him or try to rob this poor fisher boy, but nevertheless I think he was doped...The court, I believe, will instruct you that, if you have a reasonable doubt, that Hamilton was drugged and was not in his right mind, then you must acquit him."

Lindsay recapped testimony that endeavored to show that Hawkins was up all night drinking and yet, the witnesses for the state say he was not drunk. What caused Hamilton to vomit when being taken to Mount Vernon if he was not drunk?"

Lindsay asked the jury why after the shooting did Bullack and Wall board the steamer *State of Washington*. "If these men," said Lindsay, "were not guilty in some way why did they leave Anacortes so hastily after the shooting?"

Col. Lindsay closed his address as follows:

"The prosecution asked you not to give a compromise verdict, they want the boy's life, his blood. They are not satisfied to take the verdict as it may be; they say hang him or turn him loose. I can see no reason for this hatred of this unfortunate boy; can it be that these gentlemen think they will not be able to get the votes of Skagit county unless they hang this boy? I hope that is not the case of this unprecedented request. Gentlemen, there has been one life taken already in this terrible affair, my God isn't that enough...?"

Col. Lindsay did not finish until late in the afternoon. Then the court took a recess until 7 o'clock in the evening when Lieutenant Governor McBride closed for the prosecution. The courtroom and its halls were filled during the evening session. McBride took up the argument of Col. Lindsay and was said to have, "picked it to pieces in a methodical, painstaking way," said the *Bellingham Daily Reveille* the next morning. He attacked the defense's doping theory. He said how convenient a memory Hamilton had, how he remembered certain things, but forgotten others. How the accused would lie in order to save his life, and was no doubt conscious of what he was doing. "The defense," said McBride, "has been trying to furnish a peg upon which the jury could hang an excuse for not bringing in a verdict of murder in the first degree."

The Lieutenant Governor closed his address with a forceful plea for a verdict of guilty.

Day IV

Thursday, May 23, both sides had rested their case, leaving Judge Jeremiah Neterer to deliver instructions to the jury. He defined the several degrees of murder, and explained how each could be applied to the case.

At 9:00 a.m., the jury filed out of the box and retired to the jury room to consider their verdict. Hawkins was taken to his cell as it was expected to take some time before a verdict would be reached. The *Bellingham Daily Reveille* remarked how Hawkins, "displayed no concern or anxiety as to the result, and except for a slight pallor, looked the same as he did when first his trial began."

By 9:20 Bailiff Wells informed the court the jury had reached a verdict and court was called to order. Hawkins was brought up from his cell and walked calmly to his seat facing the jury.

On page 472 of the Whatcom County Superior Court Civil Case Journal[70] and the *Bellingham Daily Reveille* describe the events as follows:

Journal: "Said jury retired to the Jury room to consider their verdict in charge by two Bailiffs. And having been out 20 minutes to deliberate, returned to the Court Room…"

Daily: "Have you reached a verdict?" asked Judge Neterer. "We have, your honor," answered Foreman Charles Cissna, and the decision was handed over to the Clerk of Court (Olson J. Haier).

Journal: "In the Superior Court of the State of Washington in and for Whatcom County. We the jury in the case of State of Washington, Plaintiff, against Alfred Hawkins, informed against under the name of Alfred Hamilton— Defendant—do find the defendant guilty of murder in the first degree."

[70] Whatcom County Superior Court Civil Case Journals: Nov. 27, 1900-Jul. 21, 1901. Page 472.

MURDER IN THE FIRST DEGREE

For the Second Time a Jury Says That

HAMILTON MUST HANG

Jury Was Out 25 Minutes—An Outline of the Arguments—Hamilton Has all Kinds of Nerve—Will Move for a New Trial.

The jury was out only twenty-five minutes—Guilty—Hamilton will hang. *Daily Reveille,* May 24, 1901

Daily: "For a moment no one stirred, all eyes were upon the doomed man: not by a quiver of an eye lash or the trembling of a hand did he show that he had just heard his death sentence read. The nerve of the man is truly wonderful and the audience could not help but admire his self-possession. He had not a word to say and was taken back to his cell without even expressing an opinion as the verdict."

The first ballot taken by the jury was on the question of guilt. All twelve men voted "guilty." A second ballot resulted the same verdict. A third and last ballot was on the degree of guilt and twelve men voted "first degree."

The Long Wait

On Friday, May 24, Alfred Hawkins' attorneys submitted a motion to Judge Neterer for a new trial. The motion sited judicial error by allowing Lieutenant Governor McBride to sit on the case, arguing it was a conflict of interest and his presence tainted the jury.

The *Fairhaven Evening Herald* on May 24, quelled and greatly dampened public excitement over holding its first execution, stating a new state law now prohibited local executions, which would now only occur behind the confines of the state's penitentiary at Walla Walla as of June 14. Therefore, said the *Herald*, "if the death sentence was imposed on Hawkins it would relieve Whatcom County Sheriff William Brisbin of the unpleasant task of implementing the order." But as the trial was over, with a verdict of murder in the first-degree announced before the new law, the question of where punishment would be handed out was undetermined.

Alfred Hawkins would sweat-it-out in his cell until Monday, June 17, when

Judge Neterer overruled his attorney's motion for another trial and imposed sentence—"Death by hanging." The execution would take place at the courthouse on August 16, 1901. Bellingham was all-abuzz, and needless to say, shocked by the news of an execution-taking place in their city. In perhaps a futile attempt to stave off the inevitable, Attorney John Wight appealed to the Washington State Supreme Court, granting his client a stay of execution.

While the courthouse drama was underway, another drama was unfolding for Sheriff Brisbin. On August 15, Brisbin received word Hawkins' old "gang" was planning to break him out of the Whatcom County Jail. Not taking chances, the sheriff promptly had his prisoner removed to the King County Jail in Seattle. This being the first mentioning of such a "gang," and that newspapers didn't grasp the opportunity to sensationalize exaggerated stories of an outlaw invasion, it can be assumed Sheriff Brisbin simply wanted an excuse to get rid of his prisoner until it was decided what would become of him through the courts. A morbid side note comes when King County Sheriff Edward Cudihee invites Brisbin to attend the hanging of Charles Nordstrom, to see how a proper hanging should be conducted.[71]

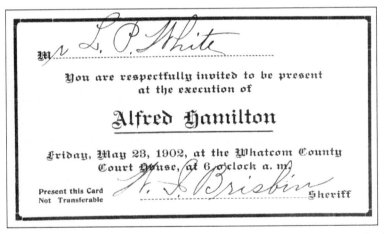

Engraved invitation to the execution of Alfred Hamilton, May 23, 1902. Addressed to Lewis P. White, President of the Bank of Whatcom. Courtesy of the Whatcom Museum

---

[71] According to Daryl McClary: Both Sheriff Brisbin and Sheriff Wells attended the hanging of William Alden Seaton at the King County Courthouse on January 3, 1902. Afterward, Sheriff Wells purchased the soon-to-be-outlawed scaffold, considered one of the most complete and substantial ever built, for the bargain price of $15. "Alfred Hamilton Shoots and Kills Attorney David M. Woodbury in Anacortes on September 7, 1899." HistoryLink.Org Essay 10004. Daryl McClary, January 18, 2012.

Hawkins' defense team failed to win him another trial. An appeal to the governor's office to reduce sentence to life imprisonment by Col. Lindsay and Wright was out rightly refused. It was Hawkins' ill luck that Governor John Rogers died in office on December 26, 1901, being succeeded by Lieutenant Governor Henry McBride. On Thursday, April 18, 1902, the condemned man was brought back to Whatcom County to eventually meet his Maker. Judge Neterer set Hawkins' new execution date for Friday, May 23, and signed his death warrant.

Sheriff Wells' scaffold was delivered and the task of erecting the device took place in the courtyard aside the Whatcom County Courthouse.[72] Apart from the scaffold a 16-foot-high cedar-board fence had to be built around the open courtyard, as only one hundred invited guests could witness the hanging.

Awaiting the Hangman's Noose

During the last few days of his life, only his jailer George Curtis and a reporter would spend any great length of time with Hawkins. Curtis kept an eye on the condemned man, making sure he didn't cheat death on the gallows by taking his own life. The unnamed reporter hoped to document any last details of Hawkins' life for readers.

What little is known of those last days are gleaned from short lines in the local newspapers. Hawkins wrote only two known letters from his cell. One was a circular letter sent to all the newspapers telling his side of events. Only the *Weekly World Herald* printed it in full:

"As I have but a few days to live, I feel justified in writing this letter regarding some of the circumstances connected with the crime which I am convicted and for which I must suffer death.

On the 7th day of September, 1899 I was in the Village of Anacortes and in a rather advanced state of intoxication having been playing cards all the previous night, in my possession during this time, I had almost $1000 in bills. I had been warned twice, that morning that two men had been watching me for the purpose of relieving me of my cash.

I did not pay any particular attention at that time, but went on playing cards and drinking until the liquor got the best of me. Then I remembered the warnings, and in my drunken way was going to see about it and demanded an explanation. Wandering about Anacortes in a dazed sort of condition doing things which I had but a slight remembrance of, I came across one of my—as I

---

[72] Today's Fouts Park is located on Ellsworth Street between G and H Streets in the Lettered Streets Neighborhood.

thought—would-be robbers going into McHale's barber shop. I followed him in and I found myself in the presence of the supposed would-be robber.

We had some words, but finally straightened the matter out, and to show that there was no ill feeling we commenced drinking a beer and to all appearances we were the best of friends. How long this lasted I have no distinct recollection, but it was suddenly brought to an end by the appearance of Charles Becker, the town marshal.

He commenced talking to me about getting a warrant and arresting me, and several other things. I remember at this time, as he stated himself, I had done nothing which would warrant any arrest, but that he thought that I would get into trouble: that is the only reason he has ever given for coming into McHale's barber shop where I was drinking and talking in a friendly way with the very man, it is supposed I started out to have trouble with. No one asked him to come in; he was not needed. We had settled our own differences: he saw through the window that there was no trouble in there and if he wanted to arrest me he could have done it right there without getting a warrant or anything else. No; he did not arrest me, but commenced borrowing trouble, as it were, by shaking the red flag in the bull's face.

It was this that drove the last spark of reason from my liquor sodden brain and made me worse than a raving maniac.

It was while in this condition that I committed the crime for which I shall soon pay the full extreme penalty. It may seem strange to some people that I should never remember committing such a crime and some other circumstances surrounding it.

The very nature of the crime speaks for itself. Is it possible for a man to deliberately, premeditatedly and with malice shoot down in a few moments a fellow man, a man who had never did him any wrong; a man to the best of my knowledge he had never seen? No, there must be something wrong; there must be some cause. He must be either drunk, drugged or insane, and I was drunk and drugged. The prosecution laughed at the idea of me being doped.

But every day men are getting drugged for less money than I had. What made me deathly sick hours after I was arrested? What made me sleep for nineteen hours right after committing such a crime? It was knock-out drops. Any man that has been drugged can easily tell it when it comes to himself, but he will never be able to prove who done it, unless he can get witnesses who will testify in his behalf.

Public opinion was very strong against me in Anacortes that I firmly believed that men who could have thrown light upon the subject have been afraid too.

Let me again return to marshal Charles Becker. Why did he interfere with me when I had done no wrong? If Anacortes had had a good marshal instead of a $30 a month makeshift, this crime would have never been committed, and Mr. Woodbury would in all probability be alive today.

So, through the ignorance of a poorly paid, incompetent marshal, two lives are thrown away, while Charles Becker still enjoys life and liberty.

I do not write these things with the idea of getting clemency from the present governor. Henry G. McBride, has been vigorously prosecuting me for nearly three years for the purpose of hanging me.

These are words of one who stands at the brink of the grave who in a short time will be lost into eternity."

Al Hamilton, Fairhaven *Weekly World Herald*, Friday May 23, 1902.

A second letter was addressed to a Captain Chase, of Tacoma. Presumably Chase was receiving Hawkins' overseas correspondence from friends and family. In his letter, he requested that Chase to never allow unopened letters be returned to his people in England. Newspapers didn't give Hawkins' alternative instructions, but that he didn't want anyone to know he was hanged for murder. It was particularly noted that he did not want his mother to know anything of the case.

The *Bellingham Daily Reveille* reported on Wednesday, May 21, that Hawkins was not inclined to talk, "but the deep lines which appeared under his eyes showed that the strain was telling on him." He remarked to Sheriff William Brisbin, "If you could come in here now and tell me I only had five minutes to live it wouldn't be so bad, but this damned waiting is hell."

On Thursday, Hawkins was informed there were two "Sisters" who would like to visit him. He declined the meeting saying: "I have no sentiment at all in regard to religion. My early religious training was very strict and I have read every word in the bible at least three times. It never had any interest for me, except from a historical standpoint. I do not want people to think that I am infidel for I have a great deal respect for my mother's religion."

Soon the reporter's stay stimulated further conversation. Hawkins was asked why he used so many aliases, to which he was agreeable to answer:

"When young I formed the idea of becoming a rover. I wanted to see the world. Signing articles on board an English training ship from Liverpool I went to Sydney, Australia, where I deserted the ship. In a few months I tired of the land and on the next vessel I attempted to ship back to England. It was then that I found that the merchant marine had a system of checking deserters and that I was unable to go again under my true name. Then I found it necessary to change my name. I repeated the desertion act again and again and accepted the first name that came handy."

The reporter learned his true name really was Alfred Hawkins. Hawkins showed him his tattoo marks on his arms. The letters "A. H.," two flags and a shield on his right arm, and a woman holding a sprig, a bracelet and an anchor are on his left wrist.

Hawkins was asked, as a criminal himself, what were his views on proper punishments for criminals. "I believe," said Hawkins, "that every time a man commits a crime he should have a finger cut off. After he had committed enough crimes to find himself without fingers he should be hung."

"How many fingers would you have left?" asked a guard.

"Oh, I would have been hung long ago," Hawkins replied.

Day of the Long Walk

"Alfred Hawkins awoke this morning," according to the reporter, "looking much less haggard than yesterday." Before going to bed he was challenged by jailer Curtis, to a game of cribbage. He was said to have played with marked interest and expressed a desire to win his last game.

At 10 o'clock, Hawkins went to bed and slept fairly well until he awoke a few hours later. Getting up from his cot he walked nervously about his cell. A doctor on hand for such a situation gave the prisoner a few drops of laudanum to quiet his nerves. It was Friday, May 23, the date set by the court for his execution. By four o'clock he was up, putting on a new set of clothes. What a waste of good garments he must had thought. For his last meal, Hawkins had asked for a breakfast of cocoa and raw eggs, he ate heartily.

At 5:45 Sheriff Brisbin came to the condemned man's cell and read the death warrant. The only effect the reading had on Hawkins was to "elicit a volley of oaths and curses." The prisoner's face was flushed, as he sarcastically asked the sheriff "if the hanging was to come off right away." The sheriff in reply told Hawkins the execution would take place promptly at six o'clock and that he, the sheriff, would come for Hawkins at 5:55.

Hawkins retorted, "Is it going to take five minutes to hang me?"

The march to the gallows indeed began at 5:55 and was not slow. Everything was in readiness. An emergency rope was provided if needed, a board and leather straps for bounding the prisoner were brought, if Hawkins should collapse and needed to be forcefully carried. Sheriff Brisbin led the way, followed by Hawkins. On his right walked Skagit Sheriff Edwin Wells and Deputy Sheriff Andrew Land walked left of the prisoner. To the rear followed officers Jensen and George Curtis. "The condemned man was braced to the straining point." Said a reporter. He came through the corridor and into the jail yard without aid. Up the gallows steps he went two steps at a time never clinging to the rail for support. "This superhuman effort exhausted his strength, but didn't weaken his nerve. He was a little wobbly physically, but strong in his purpose to die game—and he did."

Once on the gallows, Hawkins placed himself squarely upon the middle of the trapdoor that would drop him to his death. Deputies next bound the condemned man with several leather straps to keep his limbs tightly firm to his body when he dropped. "Damn it, those things are tight," he said. The deputies gave no response.

Before a black hood was drawn over his head, Sheriff Brisbin asked Hawkins if he had anything to say?

"Nothing," said the condemned man, "I am here to die, hurry up."

Then he recognized two faces in the crowd, J. W. McLeod and A. M. Clark, both men had been his jailers in the King County Jail. "Good-bye Mack," and then "Good-bye Clark, if you see any of the boys give them my regards; tell them this thing passed off good."

These were his last words, as the sheriff pulled the black hood down. Then Hawkins mumbled, "…as if he were addressing it to the air and sunshine of the world, "Good-bye," wrote the *Bellingham Daily Reveille*. The *Weekly World Herald* thought his last word sounded like a moan; "Scarcely more than audible, addressed to no one in particular…one might fancy that it were a voice raised in supplication from the depths of hell."

Whatcom County Sheriff William Brisbin did not prolong the agony and no sooner had Deputy Sheriff Land adjusted the noose around Hawkins' neck that he pulled the lever triggering the trapdoor. The depth of the drop was carefully measured; adding the proper rope-length for the condemned mere 120-pound frame. And then, the trap was sprung "Hamilton's soul went to judgment."

The *Bellingham Daily Reveille* printed an "Extra" that Friday, stating it was "Without fear, without repentance, in bravado, dying as he had lived, Al Hamilton this morning went to his awful doom." Playing the execution up to the very end the column continued:

HAMILTON EXECUTED

— —

Woodbury's Slayer Meets His Doom Without Flinching.

ASKS SHERIFF TO HURRY

RETAINS HIS COOL NERVE TO THE LAST AND GOES TO HIS DEATH AS HE HAD LIVED, COLD, REMORSELESS, UNREPENTANT, BLASPHEMING. — PULSATION CEASES 16 MINUTES AFTER THE DROP. — HIS LAST NIGHT AND STORY OF HIS CRIME.

Hamilton Executed. *Weekly World Herald,* May 30, 1902

"Up the gallows steps he bounds, and although the sheriff and deputies are strong men physically they scarce could keep pace with the murderer as he climbed the engine of his destruction. With the grin worn during his trials, the sardonic sarcastic grin that Satan might have worn after wooing Eve to her fall, Al Hamilton bade good-bye to all the bright world and stepped into the presence of his Maker, there to answer for the murder of an innocent...Woodbury's slayer meets his doom without flinching. Retains his cool nerve to the last and goes to his death as he had lived, cold, remorseless, unrepentant, blaspheming."

The execution was complete. Alfred Hawkins' neck snapped with the drop; a conclusive spasmodic shudder and all was over. The physicians gathered around and his pulse was taken. At 14 minutes after the drop, which occurred 30 seconds before 6 o'clock, his heart ceased fluttering and at 16 minutes, Hawkins was pronounced dead.

The dead man's body was quickly removed and taken by wagon to the Undertaking Parlors of Herbert S. Noice on Dock Street. He would be buried without mourners in the Bayview Cemetery's potter's field.

The hanging of Alfred Hawkins is considered the first, and last, execution to have taken place in Whatcom County[73] and the last public execution to occur in Washington State.

The present-day site of the former Whatcom County Courthouse, now Fouts Park. On this location, Whatcom County held its first, and last, legal execution. It was also the last public execution to occur in Washington State. All future executions would be performed behind the walls of the state's penitentiary at Walla Walla.
Photo taken by the author

---

[73] Daryl McClary is quick to point out the hanging of Alfred Hawkins was the first legal execution in Whatcom County since 1858, when four marauding north-coast Indians were hanged by the United States Army at Fort Bellingham.

Part II
Skagit & San Juan Counties

Chapter 9
Dead Man Walking:
The Story of Alfred Hawkins, Scene I

The murder of David M. Woodbury in Anacortes' Platt Bank Building on September 7, 1899 is reminiscent of the old west, when seedy miscreants played cards throughout the night over saloon gambling tables, with plenty of booze passing through parched lips. Tempers would often flare and gun-toting desperados at times used their six-shooters flippantly in anger. Coming out of a heavily drunken stupor with hazy heads still swirling, these mischievous individuals often asked the lawman why they were occupying a jail cell.

In the story of Alfred Hawkins, alias Alfred Hamilton, (please see the footnote regarding the usage of Hawkins and Hamilton.)[74] I have taken the liberty in dividing the following events into halves; the opening scene, below, takes place in Skagit County, while the second half finishes in Whatcom. I have also chosen to forgo much of the first trial for reasons of repetition, and that the second trial provided better information of the two proceedings.

---

[74] Alfred Hawkins had many aliases. At the time of his arrest he gave his name as Hamilton, which stuck with newspapers, and in court records. I have chosen to use Hawkins when referring to him, and "Hamilton" in quotes and other such places in the story to keep with sources of the time.

Alfred Hawkins, alias Alfred
Hamilton, notorious bandit,
pirate and murderer.
Weekly World Herald, May 30, 1902

Alfred Hawkins, alias Alfred Hamilton

On Wednesday, September 6, 1899, Alfred Hawkins (26), with a man named
Burgess,[75] his partner, moored their fishing sloop alongside an Anacortes dock
fully loaded with salmon. The haul was sold to a local cannery. In all probability,
the catch was likely pirated from fish-traps, but with no proof otherwise it was
saleable. Burgess, who stayed behind to clean the boat, was none too happy
seeing Hawkins proceed into the city to drink and gamble with a large sum of
money in his pocket. How much was made wasn't recorded, but at the time of
Hawkins' arrest his inside pocket held just under a thousand dollars.

Becoming inebriated as the evening progressed, Hawkins took sport in flash-
ing his revolver about, threatening townsfolk in the local saloons. He was eventually persuaded to return his weapon to the sloop before the law interfered,
ruining everyone's night.

Hawkins enjoyed a rowdy night at the McCracken Saloon, where he fell in
with some gamblers in the backroom tables playing cards and shooting dices.
Amongst the players were John Wall, said to be a desperate character of Anacortes, and his sidekick, William "Billy" Londerville, who was said to be an
"individual of unsavory reputation. They continued carousing and gambling
throughout the evening, but Hawkins soon became paranoid as some of the
fellows at the table warned him the two men were aware of the cash he carried

[75] Burgess is seldom referred too, and never subpoenaed as a witness.

194

and intended to rob him of it. That Wall stayed with him all night plying him with drink tended to support the warning.

Hawkins weathered the night safely, but by the afternoon of Thursday, September 7, his paranoia got the best of him. He retrieved his revolver, and searching through the city, Hawkins found Billy Londerville sitting in McHale's barbershop chair having a shave. Hawkins stormed in waving his .38 caliber Iver Johnson revolver, threatening to shoot Billy on the spot. But Londerville, playing it cool, claiming he wasn't involved in any plot to steal his money, but Wall had intended too. Tempers mellowed, as Hawkins believed the terrified man trapped in the barber chair. About this time, unarmed City Marshal Charles Becker[76] walked in, claiming later he was attempting to deescalate a tense situation between the two men.

Hawkins immediately pointed his revolver at Becker's head, ordering him to raise his hands or he would shoot the marshal. After exchanging a few words Becker slowly walked out. Noting Hawkins was obviously still intoxicated and dangerous, Becker decided to head to the city attorney's office to obtain an arrest warrant against Hawkins.

Meanwhile, Hawkins made the fatal decision to follow Becker up the city's P Street,[77] heckling, cursing and threatening the marshal along the way, all while waving his gun. Arriving at the Platt Bank Building, Becker quickly scaled the stairs to the second floor, looking for City Attorney Henry D. Allison to issue a warrant, but he wasn't in his office. Hawkins ordered Becker to halt and raise his hands, threatening to shoot if he did not comply.

Hearing a boisterous exchange of curses in the hallway, Douglass Allmond, editor for the *Anacortes American* newspaper, whose offices were on the floor, stepped out asking what was going on. Hawkins immediately swerved his revolver into Allmond's face and told him if he moved, he would be shot. The trio grew further when David M. Woodbury (50), a prominent Anacortes attorney, stepped from his office to investigate the disturbance. Hawkins, possibly feeling overwhelmed and nervous by this point, leveled his revolver at Woodbury and ordered him to throw up his hands or he would be killed.

Woodbury replied, "Here, here, this won't do young man, you'd better put up that pistol" and began to back away. Hawkins retorted, "You won't throw up

---

[76] Charles Becker was in fact the temporary city marshal, as the actual marshal was out of town. At the time, he was called away from his blacksmith forge to check on Hawkins. For this reason, he was unarmed, and knew not the arrest procedures; therefore, he needed to see the city attorney for an arrest warrant.

[77] Today's Commercial Avenue

The Platt Building was the first brick structure in Anacortes. On September 7, 1899, Attorney
David Woodbury was gunned down on the second floor.
Photo taken by the author

your hands you_____," and fired at Woodbury. The sound in the confined space
was deafening. Woodbury fell and Hawkins swiveled once more upon Allmond
and Becker. Woodbury, sprawled out on the floor staring upward in confusion
cried, "Boys I'm shot—I'm killed—why don't you summon help?" The maimed
attorney used his elbow in an attempt to drag his body toward his office.

"Lay still you_____," hollered Hawkins.

Allmond, taking advantage of the confusion, leapt back into his office and
ran to his window shouting for help below. Hawkins panicked, and lunged for
the staircase. At that precise moment, City Attorney Henry Allison was midway up the flight and became locked in a struggle with Hawkins, who attempted
to shoot the attorney.

Ernest Kasch, a street-level grocer who had heard the cry for help, came
running up the stairs, tripped Hawkins who tumbled down to the landing.
Before Hawkins could recover, Becker was atop of him. At that moment
police officer Daniel McDonald, entered seizing the gunman's right arm and
snatched the revolver away. Marshal Becker arrested Hawkins, taking him
away to the city jail. In his pockets were found $990, some silver, a pocket

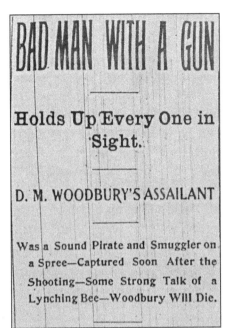

BAD MAN WITH A GUN

Holds Up Every One in Sight.

D. M. WOODBURY'S ASSAILANT

Was a Sound Pirate and Smuggler on a Spree—Captured Soon After the Shooting—Some Strong Talk of a Lynching Bee—Woodbury Will Die.

The headline: "Bad Man With A Gun" appeared in New Whatcom's *Daily Reveille*, as did similar headlines throughout region. The news was fresh and rushed to print to meet deadlines, giving limited details. *Daily Reveille*, September 8, 1899

knife, pipe, tobacco and matches. Unsure of his prisoner, he was searched again, and took his shoes away. Hawkins swore oaths at the marshal, and threatened to "fix'em" when he got out. A nervous Becker moved him to another cell, in case the killer hid something. There he remained until Sheriff Edwin Wells retrieved and relocated the prisoner to the Skagit County Jail at Mount Vernon.

Meanwhile, David Woodbury was lifted from the floor and removed to his office where he was placed upon a couch. Dr. E. Edwin Butler was the first to arrive. Dr. George B. Smith arrived on the late train after receiving a telegram to come as quickly as possible. Doc Appleby, of La Conner arrived soon after, then a telegram was sent to Doctor Eagleson, a specialist from Seattle. All the physicians expressed the opinion that operating was impossible. Nothing could be done to save Woodbury, who suffered a mortal chest wound. Woodbury was moved into the rooms of R. P. Thomas next door, instead of being taken home. The doctors advising

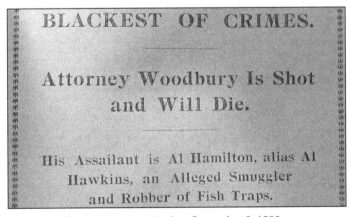

BLACKEST OF CRIMES.

Attorney Woodbury Is Shot and Will Die.

His Assailant is Al Hamilton, alias Al Hawkins, an Alleged Smuggler and Robber of Fish Traps.

Blackest of Crimes. *Anacortes American*, September 8, 1899

he could not stand the removal to his own bed. Woodbury would suffer terribly for nearly three days before succumbing on the second floor of the Platt Building at 10:15 a.m., on Sunday, September 10, 1899.

On the day of the shooting, Woodbury called on Rev. John Antle to join him for lunch at his home. An amateur photographer, Antle brought his camera to take photos of the family. One of which was of Woodbury, his wife and daughter; the last time they sat together.

Woodbury's remains were transported to Mount Vernon, where an examination was performed by pathologist Dr. Albert C. Lewis. It was revealed a single .38 caliber bullet had passed through the upper lobe of Woodbury's left lung and fractured a vertebra, paralyzing the lower half of his body.

A dignified funeral service for Woodbury was held at his home in Anacortes, with burial taking place at Grandview Cemetery. A native of Vermont, he was survived by his wife, Estelle and daughter, Vida.

Grave of David Woodbury at Grandview cemetery, Anacortes, Washington. Photo taken by the author.

The Outlaw

Alfred Hawkins was born in Bristol, England in 1872 arrived in America in 1891. He most likely jumped-ship from a merchantman in some west coast port. Seattle police held a long record on Hawkins, claiming him a well-known desperado around the sound. Records indicate he was involved in two murders, along with acts of piracy. He was known as Al Hamilton, Al Hawkins, Al Harris and Al Thomas, but to Seattle police he was, "Little Al." Hawkins started his criminal career when arrested in March 1896 for stealing "two sacks" of chickens and was sentenced to six months in the county jail.

Earning early release, Hawkins moved into a shack in North Seattle with an ex-convict named Richard Whalen. Whalen was a 38-year-old Irish laborer who usually got by with robbery and scams. In August 1896, Hawkins stabbed Whalen during a drunken brawl, being arrested by a patrolman named Corning, while on his beat. When Corning entered the shack to make his arrest, Hawkins was lying on a cot. Corning approached when Hawkins suddenly threw back the covers and swung an axe at the patrolman. Fortunately, the axe caught the sloping ceiling of the shack, thus saving Corning from serious wounds, or death. Hawkins quickly changed hands, and tried to strike the patrolman again. This time the axe got caught in a stanchion, and Corning laid the man out with his club before he had time to attempt a third swing. Whalen was taken to Seattle General hospital. Hawkins was sent to county lockup for two weeks before being released on motion by Deputy Prosecuting Attorney W. H. Morris, who said that it was merely a drunken row. Hawkins fled the city. Whalen would later succumb from complications from his wounds said to be "pericarditis," but before dying he made a statement that it was by Hawkins' hand he was stabbed. Fortunate for Hawkins, the man's dying words were never written down, signed and recorded. A halfhearted attempt was made to locate Hawkins, but failed.

Hawkins next joined a gang of waterfront thieves, and soon became a leader. Seattle police claimed the gang had secret cashes at Point No Point, an outcropping of land on the northeast point of the Kitsap Peninsula, and Point Roberts, and usually spent their time in Anacortes and in Whatcom County.

One of their largest hauls occurred when the gang stole fifteen new fishnets from the Fraser River worth $3,000. They sold five of the nets in Seattle and cached the rest at Point No Point. A Detective, Jack Williams, had been following the gang all over the sound. He believed Hawkins was the man who shot and killed a fish-trap watchman guarding a trap off Blaine. Williams thought the gang had been discovered stealing salmon, or the nets, when the guard on the trap surprised them. Only, he received the surprise, a bullet to the chest.

Therefore, it's most probable that Alfred Hawkins' September 6, 1899 load of salmon at Anacortes was the product of his pirating spree.

The Trial

On Sunday, September 10, a coroner's inquest was held at the Anacortes City Hall. Coroner James Vercoe directed the inquest, assisted by Skagit Prosecuting Attorney Maynard P. Hurd, with acting-clerk, L. H. Cowing transcribing testimony.[78] Only three witnesses were produced.

Dr. Albert C. Lewis, who performed Woodbury's autopsy, first gave testimony: "I found a bullet wound about two inches to the left of the median line...I found it passed backwards, passing through the fifth rib left of the spine, glancing between the third and fourth ribs fracturing a rib." The bullet was produced as evidence. "The bullet then passed through the upper left lung, and then through Woodbury's Vertebra, fracturing it."

Next, Marshal Becker gave testimony and identified the Iver Johnson revolver. He read off the engraved serial number-59995. Becker was followed by Douglass Allmond, baring witness to the events that took place on the second floor of the Platt Building.

A preliminary police hearing followed on Friday, September 15, a week after the shooting. It was also held at the Anacortes City Hall. Police Justice John J. See presiding. This was a short formality. Sheriff Edwin Wells led the prisoner into Justice See's chamber. Hawkins, displayed cunning enough intelligence to engage reputable Seattle lawyers, Colonel Robert H. Lindsay and John B. Wright, as defense counsel. Skagit County Prosecutor Maynard Hurd, representing the state, called forth only two witnesses. Douglass Allmond, who witnessed the shooting, and Dr. George Smith, who testified to the wounds received by Woodbury and his death. Counsel took no defense testimony, only a few flippant questions to Hurd's witnesses. Justice See bound Hawkins over for trial on a charge of first-degree murder and ordered him held without bail.

It took a month to prepare for the trial of Alfred Hawkins. Skagit County Superior Court opened in the City of Mount Vernon on Tuesday morning,

[78] Inquest jury: William A. Lowman, William Jamieson, John A. Matheson, F. W. Fry, L. A. Bishop and V. Funk.

LEFT: Skagit County Prosecuting Attorney Maynard P. Hurd. File photo: *Anacortes American*
RIGHT: Skagit County Judge Jessie P. Houser. File photo: *Anacortes American*

November 7, 1899, Judge Jessie P. Houser presiding. Former Skagit and Island County Superior Court Judge Henry W. McBride, rode second chair to Hurd in the *State of Washington v. Alfred Hamilton*. Col. Lindsay adamantly argued for a change of venue, declaring it impossible for his client to obtain a fair and impartial jury, to which Houser denied motion. It wasn't until the end of day on Friday that a jury was impaneled.

The oratory of Prosecutor Hurd's opening statement was of little surprise or dramatics. Spectators were well aware of the backdrop surrounding the killing. Hurd would bring fourth testimony from witnesses who saw the defendant deliberately shoot and cold-bloodedly murder David Woodbury. Hurd made clear the cowardly act was ruthless and unprovoked. Hurd gave a history of events leading up to the heinous crime, and how the accused threatened the citizenry of Anacortes with his revolver. "It was clearly a case first-degree murder," said Hurd, "for which Hawkins should be hanged."

Col. Robert Lindsay conceded without argument to the regrettable killing of Woodbury, but claimed the defendant was not in his right mind. Hawkins was admittedly under the influence of alcohol and was obviously heavily intoxicated, but Lindsay claimed in addition to a drunken spree, there was an even more sinister motive behind the killing. Hawkins had fallen in with a most discreditable group of men during a night of gambling, which somehow became aware he carried a large sum of money. By morning, unbeknownst to Hawkins, he had become "doped" for the purpose of stealing his money. But, argued Lindsay, the doping had quite the opposite effect on his client, turning an otherwise docile Hawkins into a violent individual with no memory of his heinous deeds. Therefore, argued Lindsay, Hawkins was wholly incapable of forming intent to commit premeditated murder. Woodbury's appalling death, although a tragic affair, was never a deliberate act, and therefore could not be deliberate. The defendant must be acquitted of the charge of first-degree murder.

Not falling for a Jekyll and Hyde defense, Hurd went on the attack, calling on the testimony of nine witnesses. Each would seriously incriminate the defendant. Two eyewitnesses described Hawkins' disposition preceding the murder. City Marshal Charles Becker testified as to his encounter with Hawkins at McHale's barbershop and the defendant's pursuing him to the Platt Building. Douglass Allmond testified to the killing outside his office. Four witnesses testified to Hawkins' attempt to escape capture. Then Dr. Smith took the stand to describe Woodbury's mortal gunshot wound.

The prosecution then rested its case.

Seattle attorney, Col. Robert H. Lindsay rose to his feet and began the defense's case by calling to the stand his only defense witness, Alfred Hawkins himself. Hawkins testified that on the night before his inexcusable act, he had been drinking fairly heavy, and was more or less, drunk all night. He had carried a large amount of money, having been recently paid off for a season's fishing. He felt the safest place for his money was on his person. During the evening, persons unbeknownst to him had acquired this knowledge and must have slipped him knockout drops in an attempt to steal his hard-earned savings. Hawkins claimed at some point all became a blur. That must have been the moment he acquired the doping, as he had no memory. He could only imagine the drug used on him sent him into an uncontrollable rage, as he was normally a very passive person. To kill an undefended man for no reason was not he. He claimed no memory of events until he awakened in the city jail unbeknownst to the reason. Hawkins declared absolutely no recollection of the incident.

Lindsay argued the effect of the drug used on his client, instead of making him unconscious, had the reverse effect, and threw him into a rage. Lindsay called four witnesses to the stand who corroborated Hawkins was indeed intoxicated all night. Next, three medical professionals testified on the effects of "knockout drops"[79] on

---

[79] Chloral hydrate and hashish cannabis indicia. "Alfred Hamilton Shoots and Kills Attorney David M. Woodbury in Anacortes on September 7, 1899." HistoryLink.Org Essay 10004. Daryl McClary, January 18, 2012.

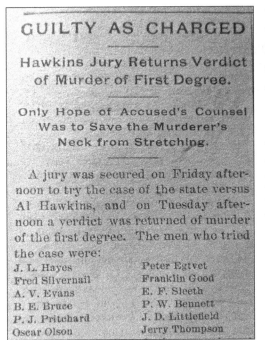

GUILTY AS CHARGED

Hawkins Jury Returns Verdict of Murder of First Degree.

Only Hope of Accused's Counsel Was to Save the Murderer's Neck from Stretching.

A jury was secured on Friday afternoon to try the case of the state versus Al Hawkins, and on Tuesday afternoon a verdict was returned of murder of the first degree. The men who tried the case were:

J. L. Hayes	Peter Egtvet
Fred Silvernail	Franklin Good
A. V. Evans	E. F. Sleeth
B. E. Bruce	P. W. Bennett
P. J. Pritchard	J. D. Littlefield
Oscar Olson	Jerry Thompson

Guilty As Charged
Anacortes American, November 17, 1899

the nervous system. The experts theorized that when mixed with large amounts of alcohol, a stimulant made Hawkins hallucinate and violent.

The defense rested.

During his rebuttal, Prosecutor Hurd called a dozen witnesses to the stand, including saloonkeepers who served Hawkins over the previous twenty-four hours before the shooting. They claimed not to have seen Hawkins overly intoxicated, nor suffering the effects of drugs as he claimed.

Other witnesses claimed Hawkins did not appear under any influence of alcohol or drugs on the afternoon of the shooting. City Marshal Becker claimed although the defendant was antagonistic and hostile he appeared sober when arrested. Four physicians contradicted the defense's theory that a mixture of knockout drops and alcohol were responsible for Hawkins' reaction.

Closing arguments followed the rebuttal, after which Judge Jessie Houser provided the jury final instructions.

The jury deliberated from eleven o'clock on Tuesday morning, November 14, reaching a verdict at 5:30 p.m. The verdict did not come as a surprise when read in the courtroom—guilty of murder in the first-degree. Alfred Hawkins was facing a mandatory death sentence.

On December 7, Judge Houser denied defense's motion for a new trial and sentenced Hawkins to be hanged by the neck until dead. The execution was to be held on Friday, February 9, 1900.

Appeal

Col. Lindsay immediately appealed Hawkins' case to the Washington State Supreme Court, maintaining that Hawkins did not receive a fair trial. As the

Skagit County court awaited the Supreme Court's decision, Sheriff Wells was ordered to place Alfred Hawkins in county lockup and to begin preparations for the execution by having a scaffold erected aside the courthouse.

The primary issues declared in the appeal process regarded a change of venue. Col. Lindsay argued that the jury was tainted with prejudice and were denied a change of venue to secure a fair trial and judgment. He argued the state could not prove premeditation due to intoxication, that the defendant should have received a lesser sentence.

On November 19, 1900, the Washington State Supreme Court ruled in favor of the prisoner and Hawkins was granted a stay of execution. The opening appeal states as follows:

The appellant was convicted of the crime of murder and sentenced to death, and judgment of death was pronounced upon him. This is an appeal from said judgment. A minute statement of the case is unnecessary, as the killing is conceded, and that it was ruthless and unprovoked. The principal defense was that the appellant was irresponsible, by reason of his having been under the influence of intoxicating drinks and drugs, which had been administered to him. The first assignment of error challenges the correctness of the overruling by the court of appellant's motion for a change of venue.

On the 11th day of March 1901, Sheriff Edwin Wells handcuffed Alfred Hawkins and the two men boarded a train in Mount Vernon. The sheriff transported his prisoner to the Whatcom County Jail where a change of venue for a second trial was to be held. Wells carried with him a single wax sealed box prepared by Skagit County Clerk J. H. Smith. Inside was a transcript of the clerk's minutes from the previous trial, together with the trial transcript, original files, proceedings and orders of the court. Also in the box were the exhibits: One .38 caliber Iver Johnson revolver, cartridges and a spent bullet.[80]

Part II of this story can be found in the Whatcom County section of this book.

---

[80] The bullet is presumed to have been the one removed from David Woodbury's body.

Chapter 10
Train Ride to Hell:
The Great Northern Massacre

The Great Northern train at Burlington station, circa 1914.
Laura Jacoby's, Galen Biery collection

Conductor Charles S. Waldron walked alongside the Great Northern No. 358 passenger train at the Skagit County Burlington Depot hollering, "All aboard!" Waldron held out his railroad watch as beaded raindrops fell upon its face showing a time close to 7:15 p. m., nearly departure time. It was Friday, February 20, 1914, and another winter evening's darkness was closing in as the No. 358 continued its Seattle to Vancouver, Canada run. It had been cold, windy and raining most of the week, with a reported gale approaching along the coast, but nothing that would delay their arrival time. The ten-wheeler steam engine had made the northerly run many times before. It would be just another uneventful journey…for now!

At 4:35 p.m., the No. 358 departed from Seattle's King Street Station with J. C. Wright in the engineer's cockpit. A coal tender was connected directly behind the engine where Fireman P. A. McIntosh worked his shovel feeding the mighty engine. Beyond was a smoking car, where most of the men retired to read the evening newspaper, smoke or converse with fellow passengers. The day-coach followed where most of the women and children were seated. A third car was a dining car where passengers could obtain simple fare. The 358 probably had a single or combination baggage car attached to the rear to carry mail or freight.

The Great Northern's Seattle to Vancouver coaches were very simple contrivances, not to be confused with the comfortable, and in many cases luxurious Pullman cars. These cars were crudely constructed daily commuters, called "four-wheelers" with few comforts. They were simple wooden structures, with little suspension, providing passengers with a rocky ride. Seating was little more than thinly cushioned reversible flip-over seats, or perhaps fixed front and back seating. In most cases the cars had drafty interiors, thin walled with single-pane glass windows, with dim electrical lamps lighting the interiors. Coal soot was impossible to avoid, leaving layers of black dust on everything.

As the 358 clamored on north, off-loading passengers along the way, the train eventually made its scheduled stop in Burlington, Skagit County at about seven o'clock for fifteen minutes. After exchanging several passengers, the engine chugged onto the Skagit flats. Among those boarding at Burlington were two men dressed in casual attire, wearing long coats and fedoras. It was nothing unusual in such wet-windy weather. Many passengers had been riding for over two hours now, and were dozing on the uncomfortable bench-seats.

Newspapers left behind were reread during the passage. In London, a young Irish woman was awarded £7,000 damages against Cunard passenger-lines after being forcibly examined on board one of their ships while immigrating to the Americas.

The ever-growing political crisis in Mexico hadn't changed. A Scottish rancher, William S. Benton, in Chihuahua, a region under the control of Mexican revolutionary Pancho Villa, was reported executed by firing squad in Juarez under Villa's orders.

Canadian businessmen were gloating over profits they were receiving from western Canada's enormous wheat harvest.

There was even an interesting news column from Bellingham. The city had just received the first of eight submarines being built in Seattle for performance trials. Bellingham Bay was chosen as the prime location for shakedown cruises and putting the boats through rigorous tests. The Iquigue, built for the Chilean navy, was the first to arrive, and hundreds of captivated spectators lined the shore each day to watch the mysterious vessel rise and dive on the bay.

One news item bound to have stimulated conversation was a daring train robbery near Birmingham, Alabama the day before. Four masked bandits boarded the New Orleans express train as ordinary passengers. They robbed the mail coach after stabbing the postal clerk in the process.

The 358 headed toward the tiny community of Blanchard, where it would begin to meander along the narrow Samish and Chuckanut Bay shoreline, snaking along through the Chuckanut Mountains towards Bellingham. The tracks literally ran along a very narrow shelf running along water's edge. A steep hillside rising immediately from the eastern side of the track had been heavily

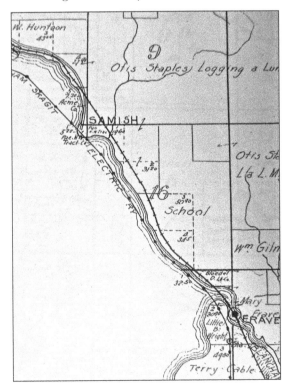

logged, and combined with its thin soil and lose sandstone made the area prone to landslides. Running west, parallel to the Great Northern, was the interurban trolley line. So, little room existed on the narrow ridge that four miles of its tracks had to be built upon offshore pilings.

Map of the Great Northern line through the Chuckanuts. It was at Samish, that engine No. 358 screeched to a halt after the killings. Blanchard can be seen on the lower right. Note: Steep cliffs offered little width for the Great Northern tracks, forcing the Interurban electric trolley railway to build upon pilings over the water. Meetskers maps.

Passengers

As the 358 picked up speed across the Skagit flats, passengers rocked back and forth in their seats. To the rear of the day-coach, sitting on the right side of the dining car door sat 38-year-old Kansan, Robert L. Lee, a timekeeper for the Puget Sound Navy Yards in Bremerton, where he had been employed ten years. He was on his way to Bellingham to visit normal school student Rose Knutson. He planned to spend the evening in Bellingham, before taking the morning interurban for Mount Vernon, where D. C. Henry, an old chum, would meet him.

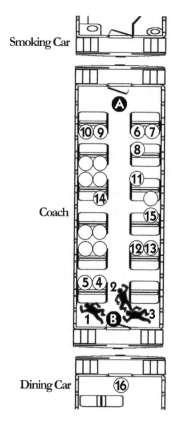

The coach layout at the time of the botched robbery, turned killing: (1) R.L. Lee (2) H.R. Adkison (3) T.F. Wadsworth (4) E.V. Derwerker (5) Edith Derwerker (6) Mary Garlick (7) George Garlick (8) Evelyn Garlick (9) Edwin Lopas (10) Edsel Garlick (11) V. Massi (12) A. Henningsen (13) Orabella Henningsen (14) M.E. Charleston (15) Mrs. Vorig (16) Charles Waldron (A) Gunman (B) Gunman.

Drawing by Brian Young

Next to Lee sat 39-year-old Harold R. Adkison, of Vancouver, British Columbia. Adkison, a high official of the B. C. Tire & Rubber Company of Vancouver, was returning home to his wife and two daughters from a Seattle business trip.

Occupying a seat across the aisle to the left of the dining car door, sat Thomas F. Wadsworth, of Vancouver. Wadsworth was a conductor for the Canadian

Pacific Railway. He was returning from a visit seeing his wife and family wintering in California. Mrs. Wadsworth had been ill, and it was thought the milder climate would do her good.

Edith Van Derwerker (34),[81] wife of a wealthy contractor/builder of Everett, sat beside her six-year-old daughter, Edith, in the seats just in front of Lee and Adkison. She was the daughter of Rev. J. Marshall Harrison, rector of St. Paul's Episcopal church in Bellingham, and was on her way to visit her father.

To the front of the day-coach, near the door entering the smoking car, sat the Garlick Family. Mary Garlick (29) sat in the first seat at the front of the coach, with her back to the door, riding backwards so that her daughter Evelyn (7), who occupied the seat directly across, might ride facing the front of the car. Next to her, was a tired and fidgety son George (3). Her father, Edwin Lopas, (67) a rancher at Mountain View occupied the beach across the aisle from Mary with her husband Edsel (35). The family was just ending a long vacation, having taken the steamer *President* south to Panama before Christmas, and now returning home to Ferndale.

The only other known male in the day-coach was Vincent Massi, an employee of the Italian Exchange Bank of Vancouver, who sat front-right of either row three or four. The rest of the men occupied the smoker in the car ahead. The rest of the day-coach consisted of women and children. Lizzie Spenger, on her way to visit her daughter Emma Rath in Bellingham. Alice Henninger and daughter Cravell, of Everett, were on their way to Bellingham to visit C. E. Stearn in Geneva. Miss Marla Lavine, of Blaine, and Miss Faulkner, a schoolteacher from Harmony, a suburb of Mount Vernon and a Mrs. Vorig and M. E. Charleston.[82]

But these were not all the passengers riding the ill-fated train north, and no recorded has come to light on how many boarded at the Burlington depot that evening. Only the two unnamed men dressed in long coats and fedoras who took their seats in back of the smoking car.

---

[81] Van Derverker, Van Dereverher.
[82] An incompleted passenger list: S. Miller, 312 Lottie Street; J. W. Saunder, F Street; W. H. Powers, Kansas City Mo., to Bellingham; Robert Nichols, 114 Franklin Street; C. D. Hunt, 1703 Champion Street; B. F. Reno, 300 Potter Street; C. E. Bell, 2010 High Street; H. F. Surles, freight conductor; F. E. Krentz, freight brakeman; Harry Edison, Mount Vernon to Bellingham; Charles E. Hildebrand, 1406 Bancroft Street; Burt Grommers, Davis Street; "Jap woman" to visit George F. Sakai, 503 West Holly Street; Mr. and Mrs. A. I. Syoddard, Spokane, to Bellingham; Mrs. William Jenkins, 1403 F Street, Bellingham; Alice Vaughn, Sauk to Bellingham; A. W. Giest Jr. and B. L. Plumton.

A Senseless Act

Before reaching Blanchard, J. F. Latham saw the men leave the smoker onto the vestibule between cars. The time was said to have been 7:35. Mrs. Vorig, who was walking down the aisle of the day-car just before the men entered, saw them standing on the vestibule tying white handkerchiefs over their faces. Before she could give the alarm, the outlaws entered the day-coach. Mary Garlick, sitting in the first seat facing the opposite direction was unaware, until one of the bandits told her to move across the aisle to another seat. He then took position in front of where Mary had been seated peering down the aisle toward the dining car door, while covering the smoking car behind. At that point, the bandit, appearing to be the leader, hollered out they were holding up the train. He demanded passengers hand over all their valuables, wallets and purses. To emphasize the point, a revolver was drawn and fired into the ceiling of the coach. The second robber ran down the aisle, where he was endeavoring to lock the door leading into the dining car.

Edwin Lopas, about 1905.
Courtesy of Center for Pacific Northwest Studies

TOP: Mary and Edsel Garlick, 1902. Courtesy of Center for Pacific Northwest Studies

BOTTOM: Lester, Evelyn and George Garlick, 1918. Courtesy of Center for Pacific Northwest Studies

Women screamed, many attempting to hide rings and valuables. The bandit called out, "Don't make so-much a fuss, you women. It's all a joke."

Edwin Lopas retorted, "It's a shame someone hasn't a gun to shoot you with." The unafraid old man stared up at the bandit, who ignored him.

With no warning, Thomas Wadsworth sprang upon the outlaw locking the dining car door. A desperate struggle insured. Lee and Adkison, who were seated across the coach, rushed to Wadsworth's aid. At this point, the outlaw standing at the front end of the coach fired his revolver, first shooting two of the coach's lights out and then firing right and left into the ceiling. Wadsworth and Lee let go of the outlaw, dropping to the floor behind a rear seat. As the two men loosened their holds the robber swung his gun into play, firing five shots in rapid succession.

According to Edwin Lopas, when the struggle commenced, "The desperado standing guard...rushed up to where his partner was being held and deliberately shot three or four times into the backs of the men holding him down. He retreated after to his original position between the first two seats in the car, and continued shooting over the passenger's heads while his partner, now freed, fired more shots into the bodies..."

The first bullet struck Adkison just over the left eye, the slug entering his brain. He dropped to the floor dead, his head and shoulders being held in a reclining position by the corner of the coach.

At the first shots, little Evelyn Garlick became paralyzed with fear. She vomited all over herself.

"My first intimation that a robbery was on foot," said Edith Van Derwerker, "came when a small man, dressed in a brown suit, his face covered with a handkerchief, stepped into the front door of the coach, fired a pistol and called in a loud voice to all of us to hold up our hands. Instantly he ran the length of the car – my seat was next to the last on the right-hand side of the car. Waving his pistol, he sprang to the door of the coach and turned the key. At this juncture, a man seated in the rear seat on the opposite side of the aisle from me, leaped to his feet, struck the bandit and attempted to imprison his arms. Two men seated immediately behind me, arose to the assistance of the passenger. The three grappled with the robber, who, when bent partly over the seat upon which I was sitting, twisted lose his right arm and with a fusillade of shots from an automatic pistol, struck down his victims. It happened so suddenly that I was paralyzed. My little girl seated beside me never uttered a word. The blood from the wound of the first man shot spurted across the back of the seat and struck me in the face."

"While the murderer was doing his deadly work, his partner, standing at the opposite end of the coach, continued to fire his pistol over the heads of the terrified passengers, and in order to avoid the danger to himself of any shot fired from the smoker, stepped in from the aisle alongside of a woman (Mary Garlick) who occupied a seat in that portion of the coach."

Lee, who was just turning to crouch behind the seat was shot in the back, the bullet entering just below his shoulder blade and passing directly through his heart. He fell on his face dead. Wadsworth was shot three times in the back, one of the bullets splitting his heart in two. Lee lay with his head between Wadsworth's legs and Wadsworth's feet touching those of Adkison.

Van Derwerker claimed one of the shots fired by the bandit in the forward end of the coach whistled past her head. Her statement was substantiated later when a lead ball embedded in the wainscoting of the car, a few inches over the rear door, was dug out. The outlaw showed no mercy once he started firing at the three men. He stood there a moment to make sure his victims were dead before heading toward the front of the coach while collecting bags.

Meanwhile, as the train approached the Blanchard depot, one story has it that the Noce brothers were playing nearby awaiting to watch the train roar by. Hearing the 358's whistle shrieking the brothers stopped their play to watch the train. As the 358 sped by the boys heard gunshots and saw muzzle flashes in the day-coach windows.[83]

As the covering bandit returned to the front of the coach after helping his partner, Edwin Lopas and Edsel Garlick frustratingly sat. One of the two said to the other, "My God, isn't there something we can do to get these fellows?" The standing bandit hearing the remark ordered his partner to check their pockets for guns.

Garlick, a "grizzled old pioneer" said the *Bellingham Herald* was "heartbroken" over the humiliation. Garlick said he had ample opportunity to kill the bandit while his back was turned, but he had no gun, and had to cowardly sit there with his hands up.

Van Derwerker continued her story:

"The three murdered men were dropped in the rear end of the coach, and

---

[83] This story comes from *Skagit Settlers Trails and Triumphs 1890-1920*. The Skagit County Historical Series, Volume 4. A note of observation: The Great Northern timetable has a stop in Blanchard, although no stop was made and not mentioned in newspapers. This brings to question why the robbery was conducted just before Blanchard depot risking the train stopping.

the robber, the objects of his terrible violation still in his mind, ordered us in that portion of the coach to hand over our valuables. I had just dropped my bag upon the floor and had placed my feet upon it. As the robber stepped over the prostrate form of one of his victims, I handed him my purse with four dollars in silver in it.

"Occupants of the seats ahead of me, seven or eight of them I should judge, handed over their purses. In the center of the car several women, hysterical with fear, were proffering their purses and jewels, calling shrilly to the bandit to come and take their valuables.

"He came down the aisle with the smoking gun in one hand reaching for purses while the holdup at the forward door repeatedly cried out, warning the passengers that they would be shot dead if they attempted resistance. Most of the passengers in the coach were women and they held out their purses for the thief to take. When about half way down the aisle, the outlaw apparently lost his nerve and broke into a run, passing by the pocketbooks and money held out to him… with a shout to his companion who was ahead of him, he dashed madly for the door and sprang off the train."

Alice Henningsen and her daughter, Orabella, were within a few feet of the scene of the killing. She thought first of her money and jewels, slipping them under the seat. Neither of the women lost any of their possessions as the outlaw broke and ran down the aisle before he had reached their seat.

Mrs. M. E. Charleston, who was seated near the front end of the coach, said she saw other women hold out their purses as the bandit passed in frantic haste to escape. He ignored the pocketbooks extended to him, but carried a number of purses and handbags in his hands.

B. F. Reno, manager of the Pacific Telephone & Telegraph Company in Bellingham, was seated in the smoking car at the time the robbery occurred. Seated with him, enjoying cigars, were Charles E. Bell, of the Schwabacher Hardware Company of Seattle, and a gentleman named Laflin, a guard from the state penitentiary at Walla Walla. Suddenly, someone in the smoker cried out that a holdup was taking place in the day-coach. A roar of gunfire followed the alert. Laflin pulled his own revolver out and prepared to fire if the outlaws were bold enough to enter the smoking car. The panicked screams of women were heard and a few men in the smoker hollered they needed to do something.

Mrs. Charleston:

"When the bandits entered the car, the train was traveling at a fair rate of speed, but within an instant after the fatal shooting, someone gave a signal and the train came to such a sudden stop that my little girl and myself were almost jolted from our places."

It was Conductor Charles Waldron who sprang into action when he heard the shooting in the car before him. He was in the dining car at the time, and quickly "cut off the air" bring the train to a halt. With the shriek of the train's breaks connecting, the men in the smoker decided to rush the day-coach, but the outlaws were already long gone before they could smash the day-coach's locked door.

Charles Bell was the first to summon up the courage to cross the vestibule and enter from the car. As he did, excited occupants raised their hands, believing one of the robbers had returned.

Samish

Victor Clarence Beecher, (16) and his buddy, Thomas Thompson were standing at the interurban station at Samish when they saw the 358 come screeching to a halt. Both boys knew something was wrong and ran over to the depot about 150 feet distant to see what the trouble was, as they thought the train would jump the tracks. Thompson climbed onto the vestibule just in time to meet the bandits, who poked a gun in his face and told him to scat. Thompson leaped off and the two bandits followed. The outlaws ran alongside the train

Samish was not a village, but a stop for workers of the logging industry, circa 1914. Courtesy of Laura Jacoby's, Galen Biery collection.

215

climbing onto the tender, possibly hoping to hide. They were apparently frightened off by Engineer Wright, Fireman McIntosh and Brakemen R. Phillips and J. J. Mingo, who were searching the exterior of the train with lights.

Jumping off the tender, the bandits started across the boardwalk toward the interurban station. On the boardwalk, they were met by the two younger Beecher girls, Hazel and Mary, who with Victor had been waiting for their father, William, a sawyer at the Samish mill to get off work. The bandits then turned and ran back toward the tracks disappearing under a platform, it was thought.

The dead men were left where they fell until the train reached Bellingham's Northern Side Station and Coroner Henry Thompson arrived on the scene. Only then did both the law and coroner approach the rear of the coach from both directions. There they discovered Wadsworth shot in his side, the bullet passing through the body; Adkison through the head, and Lee riddled with bullets. Thompson noted any of the shots would have killed Lee, but one bullet tore the man's heart apart. Examining Adkison, Thompson noted the man was shot clean through the left eye. The coroner adding, he had to have been very close to the bandit's gun, for powder burns from the cartridge blackened Adkison's face. All three men died were they fell, their lives gone before frantic passengers could be of any assistance. Meanwhile, passengers aboard the train were not permitted to alight until the train crew had obtained their names and addresses.

The dead men were transferred to the Undertaking Parlors of Anders G. Wickman at 1146 Elk Street (now State Street). On Adkison's body was discovered a letter from one of his daughters, which had evidently been given to him before leaving Vancouver. The letter asking her dad to hurry home as soon as possible as she would miss him awful. He left behind a wife and two children.

Miss Rose Knutson waited in vain for the arrival of Robert Lee. The normal school student, who had known Lee for several years, was at the depot waiting to greet him when the train arrived. Instead, she learned of the horrible tragedy that transpired a short time prior.

The following morning, D. C. Henry waited for his friend at the Mount Vernon interurban car station. But instead of it carrying his friend Lee, the car brought the *American Reveille*, telling the appalling story of the triple shooting. The headline reading, "Train Robber Spills Blood of Victims Without Show of Mercy." Henry was aghast.

From the *American Reveille*, H. H. Matteson wrote:

"With the bullets thudding into the woodwork of the car above her head, with the warm, red blood of a murdered man spurting into her face and dyeing her garments, a woman on board the ill-fated Great Northern train 358, had still the presence of mind to drop upon the floor her bag containing several hundred dollars while she placed in the outstretched hand of a triple slayer a purse carrying four dollars in silver, tells story of the killing."

The story marked one of the few occasions a reporter's name appeared in Bellingham's early papers. Matteson was awarded the byline after scoring an exclusive with Van Derwerker.

Matteson wouldn't be alone, as the same issue credited competitive reporter, Frank Downie with a column headline, "Bandit Kills Three In Daring Train Robbery South Of City: Passengers shot down as they try to overcome one of the three outlaws who rob Great Northern north bound local at Samish Station – Second desperado shoots lights of day coach out and terrorizes occupants – Women faint as men fall – Money left behind."

The Posse

News of the holdup spread through Bellingham like wildfire, with many volunteering to join a posse. Whatcom County Sheriff Lewis A. Thomas and his deputies boarded the 358 as soon as the bodies were removed and taken back to Samish. Before he left, Sheriff Thomas contacted the Monroe State Reformatory

Posses seek bandits. *Bellingham Herald*, February 21, 1914

requesting their bloodhounds be sent by rail immediately with their masters. Thomas also contacted Skagit County Sheriff Edwin Wells, informing him he was leading a posse from the north, and with rapid measures from the south; they could capture the killers presently trapped within an inescapable location, if they hurried.

Thomas realized at once the bandits could easily escape by water, if it had been their original plan. Thomas was of the assumption the robbers may have intended to rob the train around Blanchard, as they had done. By the time the robbery was completed the 358 would have been in the Chuckanut Bay area. How they planned to get off the train, he did not care, but it was the perfect location for a hidden launch to get them away.

A posse of about fifteen heavily-armed volunteers, under the charge of patrolman Wallace Nugent, boarded the motor launch *Wasp* and was plying the waters south along the shoreline. *Wasp* would conduct a comprehensive search of any boats encountered along the way. The U.S. Revenue launch *Scout* was dispatched from Friday Harbor at once to take part in the manhunt.

Samish, located at Pigeon Point, had no population. The depot servicing the stop was for workers of either the lumber mills of the area, or the Pearl Oyster Company. Sheriff Thomas looked over some maps he brought on the train. There were extremely steep hillsides at Samish he considered inaccessible at night. If there were a boat on shore, which was more than probable, the two outlaws could escape by water. Just a few hundred feet up the tracks was railroad tunnel 18; beyond would be very difficult to escape from the tracks. Retreating south would lead to the open flats and capture. Thomas shook his head. "The bandits hadn't intended on this," he thought, "neither the killings nor abandoning their original plan." They were in a most desperate situation. Thomas' fear was that once cornered, the bandits would shoot it out to the death, and more innocent lives may be lost.

In Mount Vernon, Skagit County Sheriff Edwin Wells had formed a posse of volunteers and was presently heading north along the tracks toward Blanchard. Once there, Wells intended to headquarter Deputy Sheriff Charles Stevenson and several other men, who would watch over the Blanchard Slough in case the fugitives should break through to the south. Meanwhile, Wells and his men would fan out scouring the woods, hillside and the water along a broad front.

The night was intensely dark with a waning crescent moon overhead, hidden by thick rain clouds. All of the uneven footwork had to be done by the glow of lanterns. But even under those horrid conditions, Whatcom Deputy

Looking south toward Samish from tunnel 18 in 2017. The cliffs of the Chuckanuts rise to the left. Only a narrow shelf exists for the Great Northern tracks. Taken by the author.

Sheriff Larry Flanagan found fresh tracks running along the muddy beach. Flanagan felt they were undoubtedly those of the bandits. He succeeded in tracking the prints to water's edge where he feared the outlaws made their escape. But the idea didn't entirely sit with him. Like his boss, Flanagan believed the outlaws had a preplanned means of escape. The deputy was willing to lay odds on the fiends running the short distance to Chuckanut Bay, about 4 miles distant, where he believed a boat was waiting, and possibly a third man.

As the Whatcom posse combed the region north of Samish, Sheriff Thomas set-up headquarters at the Pearl Oyster Company near the Samish depot with his underling, Larry Flanagan. Thomas would retain the 358 at Samish until it was recalled by the railroad, which would be soon. William A. Barnes, a reporter for the *Bellingham Herald*, followed the posse. He also set up a desk at Thomas' makeshift headquarters. The men discussed various theories of escape taken by the bandits. Some thought the bandits somehow reboarded the train and rode it into

Whatcom Deputy Sheriff Larry Flanagan. File photo: *Bellingham Herald*

Bellingham. It was acknowledged that they could have hidden in a tight corner or possibly beneath the train. Bellingham Police Detective Thomas Nugent denounced the theory sighting, "That would have been to exhibit headwork. The bandits certainly didn't show any headwork in their methods up to that time."

Sheriff Edwin Wells arrived at Samish with a few of his deputies to talk further theory and strategy with Thomas. There was an opinion the men had fled south from Samish with the purpose of avoiding the almost impassable country north. Sheriff Thomas told Wells his priority was to cutoff every possible means of escape north into Whatcom with eighteen able deputies and a posse of volunteers. Sheriff Wells concurred he was performing a similar tactic to the south with thirty-five heavily-armed deputies. The sheriffs both voiced concerns that time would eventually wear down their citizen volunteers, who were not used to beating the bush, or standing silent in the windy rain and winter's cold. Once the euphoria and excitement of the evening wore on they would retreat and head home to their warm beds.

Saturday

After interviewing all the passengers aboard the 358, descriptions were released to the press. It was determined the bandit standing in the forward end of the day-coach was about 5 foot, 9 inches tall; weight, 140 to 150 pounds; about 25 years old; of slender build, smooth shaven, with high cheekbones, and a thin pointed nose. His complexion and hair were said to be "medium dark." He wore a soft, dark hat, which was telescoped during the time of the holdup, but worn down while he was in the smoking car. He wore a brown coat and gray overcoat.

The bandit who struggled with the three men before the fatal shooting, was about 5 foot, 6 inches in height; 140 pounds; and aged around 25 years. He was also smooth shaven. He had sharp features, dark hair and dark snappy eyes. He wore a blue-black serge suit and a black soft hat. Witnesses claimed both men's faces and hands were pale white, giving thought they had been recently confined or were drug users. Each carried light caliber, blue steel barrel guns.

The Great Northern Railroad released a notice in the morning, offering a reward of $5,000 for each man captured, dead or alive. It was expected the reward would be greatly increased if the robbers were not captured immediately.

Meanwhile, the manhunt continued as morning dawned over Samish. "There is no especial fun, when you weigh 225 on the hoof, to don a pair of rubber boots and wade thigh high in the mud of Samish Bay man hunting," wrote *Bellingham Herald* reporter William Barnes. Saturday morning, he followed Deputy Sheriff Flanagan wading out into the mudflats in search of tracks. "Flanagan wasn't afraid to take a chance, and for the sake of reputation...the writer waddled along."

Overnight, tugs *Reliance* and *Warrior,* in the charge of Whatcom Deputy Sheriff Bowden, arrived to reinforce *Wasp* and *Scout* in their efforts to blockade Samish and Chuckanut Bays. A boat would periodically peel-off to patrol the islands off Samish Bay, in hopes the outlaws were in a temporary hiding place and would attempt to move.

USRC *Scout*, circa 1900s. The revenue cutter patrolled the Chuckanut shoreline, suspecting the killers would escape by night in a hidden launch.
Courtesy of Coast Guard Tugboat Association

In the morning, despite heavy rain, large posses left both Bellingham and Burlington amounting to a reported 500 men supplied with provisions to relieve the posses from the night before. Several grand sweeps of the Chuckanut Mountains were undertaken throughout Saturday, but as evening approached both sheriffs agreed the outlaws had slipped through before they could close a noose on the hilly region. Deputies still remained posted to cover potential escape routes, but the main force of volunteers returned to their respective cities. Soon, undaunted by the weather, bounty hunters appeared in the Chuckanuts armed with an assortment of weapons. Once the $5,000 reward was posted every amateur with a gun hit the woods.

Bellingham Police Captain Alexander L. Callahan returned from a trip into the hills above Samish, stating to the *Bellingham Herald* to have seen "...a bandit hunter hidden behind every tree and bush within miles of the scene of the hold-up..." and that he fled from the vicinity for fear of being shot himself. Callahan was convinced "the outlaws can not escape by way of the route he followed unless they are bulletproof." The captain also pointed out his fear it was only time before an innocent was gunned down in the Chuckanuts believed to be an outlaw. Everyone wanted to secure the bounty, and many trigger-happy men were out there.

As expected, over a hundred railroad detectives, Pinkerton's and other agencies were about to descend on the region and push out the local boys for the bounty.

William Barnes wrote in Sunday's column:

"One thing alone seems inevitable. These wretched murderers will be caught, perhaps not without desperate expedients, but caught they will be.... Society, outraged, eventually will murder them in reprisal. It may not be popular, it may not be just, but, without losing sight of the pall, which has descended over three wretched, sorrowing households, the writer feels a mighty pang of pity for those hunted creatures."

Roundup and Folly

Bellingham was soon invaded. James J. Hill, owner of the Great Northern Railway, sent his own man, Special Agent Al G. Ray from headquarters in Saint Paul, Minnesota, along with Assistant Special Agents James J. Davis from Seattle, Charles McShane from Chicago, and James A. Dundon from Columbus, Ohio to direct the investigation. Newspapers claimed over 150 railroad detectives and Pinkerton agents would participate in the manhunt. Special Agent Ray made his headquarters in Bellingham's Leopold Hotel, on Sunday, February 22. His first act was to appoint Detectives James J. Davis and Lee Tegner to direct all railroad operatives between Burlington and Bellingham in the search.

Hill increased the reward to thirty thousand dollars for the capture of the bandits, dead or alive. If any man should be slain by the outlaws while trying to affect their capture, his heirs would be paid the sum of $15,000.

Special Agent Davis posted in the *Bellingham Herald*:

"Any evidence or information given us will be strictly confidential. No one need hesitate telling us what they know about the identity of the outlaws or giving us their own names, as their identity will be divulged to no one unless they desire that their names be made known. Any one who gives information to us, which will lead to the arrest of the proper person, will receive the reward just the same as if they had affected the capture themselves."

Bellingham Chief of Police Horace C. Byron issued orders to his officers to keep a sharp lookout for suspicious characters in the city. He and railroad detectives believed the bandits were amateurs and their homes discovered within the two counties. It wasn't long before lawmen from Seattle to Vancouver, B. C., were arresting anyone deemed suspicious. Most of which constituted unfamiliar faces. Hundreds of calls were coming into police departments creating a backlog. Citizens reported on every stranger they encountered with obvious hopes of getting the reward.

One report came from Hanna's café at 307 West Holly Street. Mrs. Hanna and her waitresses opened the restaurant about 8 a. m., and a few moments later a man of medium height and slender build entered asking for a cup of black coffee. He wore a fedora pulled down over his eyes, and appeared so nervous he at once drew the attention of the waitress.

The stranger started a conversation, saying he had come from Seattle on the train following the one just robbed. He seemed eager to talk about the robbery, but was so nervous his teeth chattered as he tried to speak. (It wasn't mentioned how he came out from a cold February gale) The stranger's actions aroused suspicions, however, and Mrs. Hanna feared he knew more. The man declared he was in search of a room and asked the location of a hotel. He claimed to have been in a number of train robberies and did not care to be mixed up in another. Hanna directed him to the Leopold Hotel, but police failed to locate him.

Charles Bell, who was a passenger in the smoking car, thought he had identified the man who did the killings in Bellingham. Bell was standing in the Pickering Hardware store at 1317 Commercial Street talking with J. L. Pickering when three shabbily dressed men entered and asked for ammunition for a .44 Colt revolver. Pickering informed the trio he did not have the shells in stock.

As soon as the men left, Bell informed the hardware man that one of the three was the fellow who had fired the fatal shots on the Great Northern train. The police were notified. Bell trailed the suspects to the Stanbra gun store at 1315 Railroad Avenue, and seeing no officer in sight, left the trio there and started for police headquarters.

He soon returned with a squad of officers, but the men had left. Half-hour later, Bell spied one of the young men walking down Dock Street near the Leopold Hotel. The officers trailed the suspect to a coffee house in the basement of the Alaska Building. A moment later he found himself looking down the barrels of several revolvers. He submitted to arrest quietly and was taken to headquarters. The young man explained that he and two other friends were securing a supply of ammunition because they were going to get the reward for the bandits, when they found them. The story was accepted by the police and the men released.

A report from Mukilteo brought the news of the capture of the robbers. There were four in all, who were overpowered when they came to the wharf of the fishing village in a launch. It later developed the party were actually fishermen who went to Mukilteo to secure medical aid for one of their friends.

Bellingham's Lynde Williams and Garnet Crews placed Art Shelton under citizen's arrest when he was found crawling up a steep bank leading from the Great Northern tracks to the interurban line. Shelton's clothing was soaked through from rain and mud. Nothing was mentioned regarding Shelton's beaten condition when brought in. He told the deputies he was looking for a logging camp, but could not name the camp. Shelton was held at the city jail.

The Pinkerton Detective Agency placed a large force in the field, although they were most secretive, never disclosing their operations. The *Bellingham Herald*, claimed many of the agents were disguised as "hoboes riding the rods of coast trains and sleeping in box cars with tramps in an effort to secure some clue as to the identity of the much wanted robbers." The agency wouldn't confirm, nor deny this, but local police noted the once "seemingly endless string of hoboes that called on the city jail nightly in search of a bed had suddenly vanished." It was also noticed that the city had lost most of its questionable characters, as they evidently deemed it best to leave while the leaving was good.

Circumstances were no different in Skagit County, where mass arrests took place as well. Deputy Sheriff Stevenson arrested Frank Holton, alias "Cincy Jack," in Anacortes on suspicion of knowing something of the train robbery. Holton had made several wild remarks at Burlington, which led persons to suspect him of being connected with the robbery. Deputy Stevenson was informed, but before he could locate Holton, he had taken a train for Anacortes. The officer secured an automobile and followed, locating Holton soon after arriving. When interviewed by the *American Reveille*'s correspondent at Anacortes, Deputy Stevenson would not divulge the nature of Holton's remarks, but that he was being held.

Ada H. Durdle, who lived in Whatcom County, reported news that had the attention of all law agencies on February 25. And it was big news! Ada was forced to feed three men at gunpoint who entered her home without warning. "Get something for us to eat and be quick about it," one of the trio remarked as they seated themselves at the dining room table and laid their guns down. She informed them there was very little food prepared in the house. This seemed to make the taller of the three angry, who sprang up from the chair. He told her to "get something to eat and be quick about it." On returning to the dining room with some of the victuals, she heard one of the men remark: "Well, we have plenty of ammunition now anyway."

Ada told Police Chief Byron, before leaving her home one of the three turned to her and said: "If you tell the police we were here you will be shot dead." Ada watched the men until they had disappeared and then ran straight to the police. But the men had made good their escape. Chief Byron believed the men had been in hiding somewhere in the vicinity since the night of the killings and probably ran short of provisions. He was certain now they were making for the Canadian border. Word was sent to Blaine, Ferndale and other places in the probable path taken by the men in the hope they might be apprehended before reaching the Canadian line. The description of the two train robbers fit two of the men who fled the Ada's home.

Unfortunately, the mystery of the trio was never solved.

The Case Against George Ball

On March 26, Special Agent James J. Davis announced a man was in Canadian custody and another, believed to be Harry Mathews, alias McAvoy, had escaped police surveillance. George E. Ball was arrested at Calgary, Alberta. It was claimed Ball had been in Bellingham on Wednesday, February 18, and again on the morning after the killings. Chief Special Agent Ray announced he was in possession of an unbroken chain of evidence showing Ball's movements from the day preceding the shooting to the time of his arrest. Harry Mathews, who railroad detectives declared without doubt to be the other man with Ball, was in Bellingham the day before the crime.

Railway operatives claimed on February 18, two men, said to be Ball and Mathews, entered a Seattle store and purchased two revolvers. The second-hand dealer recognized photographs of Ball and Mathews as the men who visited his store.

On February 19, the two men arrived in Bellingham where they visited two local drug stores trying to purchase morphine, both being users of the drug. Later they went to a pool hall and played several games. The druggists and billiard hall proprietor picked the two suspected men from fifty photographs of convicts.

On February 20, the day of the fatal shooting, the two appeared in a Mount Vernon drug store asking for morphine. They walked from Mount Vernon to Burlington and boarded the ill-fated train at Burlington depot. Thirty-five minutes later three passengers were shot to death. Ball was alleged to have reached Bellingham by riding the brake beams of the train. Detectives were unsure the route and method taken by Mathews.

A Seattle railway detective who happened to be in Bellingham recognized Ball the morning after the robbery. He followed Ball to a northern bound passenger train at 12:35 p.m. They got off the train at New Westminster, Ball securing a logging job; the detective doing likewise. The detective was advised not to take the arrest by his superiors, as it was hoped Ball would soon leave the camp and join his companion at a previously agreed location. Ball did not remain at the camp long, but went to Vancouver. Six other railway operatives joined the railway detective in shadowing the man. Later, Ball went to Calgary and the party of detectives rode the same train.

They watched Ball closely. News leaked out of Seattle that warrants had been sworn out for the arrest of two men suspected of the robbery. Ball began to act suspiciously and the operatives feared he was aware of being shadowed. On March 25, Ball walked into a telegraph office and sent out a telegram. As he came from the building Canadian police placed him under arrest. It was the belief of agent Ray, that Ball realized he was being watched and warned his partner not to join him.

With Ball behind bars an effort was made to have him identified by passengers aboard the ill-fated 358 and those who believe they had seen him in the vicinity on the days prior and after the robbery. Ball was taken to Mount Vernon for lockup.

Ball's Trial

By Wednesday, April 1, 1914, George Ball was standing in Mount Vernon's Skagit County Superior Court before Judge Egbert Crookston (58), charged with train robbery and the first-degree murder of three passengers. Ball swore he was not guilty of the charges, and had an alibi to prove it. Chief Prosecutor Charles D. Beagle put forth the information, but he and Sheriff Wells were not satisfied they had charged the right man for the crime. Feelings of this uneasiness were never disclosed, but the two, along with Detective James Davis, would travel to British Columbia to investigate Ball's alibi.

On Friday, April 10, Ball entered a plea of not guilty at his arraignment. A preliminary hearing had produced testimony from three Bellingham witnesses. Edward G. Fremming (34), proprietor of Fremming's Drug Store, said he had no reason to believe Ball was the same man in his store asking for morphine. Spencer B. Weiser (41), proprietor of the Weiser Drug Store claimed the same. Sadie J. Knowlan (40), landlady of the Butte Lodging house at 303 1/2 West Holly Street was asked if a man matching Ball's description spent a night at her lodging house about the time of the holdup. If so, could she identify Ball as that man; she could not.

Passengers Edwin Lopas and the Garlicks appeared as witnesses against Ball. Their testimony was the strongest in their identification of Ball, as being the man who stood guard and fired several of the shots during the holdup. Edsel Garlick and his father-in-law Lopas claimed to have had a good look at the man and knew his features. Mary Garlick said she got a good view of Ball's face, where it was exposed under the handkerchief, and swore she knew Ball was the man.

Meanwhile, things became complicated when Prosecutor Beagle, Sheriff Wells and Detective Davis returned from Canada. They had become convinced the Great Northern detectives had arrested the wrong man. But railway officials ignored the assertion and continued to pursue the case against Ball. Beagle, in an unprecedented move, paid to bring three witnesses from Port Coquitlam, B.C. to Mount Vernon to testify on Ball's behalf.

On Saturday, after four hours spent in the examination of witnesses, the Ball case stood practically as it had before the preliminary trail. Seattle defense attorneys John F. Dore, and Robert Welsh, believed the case would never go to the jury. However, rail officials believed otherwise.

Spectators were full of anticipation to see the killer. Entering the courtroom walked attorneys Dore and Welsh, surrounding George Ball on each side. Closing the gap behind followed Sheriff Ed Wells and Prosecuting Attorney Beagle. They passed through the crowded corridor and took their places in Judge Crookston's courtroom. Sheriff

Skagit Prosecutor Charles D. Beagle.
File photo: *Anacortes American s.*

227

Deputies Charles Stevenson, Shell Elkins, William Beardsley and Gilkey were seated in the courtroom in case the crowd got out of hand. Also present were Deputy Prosecutor Lester Whitmore and Court Stenographer John Begg.

The first few witnesses testified to having seen Ball in Burlington.

Marshal G. C. McDaniels of Burlington, claimed he saw Ball, or a man whom he believed to be Ball, near the depot about 6:30 on the evening of February 20. McDaniels thought another man with Ball resembled a photo shown to him of Harry Mathews.

Harry Robinson, station engineer at Burlington, next testified he had observed two young men about the depot on the night of the holdup, and was positive Ball was one of the two.

Thomas Macintyre, assistant road master at Burlington station, stated as he stood at the conductor's window two men approached and he directed them to another window to purchase tickets. He was positive Ball resembled the smaller of the two men he saw that night.

Vincent Massi, the Italian Exchange Bank employee, gave his account of the holdup. He sat three or four seats from the door through which the bandits entered. He witnessed the two men in conversation on the vestibule, and claimed to have seen their faces before they tied handkerchiefs over their faces. He thought Ball was one of them.

The next witness called was Edith Van Derwerker, of 1222 Rucker Avenue, Everett. She heard a loud crash and then heard someone yell, "Hands up." Edith thought she was dreaming, as she had been dozing. Then she heard someone from behind say, "It's a holdup." Three men jumped on one of the bandits and she heard gunshots. She thought Ball resembled the general build of the man who walked down the center of the coach and took her purse.

Edsel and Mary Garlick gave the strongest testimony that Ball was the man in the holdup. Edwin Lopas took the witness stand, but he could not swear positively as to Ball being the man.

Marla Lavine, of Blaine, and Miss Faulkner, of Harmony, could not swear Ball was on the train. Even Conductor Charles Waldron thought Ball was the man, but would not swear to it.

Scapegoat and Alibi

Next taking the stand were the three witnesses Prosecutor Beagle brought from Port Coquitlam, B.C., to establish Ball's alibi. The first, Walter R. Russell, a

228

machinist on the Canadian Pacific Railway, stated he saw Ball on the night of February 20 at Coquitlam. Russell was leaving the post office about 7:30 p. m., when Ball tried to sell him a raincoat, as he needed quick money. Russell remembered the date, as he was on his way to a dance. He considered purchasing the garment and was later sorry for not doing so. When asked why he was sorry, Russell said on the way to the dance his friends were wearing similar garments and regretted his not taking Ball up on his proposition.

John St. Pierre, of Coquitlam, testified to having been approached by Ball to purchase his raincoat the same evening. St. Pierre, who ran a pool hall, was able to confirm the date as Ball offered to sell his coat to a customer. St. Pierre had just cashed a check for the same customer who was pocketing his money in Ball's presence. Ball sold the coat. St. Pierre looked up the check and learned he had cashed it on February 21, and concluded Ball had been in his place on the night of the 20th.

J. W. Lowe, a switchman on the Canadian Pacific Railway, swore he had played three games of pool with Ball on the evening of the 20th at Coquitlam.

George Ball was then called to the stand and the courtroom fell silent. The *Bellingham Herald* reported Ball, "...talked rapidly and was very sure of his dates and very positive in his statements. He made no contradictory assertions and appeared at ease except for a slight nervousness." He gave his age as 26, and Winnipeg as his home. While in Vancouver, on the 18th, he registered at the Royal City Hotel, room number 13; got up on the morning of the 19th and walked to Coquitlam, a distance of seven miles. He said he got there about 2 o'clock in the afternoon and stayed about the pool halls until suppertime. He then went to the rail yard expecting to hop a ride to Calgary. He stayed in the neighborhood of the depot until midnight, when the yardmaster drove him out. Then he met his friend George Bell, and the two spent the remainder of the night in room 5 of a rooming house. The following day, he spent the afternoon in the pool halls, and bought a ticket that carried him twenty-six miles, and from there "bummed" his way until he awoke at Kamloops, B. C., on the morning of February 21, and registered at the "Time to Eat" hotel under the name of George E. Ball.

Ball claimed he had not been in the United States since November 1, 1913. He added he did not tell the officials about the pool halls he had visited in Coquitlam, as he was so full of "hop" that he could not remember. He admitted "...he used what he termed as hop, and says he has been using the drug for seven years." He declared he never committed a felony, robbery or burglary;

never has been in the penitentiary. He had served time for being a vagrant as follows: "Three months in Vancouver, two months in Calgary, thirty days in Mission, six months in Mission at another time; a few days in Seattle."

Great Northern detectives continued to push their case against George Ball. Skagit Prosecutor Beagle, beginning to feel the weight of forces larger than he could handle, requested that Washington State Attorney General William V. Tanner conduct an independent investigation of Ball's alibi. During Beagle's investigation, he had also turned up evidence regarding one of the railroad detective's informants who had it in for Ball over a woman. He gave Tanner his complete investigation files and sources.

Beagle told Tanner he believed railroad detectives were framing Ball in order to collect the $30,000 reward themselves. Tanner put the matter in Assistant Attorney General Scott Z. Henderson's hands, who engaged the Burns Detective Agency to investigate the Skagit prosecutor's findings. In short order, it was determined Beagle was correct in his assumptions, and Ball was innocent of the charges.

On Monday, June 15, 1914, the case against George E. Ball was dismissed on a motion by Prosecuting Attorney Beagle, that state's evidence was insufficient to sustain a conviction. To this day, no one knows who the two outlaws were who robbed the Great Northern No. 358 train, taking three innocent lives.

Chapter 11
Battle of Samish

Two steamboat owners were in competition for transporting goods up the Edison slough in the 1890s. Above is the only known photograph of one of the unnamed steamers docked in Edison, 1892. Courtesy of Skagit County Historical Museum

Few remember Skagit County was once highly dependent upon the Skagit River, and the sloughs cutting across the flats, to transport freight and passengers into the interior. Nothing moved inland without the navigation of a tiny fleet of stern and side-wheelers. Hay, oats and livestock, machinery, building materials, mail—every imaginable item moved afloat.

Life along these waterways were reminiscent of wistful old Mississippi River days. A glimpse of funneled smoke in the distance, coupled by the screech of a steam whistle, meant the approach of a paddle wheeler rounding the bend carrying mail and visitors. Children ran along the upper banks hollering and waving; gesturing for the wheelman to toot the whistle. Once landed, activity would accelerate along a wharf or small landing, transferring cargo.

The river boat was king, until the 1890s when rails were laid and automobile roads cut. Until then, everything traveled upon the waters of Puget Sound and elsewhere toward Skagit County's city of Anacortes, or to an exchange wharf on Samish Island. At Samish Island, freight and passengers offloaded from the larger steamers to be reloaded onto small privately owned boats and transported to Edison further up the slough.

Many challenges met those traveling by river or slough. Tidal shifts inhibited movement, as well as times of flood and drought affecting the rise and drop of waterways. The primitive steamers were prone to fire from embers carried from their wood burning stacks, especially those with flammable cargo, such as hay. Snags and groundings sunk their share of the fragile and often overloaded little vessels. And as competition cut rates, berthing at docks and wharfs were contested, tempers flared, rivals clashed and at times this escalated into violence. So was the case on Samish Island on August 9, 1895, with the beating and shooting death of Alonzo Wheeler. The episode became notoriously known, if not exaggerated, in the region's newspapers as the "Battle of Samish."

The origins of this savage encounter are rather murky. This was likely due to the island's close-knit community, which didn't speak against their own. Furthermore, the principal participants were bound by blood and marriage—united in an apparent long simmering conflict. The question stands—who was the aggressor, and who the victim in this bloody affair? The best offering is to tell the story, as it is known, and sort fact from fiction, and legend and lore.

An official record of events was chronicled in *An Illustrated History of Skagit and Snohomish Counties*, published in 1906 (11 years after the event). This immense volume, along with local newspapers of the day, faintly gives impression of Alonzo Wheeler being a sword-wheeling veteran of the former Confederacy. And Wheeler's adversary, Edwin Baldwin, a staunch veteran of the Grand Army of the Republic, and local leader of the so-called, "gang of thugs" who dispatched him.

It is true an attempt was made to form a community on the island for drifting confederates called "Atlanta," but that is where the legend begins and ends. Wheeler was born in 1862, a native of Polk County, Oregon. Barely out of diapers, Wheeler wouldn't have made a very formidable "Johnny Reb."

Edwin Baldwin on the other hand was born in 1845 and may have been a scrappy young teenage soldier. He was a pensioner of disabilities, granted by the government for "services rendered and wounds, exposure and disabilities received and incurred" during the war of the rebellion.

Alonzo Wheeler

If Alonzo Wheeler wasn't a son of the Confederacy, then who was he? Alonzo was one of thirteen children sired by James Wheeler. James, born 1820 in eastern Tennessee was a pioneer, reaching Oregon Territory in April 1849, settling a farm near Corvallis. He died aged 82 on November 14, 1902, after walking through a door to nowhere of the second story of the Farmer's Hotel, at Corvallis. With no stairs attached, he plummeted to his death.

Alonzo Wheeler first appears in Colfax, Whitman County, Territory of Washington, in 1887. On June 13, Colfax Constable J. W. Steward apprehended him for the crime of grand larceny. Wheeler was accused of rustling a two-year old steer belonging to C. R. Mooney, valued at $30.00. The steer was identified by a 'OO' brand on the left hip. He was slapped with a $500 bond, and to appear before a grand jury. Unable to pay, Wheeler was jailed and further ordered to pay court costs of $28.80.

It was a bad day for Alonzo Wheeler. After his hearing, he was re-arrested by Whitman Justice of the Peace, William A. Inmau and Sheriff L. P. Berry to appear the following day before Judge William Longford. The crime? Stealing two head of cattle from Andrew McNeilly of Whitman on May 31, 1887. Both branded on the hip with a cornered star. This time seventeen witnesses, including his accomplice, Harry Ham who was also captured took the stand. Both plead guilty, receiving 18 months in the penitentiary with fines. Wheeler and Ham would serve one year and a day each.

Wheeler goes into obscurity, reappearing in Seattle in 1889, living at 412 Terrace. Soon after, he meets Ohioan Rebecca Jane Ray (44), and the two marry on February 8, 1890. The couple eventually move onto Samish Island, where Rebecca became owner of the Samish Hotel. Their union was short-lived, divorcing for reasons unknown. Wheeler was often penniless, and held jobs for short periods, which likely contributed to the breakup. Tragedy struck in March 1895, when Rebecca succumbed to heart failure. Her holdings were large: four lots of land held the hotel and outbuildings, 6 acres of land, 5 head of cattle, 18 chickens and a pony. Personal property was valued at $3,000. None of the estate going to her ex-husband. The hotel was purchased by John M. White, who will be discussed later.

Alonzo Wheeler, who never stopped loving Rebecca, would publicly lay blame for her demise at the feet of Edwin Baldwin. The accusation would appear in newspapers and during the trial to come, but no explanations were given to his claim. Needless to say, bad blood existed between Wheeler and Baldwin. The situation would come to a climax with a dispute between the two men.

Scene of the Crime

The scene of the row occurred on Samish wharf, where freight for the town of Edison was landed from the larger Puget Sound steamers. Reloaded, it was then ferried by small paddle wheelers up the shallow slough. The wharf was rather large, extending northward from a long, narrow neck of land from the mainland called Samish Island. On the southerly side of the island mudflats stretched for miles. The shore on the north side being more abrupt; the wharf dock extended out into the bay 150 feet. At high tide, both the north and south shores rose twenty feet, and in some places considerably more.

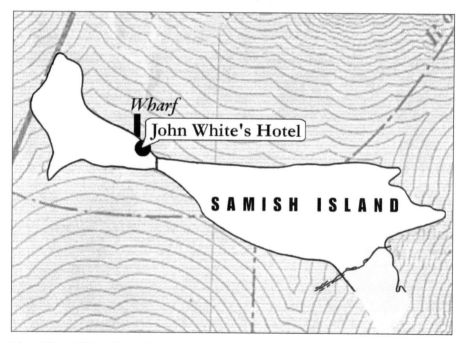

Map of Samish Island, Skagit County.
Drawing by Brian Young

On a bluff high above the wharf, John White's home and hotel (formally Rebecca Wheeler's Samish hotel) were located. White, who had lived in the region for over thirty-five years, was originally from Virginia. He came to the northwest before 1860, as a 29-year-old naval lieutenant serving aboard the Revenue Cutter *Jefferson Davis*.

White's hotel had a glorious view overlooking both Samish Bay and further to the north, Bellingham Bay. During the dark winter months, the northern exposure made the home a chilly affair as powerful gusts slammed against the bluffs. White had fewer boarders during the wet winter months, unless they were awaiting a steamer. During summer months, there was a swell of activity on the island and White saw a modest increase in guests. Summers were vibrant, with green foliage shading the house; his wraparound porch was a fine sitting area for guests sipping ice teas, or perhaps something a little stronger. A growth of thick bushes ran westward, along the length of the bluff toward a stairway leading down to the wharf. This provided a strong barrier and guests enjoyed walking its length.

Samish wharf would have been located along this shoreline, with John White's hotel on the bluff above, as it looked in 2017.

The Edison slough as it looked in 2018. Photo taken by the author

Less than a quarter mile to the east lived Edwin Baldwin, in a building he formerly operated as a saloon. A number of buildings were scattered about the property, some occupied and some vacant. Baldwin also operated a small hotel establishment, in direct competition with White for lodgers. It was claimed that he was not a pleasant man, having few respectable friends. Baldwin was reported by neighbors in the *Anacortes American* "...to be of a quarrelsome disposition and the chief cause of the feelings that have existed in the little community of Samish."

Edwin Baldwin was born in Maine. An imposing figure, Baldwin, and his clan were known to carry a certain amount of "bullish" weight on the island controlling several enterprises, primarily cornering two drinking establishments. Standing at five foot-seven, he had a large barrel chest, which complemented a wide girth. Of lesser intimidation was his balding egg-shaped head with patches of grey hair rounding his ears. Baldwin's face had a drooping appearance with sad blue eyes; not enhanced by his long, thick walrus mustache.

For several years, White and Baldwin were engaged in competing businesses running freight and ferrying passengers between Samish Island and Edison.

Baldwin hired his stepson, Ozro[84] Perkins as his mate on the boat. White had engaged Alonzo Wheeler as a partner, and perhaps feeling sorry for the man offered up lodgings at his home as well. The competition caused unpleasant feelings between both parties. In the fall of 1894, Baldwin abandoned the freight run, giving White a monopoly of the waterway. Months later, Baldwin and Perkins decided to resume operations and the rivalry intensified. The *Anacortes American* claimed, "The previous ill-feeling seems to have rapidly grown to bitter hatred." Wheeler, with his own troubles with Baldwin, only exacerbated tensions on the wharf.

Over time, Baldwin's insults and threats are said to have been too much for White. Eventually, White traveled to Mount Vernon to consult with Prosecuting Attorney George A. Joiner, with the expectation that something might be done toward the preservation of the peace on the small island. Joiner advised White it would be necessary to show cause for Baldwin to be arrested and placed under bonds. Disappointed, White returned home. A few days later, the conflict took place.

Early morning, Friday August 9, 1895, about the time the steamer *State of Washington* set course north for Bellingham, an exchange of words took place in front of White's hotel. Wheeler was sitting on the front porch, when Baldwin and his cohorts came along the path on the bluff. After a wordy argument progressed some time (possibly regarding either the Edison run or Rebecca), Wheeler called White to his assistance. Before White's arrival, Baldwin had left. It appeared Baldwin was instigating a showdown. With tensions escalating over the past month, both quarrelling parties had now strapped on their guns whenever leaving their homes.

White had a few chores requiring his attention before he and Wheeler ate an early lunch. Afterward, the two were to prepare the boat, as the *State of Washington* would be returning from Bellingham with a load of freight.

Battle

Captain George Dean (42), a Scotsman by birth, had been at sea most of his life. Residing on Samish Island for the past eighteen years, he was now employed as a 'Wharfinger,' charged with Samish wharf, the freight, passengers, mail and the visiting boats that tied up to its docks.

---

[84] Perkins' first name has appeared as: Ozio, Ozora and Ozro. The latter has been chosen in this story, as it appeared most often in legal documents.

Late Friday morning, Dean was awaiting the return of the *State of Washington* sitting in his room reading papers. Dean had quarters in the wharf's warehouse, which operated as his office, and at times a place to sleep. His quiet morning was soon interrupted by the sounds of footsteps coming down the wharf. He figured it would be White preparing for the inbound steamer. Dean got up from his chair and walked to the doorway peering out toward the stairway. He saw Ozro Perkins (Baldwin's stepson) about half way along the wharf, east of the stairs. White and Wheeler followed several feet behind. White carried a large block and tackle over his shoulder. Further back, Baldwin, Ulysses Loop (Baldwin's son-in-law) and A. Worden (husband to Baldwin's stepdaughter) were making their descent.

Ozro Perkins (30), was born in Skagit County; his father died soon after his birth. Perkins spent most of his youthful years on workboats or working as a logger in the region's thick forests. He wore the marks of his trade, cut scars on the right knee and another on his leg, along with many other healed wounds. Perkins married August 14, 1886, at Ferry, in the county of Oceana, Michigan to one Myrta Maud Inman. By the summer of 1895, he was a father of four, with another on the way. Perkins was a lean muscular man, five-foot five in height, with black greasy hair, bushy eyebrows, lacking ear lobes, with a long dropping mustache. He held an intimidating expression, with piercing steely eyes, which bore through a person.

Born in Pennsylvania, Ulysses Loop was the youngest of the men, at twenty-nine. He was also the smallest, standing at five-foot four. Broad shouldered, thick neck and heavyset, Loop wore a bushy mustache over his thick lips; groomed with waxed ends. He wore his black hair cut short, making his brown eyes more pronounced. Loop did not live on Samish Island, but with his wife Katie and son Darrel in New Whatcom, to the north on Bellingham Bay.

No description or history is known of A. Worden.

Worden walked with a long iron crowbar over his shoulder. Sensing trouble, Dean stood watch as the men came along. At the foot of the stair ramp, White turned off toward his boat, while Wheeler continued down the dock following Perkins. As the trailing three men reached the dock, Worden stopped where White veered off and just stood in place. The other two men followed Wheeler. Dean knew tempers had been accelerating all week, and thought it queer the men were hustling to catchup with Wheeler. Dean turned looking out over the bay and could now see the steamer approaching in the distance. It would dock in fifteen minutes.

At that very moment, Perkins went around the east side of the warehouse, followed by Wheeler. Out of his sight, Dean heard a shriek from around the corner and started running in that direction. "Everything happened fast," Dean would say later. As he ran toward the commotion, he glanced thirty feet down the south side of the dock where the men had come from. He could see White coming along fast with his sidearm drawn, when he heard gunfire erupting from around the corner. Dean said later, "I heard a scuffling and then the shooting commenced from behind the warehouse, toward the shore from where I was." Dean lurched back, not to be caught in crossfire. White's pistol discharged, but at what Dean could not tell. The shot went wild, as Worden swung the crowbar down on White's head, tearing the scalp back from his skull. White collapsed onto the dock, the blow causing him to remain unconscious in a pool of blood.

Dean hollered at Worden, commanding him not to hit White again. Worden hollered back, "If he did not stop bothering them, they would kill him." Re-rounding the corner, Dean could see Wheeler down on the dock with a revolver in hand. Baldwin stood over him with his own revolver drawn. The other men were locked in furious battle kicking and beating the down man. "He was down then," said Dean, "Perkins was trying to strike him with a club and Loop tried to strike him with his feet."

Wheeler miraculously got to his feet and started running north again, with the three chasing after him. Dean claimed later, "I tried to check them, but they went too fast. I couldn't do it." Dean gave chase, again hearing gunshots before he made the northeast corner of the warehouse.

Again, a beating incurred. A bloodied Wheeler moved on around the building, only to be cutdown by Baldwin with a shot to his side and another to the ankle. "I saw him point his gun at Wheeler and heard the gun go off." said Dean.

Threatened the same could happen to him, Dean moved off toward the southwest corner hoping someone heard the shots and was responding. Wheeler broke loose once again and came racing around the front corner of the warehouse, darting behind Dean for protection near a rain barrel. He fell there in a heap. "I tried to protect him, but they threw me off. They swung me around back from him; (Perkins) told me to keep away from him, they wanted to kill him. I said, you have done enough now." Baldwin took aim and shot a last time, the bullet passing through Wheeler's abdomen and into the fir dock.

"I told Baldwin to get off the wharf. He said, 'Let us go, we are ordered off the wharf.' He went ahead and the other two stayed there and tried to beat

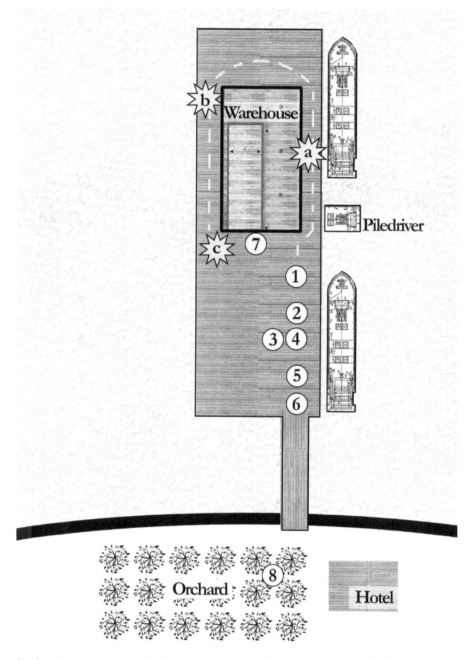

Samish wharf. Illustrating the fight on August 9, 1895: (1) Ozro Perkins (2) Alonzo Wheeler (3) Ulysses Loop (4) Edwin Baldwin (5) John White (6) A. Worden (7) Capt. George Dean (8) Daniel E. Douty. (a) First time Wheeler goes down. (b) Second time Wheeler goes down. (c) Third time Wheeler goes down. Drawing by Brian Young

Wheeler to death. They went back to pitch on him again and told me if I resisted I would be killed too."

Once more, Wheeler was plummeled by the men's heavy boots. His body a bloody mass of torn flesh and mashed meat. Blood was flowing onto the dock. Captain Dean's yelling finally persuaded the men to depart. They may have had further incentive to leave, as the steamer *State of Washington* was fast approaching the wharf with her whistle blowing. No doubt the passengers and crew saw what was amiss and tried to break up the brawl with whistle blasts.

The scene on the wharf after the mêlée was a bloody affair. Wheeler lay

The steamer *State of Washington* was returning from Bellingham and preparing to dock. The crew, witnessing the fight, blew the ship's whistle as it approached. Alonzo Wheeler was swiftly carried aboard and taken to Anacortes for medical attention.
Laura Jacoby's, Galen Biery collection

motionless, nearly dead with three devastating bullet wounds fired at close range and heavily beaten. His head was a mass of cuts and bruises. His body scarred with blackening bruises from kicks, clubbing and gunshot wounds. One bullet penetrated his ankle shattering it; another entered his right side above the sixth rib, ranging downward (through the right lung) and out through the back; a third entered the abdomen "midway between the anterior superior process of the ileum (small intestine) and the median line, ranging down through the pelvis from right to the left buttock."

Alonzo Wheeler was not alone in the carnage of the battle. John White's scalp was torn open by the blow to his head. He was on his feet again, but dazed. Two bullets struck Baldwin, one to the forehead above the right eye, which fortunately for him veered off his skull. The other bullet struck his left wrist. Perkins carried two bullet wounds, both mere scratches. One struck the top of the head, the other his breast.

When the steamer arrived, crewmembers rushed off with a mattress, building a makeshift stricter-bed. Wheeler was placed on board and taken immediately to Anacortes. On arrival, the crew carried Wheeler to the Wilson Hotel, where Dr. George B. Smith announced his recovery as doubtful. The other injured men remained on Samish Island, attended by a Dr. Shore of La Conner.

Much of the time, Alonzo Wheeler remained unconscious. Occasionally, he would attempt to speak—sometimes commencing, "My father lives at the old home—." Then lapse into unconsciousness. During one lucid day, Wheeler realized his impending death was near, and made a legal statement to authorities of the facts leading to his death. He survived only a few days, dying on the afternoon of August 15, at 1:15 p.m.

The story of the fight on the quiet island quickly made the region's newspapers, the *Weekly Anacortes American*.

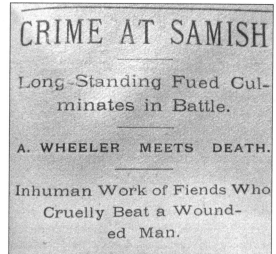

Crime at Samish.
Weekly Anacortes American

Arrest

The day after, Skagit County Sheriff W. E. Perkinson arrived on Samish Island, where he rounded up all parties involved and brought them to Mount Vernon. The men were held for assault, but Perkinson waited on filing formal charges until Wheeler was out of danger. However, recovery was not in the cards for the dying man. Sheriff Perkinson finally charged the men with murder in the first-degree, filing a complaint on August 16, 1895.

Skagit County Prosecutor George A. Joiner represented the state. Attorney B. B. Fowles represented the defendants. A preliminary hearing was held in Justice Court on August 17, before Justice of the Peace John L. Anable. Witnesses included: George Dean, James Dean (brother) and John White.

Attorney Fowles asked the court to dismiss all charges, and discharge each of the defendants on the grounds the complaint did not state facts sufficient to constitute a crime. The state had not established a case.

"I desire at this time before the arraignment of these parties…to require the state to elect as to which of these complaints they will stand upon," demanded Fowles. "We have in the first place a complaint filed charging Baldwin with assault and intent to do worse; Loop and Perkins are charged with malignant assault and Worden is charged with assault with a deadly weapon. Then there is a blanket complaint filed afterwards charging each of these defendants with murder in the first degree."

Anable turned to the prosecutor and asked, "Which complaint will you stand on, Mr. Joiner?" To which Joiner exclaimed, "I will stand on them all. I will try the last one filed. I want it understood I am not dismissing these other complaints."

"You will try the four of them on the charge of murder in the first degree?" asked Anable.

"Yes sir."

Anable scratched his head regarding the charges of assault and murder combined, as the victim was now dead. "For the purpose of this examination and this examination only, it is admitted that Wheeler, the party upon whom the assault is alleged to have been made has since said assault died from the result of his wounds."

Fowles confirmed his charges again.

The case was continued to August 18, at 10:00 a.m., with the judge's decision.

The next morning the sheriff brought each of the defendants into court. Judge Anable determined that John White, who had taken no active part in the quarrel, would be discharged. Worden was charged with assault with a deadly weapon upon White and the murder charge was dropped. Since the death of Wheeler, the assault charges would be dropped against Baldwin, Perkins and Loop and the complaint amended to murder in the first-degree. The defendants were bound over in the sum of ten thousand dollars each.

Trial October 23 – October 27

The case of the *State of Washington v. Baldwin*, Perkins, and Loop, opened on Wednesday October 23; Judge Henry W. McBride presiding. Nearly the entire population of Samish Island came to Mount Vernon, along with many from Edison and Anacortes.

Renowned lawyers appeared on both sides of the aisle. Prosecuting Attorney George Joiner would prosecute the case for the state, assisted by James T. Ronald. Ronald, a former Seattle mayor, was a formidable man whose appearance alone was intimidating in any courtroom. He displayed a solid physique, topped with a rounded bald head, which with his small-rimmed glasses, goatee and mustache held the appearance of a professor. Ronald was an upstanding attorney with a high regard for ethics. He had taken a stand against Seattle's anti-Chinese riots and fought political corruption.

Skagit attorney B. B. Fowles led a defense team made up of George Sinclair, assisted by Colonel Robert H. Lindsay and Judge Turner of Seattle.

Two days were consumed in securing a jury. Three special venires were issued before twelve men could be secured. The first venire called for 24 men and the second and third for six each.[85] Opening statements began on the

LEFT: Skagit County Prosecuting Attorney George A. Joiner. File photo:
Weekly Anacortes American
RIGHT: Attorney James T. Ronald, for the state, was a formidable man whose appearance alone was intimidating in any court of law. Courtesy of Washington State Digital Archives

[85] Juries selected: Andrew McCutchen, W. A. Hawkins, Napo Brunett, A. J. Porter, Edward Thomas, J. McElreath, Wiley Roach, Joseph Boswell, L. C. Porter, E. S. Stewart, G. A. J. Burch and Joseph Dodson.

morning of Friday the 25th. At 6:00 p.m., the state still had possession of the court. Judge McBride ordered opening statements to conclude Saturday. Testimony would begin Sunday.

Prosecuting Attorney George Joiner opened his case reciting the crimes committed by the accused on the 9th day of August 1895. He accused all three defendants of "purposely and of their deliberate and premeditated malice killed one Alonzo Wheeler...striking and beating him with a cane, kicking and stamping him with the heels of their boots...shooting him with a revolver...of which wounds he died."

After state's opening statement the testimony of witnesses commenced. At first, Joiner placed character witnesses on the stand to humanize Alonzo Wheeler. Then Joiner called George Dean and John White, who testified to having heard Perkins and Baldwin make threats against the life of Wheeler. Numerous other witnesses would testify to the bad feelings between the men. A surprise witness, Daniel E. Douty of Seattle, was subpoenaed to take the stand. Douty was a guest at White's hotel at the time.

George Dean stated as previously known. He observed the defendants and Wheeler coming down the wharf, and then a desperate fight commenced. He testified White attempted to stop the fight by firing off his revolver. Worden struck him on the head with an iron bar, knocking him out. Dean declared, "...he did not shoot any more. White just laid there." All this time, Dean stated, the other three men were beating Wheeler. "Worden stepped back around a piece, stood and looked at them and didn't do anything else. Later, he picked up White's gun and came around to the front. He said to me I was in a critical position...a dangerous position, with these parties pulling guns; that I ought to quit it."

The prosecutor asked Dean if Perkins had a revolver. "No sir; not until it was over; he showed me Wheeler's revolver. Wheeler had no other gun. I would have seen it; he was lying right at my feet."

Daniel Douty (61) testified for the state, being first sworn. His testimony was the most damaging to the defense, as Douty was the only unbiased witness to take the stand. He had been on Samish Island eight days conducting business in Edison and was waiting transportation back to Seattle.

Douty gave testimony:

"At the time...I was in the hammock in the orchard reading. As soon as I heard the noise, I started for the wharf. I had to climb the fence surrounding the orchard. When I got across the fence I could see over the brush; [I] saw the men on the wharf. In my hurry, I couldn't tell them apart. When I got to the top of the stairs I saw a man in black clothes lying on the wharf and another man a short distance from him, and four men going around the west end of the warehouse disappeared entirely. The man that was standing near the man that was down was the only one who didn't pass out of sight. I hastened down the wharf. The man standing on the wharf was Worden. He was standing by the prostrate man and that was White. The other four men were running around the warehouse.

"White raised himself on his elbow. I heard White talk to Worden about the gun he was holding in his hand. White told Worden that was his gun. Worden told him he took the gun from him and that he had struck him. When I came up, Baldwin, Perkins and Loop came back around the warehouse. Baldwin was holding a gun in his right hand and a splintered cane in his left. I didn't see any weapons in Perkin's or Loop's hands at the time, although they were badly covered in blood and showed a few injuries. I was curious to see where the other man was and walked around the warehouse and saw Wheeler lying in the corner between the warehouse and the water barrel that stood near the door. He said he was dying. Baldwin, Loop and Perkins came back around the warehouse and they attempted to get to Wheeler who was lying down, but Captain Dean interfered and kept them off. By this time, White had got up and asked me to examine his wounds. I said when the fight was over I would, that I was a disinterested party; I didn't want anything to do with it. Captain Dean tried to get them to leave. Perkins started to go. Perkins then discovered there was a bruise on his abdomen and he came back and wanted to get at Wheeler again but Captain Dean wouldn't allow it."

Defense attorney Fowles cross-examined the witness. He asked if either Worden and White talked in a peaceable tone once he arrived on the scene. "I don't think the tone was peaceable," said Douty, "Worden was excited and used a great many disagreeable oaths toward White."

Fowles then asked how Dean managed to get the men off the wharf. The witness said, "He promised them he would take care of Wheeler. One of them (possibly Perkins) said, "If you see he doesn't leave the wharf we will go."

Fowles asked if Worden left with the others. "Worden stayed with the group. He made several remarks to Wheeler. He swore he wanted to see Wheeler killed. He didn't want to see Wheeler back on the island."

George Sinclair stood and suggested Worden may have simply been preventing bloodshed, and met no disagreeable harm. Douty thought a moment, and replied: "When White was down Worden's remarks were very harsh. He swore at him; called him a great many disagreeable names. He said he had taken the gun away from him. He was telling White he had done it for his own good, because he would hurt someone. Tried to pretend he was friendly towards White. It wasn't a reasonable conversation. It was bad language."

Douty was excused.

Joiner called John W. White. White's story differs in chronology and claims he saw all that occurred:

"I left the hotel to go down and meet the steamer *State of Washington* and took with me a block and tackle I used for hoisting and lowering freight. I noticed Perkins was coming down the hill that leads to the wharf ahead of us…I noticed Worden, Baldwin and Loop coming up the road beside my house, which left them behind us. Wheeler was close behind me. He caught up with me shortly after I got on the wharf and we walked together. I remarked to Wheeler there was quite a crowd of them. We talked but very little when going to the wharf. We walked together that way until we got to the head of the steps used for the small boats. There I turned to the right and laid my block and tackle down. Wheeler kept on a little ahead. I heard a scuffle…Baldwin rushed on him with a club he used as a cane. Loop closed in on him at the same time and Perkins closed in from the other way. The men scuffled and got considerably further away from me. Baldwin struck at him. They got further away from me. I heard shots fired…then Wheeler broke free and ran around the warehouse. Perkins and Loop followed after him. They went clear around the warehouse before coming in sight of me, and shortly after that, Wheeler fell and when he fell they were all there Baldwin, Perkins and Loop. Loop was using his feet. Perkins was jumping at him with something."

Joiner asked about the first and second time Wheeler went down and White's efforts to intercede.

"There were shots fired after Wheeler broke away after the first scuffle and was running. I didn't hear any more shots fired until Wheeler was down. Three shots rapidly by Baldwin. Wheeler was on his back; sometimes on his side and Baldwin was nearly over him pointing his revolver at him and the other two helped beat him. Wheeler called to take them off, "They are killing me; they are killing me." I advanced toward where he was and it was then I pulled my gun and fired in the air with the intention of scaring them until I got close enough to prevent them from killing him. Just as I fired that shot I was hit from behind by Worden with a crowbar. I knew nothing more about the affray until it was over."

Joiner asked what the feud was all about.

"Ill feeling over the route to Edison and boarders at the hotels," said White. "Baldwin was engaged in the same business. Hard feelings existed. I started wearing a gun because of threats against me by Baldwin and his crew. I carried it to protect my person."

Joiner asked, "Wasn't it true that there was trouble between some of the parties and Wheeler and yourself up at your house on this day?"

"Yes sir, there was a quarrel between Wheeler, Perkins and Baldwin. I understood it was somewhat bitter for the past several years between Baldwin and Wheeler."

Under cross-examination Fowles asked, "Didn't you know that Wheeler swore dire…against Baldwin recently, within the past few weeks…claimed Baldwin circulated a report that he was the cause of his wife's death? Didn't you know as a matter of fact that Wheeler, while he was staying at your house, within a week prior to this fight on the wharf, had sworn dire vengeance against Baldwin?"

"No sir," claimed White. "I know nothing."

Fowles had no more questions for the witness.

Remembering the trial and their testimonies years later were witnesses Roland L. Lewis[86] and George Hopley.[87] Both were youngsters at the time.

Lewis remembered: "It (Samish Island) was a wild place…they chased him (Wheeler) clear out to the end of the dock…Boy, they was just cuttin' him all to pieces and jumping on him with cork shoes. Got him in between a couple of barrels. There was a Seattle steamer coming in but they couldn't get there quick enough…They could see what was goin' on, but by the time they got there it was too late."

Hopley, was a boy at the time, when he was sworn in to testify:

"I was a young man. I didn't like to go into the courtroom. I was subpoenaed. I am sorry I was there. I went down to the dock that night, my brother and I, after we heard. We should have kept away. We went down to the dock, like kids will… My brother wasn't a kid but I was, and I wanted to see what was going on. One fella, he took bullets out of his vest pocket, (Ozro) Perkins did. He told me about when he shot him (Wheeler) and said, 'Here is one of the bullets.' I had to say that on the witness stand. Then I said, 'If it will be all right, I will sit down and hear the rest of it.' Didn't more than sit down and they kicked me out of there. They didn't want me to hear it that way."

[86] Skagit County Oral History Preservation Project. Interviewee: Roland L. Lewis by Barbara Heacock and Peter Heffelfinger Dec 1, 1977.
[87] Irene Pike, "An Early History of Samish Island and its Pioneers." George Hopley, *Burlington Journal.* June 12, 1952.

The state next introduced evidence. Most telling, was Wheeler's heavily bloodied clothing. Joiner then entered into evidence the crowbar, which came so near killing White in the battle. A piece of the splintered cane, used on Wheeler, was introduced. The cane itself having disappeared. Then medical testimony was introduced. Elmer C. Million testified Wheeler had come to him several days before his death to see if he could get legal relief from Baldwin, who was claiming he had murdered his wife. Upon being told there was no legal relief for him, Wheeler declared he would get relief in some other way.

Before closing his case, Joiner presented Alonzo Wheeler's dying statement. It was the prosecutor's last effort, by ending his case with Wheeler's last words echoing in the jurors' ears. Joiner read the document with dramatic flair and enthuses to the combat on the wharf:

"Ed Baldwin, Ozro Perkins and Loop ran up to him, Wheeler, and began to strike and beat him on the head with canes and a club; that he tried to escape but they pressed upon him and Baldwin struck him with a heavy cane and tried to hit him again when he, Wheeler, drew his revolver and fired at Baldwin and thinks he hit him in his forehead but was too dazed by the beating he had received to be sure where he did hit Baldwin; that he, Wheeler, then ran around the warehouse with Baldwin, Perkins and Loop in close pursuit and as Wheeler turned the corner of the warehouse Baldwin shot him in the side, then he fell down and Baldwin shot again and hit him in his foot then he, Wheeler, fell again and Perkins and Loop kicked him in the side and abdomen and over the eyes and said they were going to kill him and threatened to throw the wharfinger, Dean off into the water if he interfered. Baldwin, who had been around to building out of sight for a time, returned and as he, Wheeler, lay on the floor of the dock and Perkins and Loop beating him, Baldwin fired at and hit him again; this last wound was in his, Wheeler's abdomen and the ball seemed to go through his body. After this he became faint and dazed and is unable to tell or remember distinctly what did occur till he found the boatmen pulling him upon the boat that brought him to Anacortes, and he further says that in this solemn moment when he faces death and expects to die he solemnly swears by the God before whom he expects to soon appear that the above is a true statement of the affray which ended so seriously for him."

Then Prosecuting Attorney George Joiner said the state rests their case.

The *Bellingham Daily Reveille* reported testimony thus far introduced was similar in drift to the published reports of the tragedy. Still, it was damaging to the accused, showing among other things they brutally beat and shot Wheeler after he had tried to escape and even after he had fallen helplessly to the ground.

October 28 – November 2

Defense attorney B. B. Fowles opened his defense with a motion for the court to discharge the prisoners as a matter of formality.

Judge Henry McBride gruffly overruled the motion.

Fowles fired back, "I desire to move the court for the discharge of the defendants…first upon the grounds that the complaint does not state the facts sufficient to constitute an offense, and second that the evidence introduced by the state has not been sufficient to establish the guilt of anyone of the defendants as charged."

"Motion overruled." McBride answered with little thought.

Not letting go, Fowles, attempted another approach. "Before proceeding to offer any testimony, on behalf of the defendants I move for the discharge of the defendants for the reason that the evidence has not shown in any particular that anyone of the defendants is guilty of the offense of murder in the first degree."

This time Judge McBride pondered the motion before delivering a surprising ruling. "I will abstain the motion as far as Mr. Worden is concerned, but deny it as to the other three."

For a moment, Fowles was flush by his small victory. Fowles asked the court for a moment to confer with his defense team, George Sinclair, Colonel Lindsay and Judge Turner. Worden's defense was eliminated. It was decided to target Alonzo Wheeler's history, which was easy, as the man could no longer defend himself.

In trying to prove the bad character of Wheeler, defendant's attorneys attacked Wheeler's criminal past. He had been convicted of cattle stealing in the eastern part of the state. The defense tried to prove Wheeler was the aggressor on Samish wharf and that Baldwin fired only in self-defense. The defendants all testified Wheeler fired the first shots, claiming there was no reason for them to attack Wheeler.

Baldwin was placed on the stand on Tuesday, October 29. He said little in his defense, not wanting to open an avenue for the prosecution. Baldwin testified the trouble was commenced by Wheeler. Baldwin claimed he and his wife were living in deadly fear of Wheeler. Proving Wheeler's aggression, he pointed to the bullets he had taken in the head and another in his arm as a result of the fight. He was alive only because he was armed, and could defend himself. Baldwin claimed he was so stunned by the attack, that only the actions made by the other men stopping Wheeler allowed him the time to recover and defend himself.

Under cross-examination by James Ronald, Baldwin answered the state's questions with only a simple yes or no. Baldwin would claim the outcome could be no different in their defense for their lives.

Ozro Perkins, stepson to Baldwin, approached the stand after Baldwin was excused. Perkins first gave a little history of his life. He stated his biological father died while he was an infant. Baldwin soon after married his mother, Harriet, and raise him, knowing no other father. Perkins claimed the quarrel between Baldwin and Wheeler was long standing. Wheeler repeatedly threatened the life of Baldwin. He blamed his stepfather for the death of his ex-wife, Rebecca. Perkins told the court that Wheeler was a strong and able man, of desperate character, who intended to drive Baldwin from his home, ruin his business and kill him.

Perkins claimed on every occasion where contact was made between Baldwin and Wheeler—Wheeler was the aggressor. On the occasion of the alleged murder, they were simply pursuing their vocation as ferrymen. He said the quarrel was not his, but he was protecting Baldwin from Wheeler. He claimed he had no pretense to kill Wheeler, or held any part in a killing, except as it became necessary in their own defense.

Ozro Perkins' four children were in the courtroom watching the trial of their father. A move the defense thought would have great effect. Perkins' wife, Myrta, advanced in pregnancy became overwhelmed in a whirl of anxiety and fell to the floor in a faint. With great difficulty, she was restored to consciousness. Court was adjourned for the rest of the day.

Wednesday was occupied in hearing arguments. The defense closing their case well into the evening.

James Ronald, was the last to make closing remarks, closing the case for the prosecution with a lengthy speech. The case going to the jury on the night of Thursday, October 31, Halloween. The following day the jury brought in a verdict. Foreman, E. S. Stewart, stood before the court. "We the jury in the case of the *State of Washington v. Edwin Baldwin, Ozro Perkins and Ulysses Loop* defendants, find the defendants guilty of manslaughter."

The courtroom room couldn't have been more electrified. Judge McBride fought to regain order of his courtroom. Residents of Samish and Edison, were relieved to hear of a lesser murder charge. While those from Mount Vernon, Anacortes and elsewhere in Skagit called the verdict a sham. Three men had gotten away with murder, with no attempt to even hide their actions from the public.

A motion for a new trial having been written and filed was denied.

The *Anacortes American* stated: "Extremists may look upon the verdict as not being sufficiently severe, while sentimentalists will doubtless claim that the men are doomed to a punishment that is too severe. Twelve men have meted out justice as they understand justice to be, and the criminals must pay such penalty as the court may impose."

The *Daily Reveille* related the verdict would divide the people of Skagit County. The maximum punishment in the state for manslaughter was twenty years in the penitentiary and a fine of $5,000, and the lightest given was one year in the penitentiary. How heavy would the court come down on such a vicious attack, as the slaughter occurred on Samish Island?

On November 12, Judge Henry McBride imposed sentence. Baldwin was sentenced to confinement and hard labor for ten years and fined in the sum of one dollar. Perkins, sentenced to confinement and hard labor for five years and fined one dollar. Loop, sentenced to confinement and hard labor for one year

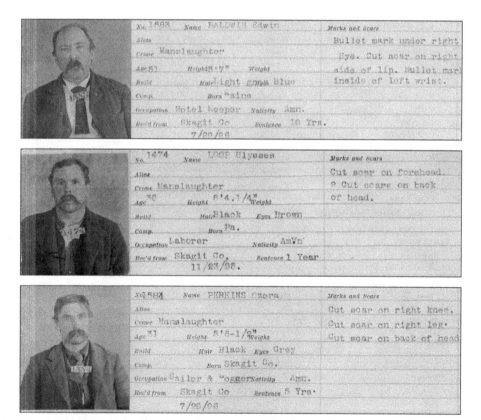

The murderers of Alonzo Wheeler. Courtesy of the Washington State Archives, Olympia

and fined one dollar. The cost of the case amounted to $2,450.05.

On Reflection

Ulysses Loop was received from Skagit County to the Washington State Penitentiary at Walla Walla on November 23, 1895. As prisoner No. 1474, he served out his sentence of a year, and was discharged September 23, 1896. He was a model prisoner.

Edwin Baldwin, prisoner No. 1583, was received at the penitentiary, July 29, 1896. His prison entry records indicate bullet marks under his right eye, as well as that incurred to his forehead during the battle of Samish. Could the second head wound have been inflicted during the Civil War? The record also records a "cut scar on right side of lip. Bullet mark inside of left wrist."

Ozro Perkins followed his stepfather to Walla Walla. His prisoner number being No. 1584, one digit following that of Baldwin's.

Within eighteen months, a movement was underway seeking pardons for Baldwin and Perkins. James Ronald, former mayor of Seattle and attorney for the prosecution, was one of the first to take up the cause, forwarding correspondence to Governor John R. Rogers. The movement expanded to most of the prosecution team and the residents of Skagit County.

On June 19, 1897, Ronald indicated in his recommendation to the Board of Pardons, that the daily press "published the most sensational, exaggerated, and in some cases, many false accounts of the murder." The published articles served in prejudicing the minds of the jury against the accused. Ronald claimed the "locality of the offence was Samish Island, a place remote from, isolated and unknown to the great bulk of Skagit County people, who in the absence of other information, formed the opinion of guilt." They were already convicted of the offence long before the trial. Therefore, it was impossible to receive a fair and impartial trial.

Ronald, in his correspondence, enclosed affidavits taken April 15, 1897, in New Whatcom from Katie (43) and Darrel Loop (15). Neither taking the stand during the trial. The affidavits were meant to offer another side of Alonzo Wheeler:

"I remember on or about, the month of June 1895," said Darrel, "I went with Mr. Baldwin and Ozro Perkins to the village of Edison…while in Edison we went to the wharf where Mr. Baldwin had some business to look after; and while at the wharf we saw Alonzo Wheeler. We left the wharf and went up into the village. Every place we went to, while there, Wheeler followed. Keeping his right hand in his coat pocket all the time, and would frequently make ugly faces at Mr.

Baldwin…I saw Alonzo Wheeler holding his revolver in his right hand, which he still kept in his coat pocket. I saw the butt of his revolver as he held it in his hand partly concealed…Mr. Baldwin tried to keep away from Mr. Wheeler by going from one place to another, but Mr. Wheeler would follow us every place we went. We finally left Edison and Mr. Alonzo Wheeler followed us to the wharf."

On January 5, 1898, attorney Ronald wrote another appeal to the governor. This time writing on behalf of the convicts' wives: "I am sure that while (Ozro) Perkins deserved punishment," admitted Ronald, "he has felt and realized his punishment now as sorely." Ronald requested early release due to "humanitarian" reasons being the care of his wife and children. Myrta Perkins by this time was destitute and filed for divorce. "Although Perkins' wife is a superior little woman…she and her children have been entirely dependent upon the county. That is cold charity indeed." Ronald added Myrta needed her husband more than ever. The family consisted of his wife and five children, the eldest being seven years old and the youngest born while he was in jail awaiting trial. "There is no means of support… his family have been, and are now, in a starving condition. His wife is now a weak woman, and physically unable to feed the children…they will become paupers."

As for Edwin Baldwin, Ronald said, "…he is an old man and cannot live to see the end of his term." Ronald acknowledged although he prosecuted Baldwin he admits now that:

"He was very much afraid of Wheeler, who was to a great extent a bluffer and an intimidator. He had been for some time imposing upon and threatening old man Baldwin. This weighted upon the old man's mind until life became almost a misery to him. In an unfortunate hour, the men met, and as claimed by all the defendants, the deceased commenced the attack by shooting. I cannot dispute this…the defendants, having their blood worked up, and their passions, failed to cease fighting when they ought to have ceased, and pursued operations too far. Of course, they all lost their heads at that time…I do not believe the old man mediates, or under circumstances or occasion of provocation now if released, would ever allow himself to be again goaded or irritated into a fight."

In closing, the attorney told Governor Rogers that Harriett Baldwin was now fifty-five years of age, with few years left in her. The verdict deprived her of her husband, son and brother. Ronald ended, adding, "No one would hold it against him [Governor John Rogers] should you make it possible for this old couple to go hand and hand down the remainder of the hill together."

Persistence, and the actions of a liberal minded governor paid off for the convicts. On May 6, 1898, both Edwin Baldwin and Ozro Perkins stepped out-

Chapter 12
Bloody Revenge at Mount Vernon

#159, Mt. Vernon, Wash, Taken from midway between Myrtle & Gates Streets, on First Street, looking south on First Street.
J.0.842   2-10-1912

Mount Vernon's First Street looking south toward Cleveland Avenue at the end of this photograph—entering the Riverside Addition, February 10, 1912. The Lincoln Theater will be built on the left in 1926. Courtesy of Whatcom Museum

side the prison walls as free men.

William Gorsage is Dead! Shot through the head read Skagit County newspapers. The bloody story picked up by the *Seattle Daily-Times* would make front-page news clear down to California. Readers paid five cents a copy for the *San Francisco Call* to read of the happenings in the Pacific northwest.

Gorsage was a Civil War veteran, fighting in the Grand Army of the Republic. He had been a semi-productive farmer in Avon, Washington. His wife Jeannie, twenty-four years younger, had borne him three children. But under this veil of tragedy the city of Mount Vernon rejoiced, for as far as anyone was concerned he was a viciously cruel son of a bitch. Gorsage was dead, and rounds of beer flowed in the saloons. The only sadness felt by the community was in the way of which his death transpired. If only it had occurred under different circumstances. If so, the city marshal, county sheriff, prosecutor and the court would have turned a blind eye and all would have ended there. And it wasn't as if there was lack of opportunities. "Revenge is a dish that should be eaten cold," so the saying goes.

What could possibly make a human being so cruel, brutal and sadistic? Could it have been a genetic flaw, a violent upbringing or perhaps a horrific life-altering event? Did something happen to William Gorsage, or had he always been vicious? Did it have something to do with losing his father at an early age and his mother remarrying soon after his death? Was it the horrors of war? Did nightmares transform him into a drunk? Maybe he just wasn't cut out for family life; forced into a world he never wanted. A more likely answer is William Gorsage was just a mean bastard!

Civilized people would like to believe there is no place within our society for such temperament, as the abusive nature and physical violence existing toward women. Such grotesque brutality cannot be tolerated, but as sure as the sun rises and sets, such abuse is a dark reality existing amongst us. The Gorsage family gives interesting insight as to how one community dealt with spousal abuse at the turn of the last century.

Gorsage

William G. Gorsage was born February 1840, in Johnstown, Fulton County, New York about 20 miles northeast of Schenectady. At age six his father died and his widowed mother, Margaret immediately remarried to William H. Talmadge, a carpenter, 28 years her senior. In 1860, it is documented Gorsage had one biological sister, Eliza (16) and a half-sister Margaret (17), a glove-maker, and a half-brother named John (13).[88]

By 1861, Gorsage was living only a few miles away in Amsterdam working as a laborer, when the War Between the States broke out on April 12. Thirteen days later, perhaps naïve to the "glories of war" Gorsage enlisted as a private

---

[88] August 1860 Census. William H. Talmadge was 68 and Margaret (Gorsage) Talmadge 45.

into the newly forming New York 32nd Inf. Regt., Co. B at Amsterdam. No doubt, Gorsage knew everyone in his regiment, and would likely see many of his friends and neighbors killed or horribly mutilated over the course of the next twenty-six months.

A competent Colonel F. Pinto commanded the regiment, while Company B was led by an equally intelligent, Captain Charles Hubbs. But fine officer-ship wouldn't protect their men from the horrors at Manassas. The Peninsula Campaign followed where 19,000 Union casualties would mount. At the Battle of Gaines' Mill, (First Battle of Cold Harbor) Union casualties would reach 8000 during the engagement. Following a defensive rearguard retreat back down the peninsula, and after much needed rest, the regiment was flung into the Battle of Antietam, a meat grinder claiming another 12,000 Union casualties. It would be the regiment's last major engagement. The New York regiment mustered out on June 9, 1863, three weeks before the climactic Battle of Gettysburg.

Gorsage ended his war physically unscathed, but what about mentally? His military record indicates he served over two years of tough campaigning, but without promotion. This gives some credence that Gorsage may have been a troublesome individual while in uniform. Did he have disciplinary or anguish issues preventing advancement? If so, were these issues pre-existing before his enlistment?

Fear of being forced back into the war may have been a deciding factor for Gorsage leaving New York. Under the new Union draft acts men faced the possibility of conscription in July 1863 and 1864. Hitting close to home were the 1863 New York Draft Riots. With tension and fear on the rise, Gorsage may have decided not to take chances and left, one day arriving at the banks of the Skagit River, where he is first mentioned in newspapers dated 1875.

Within five years of his arrival, William Gorsage married in 1880. Her name was Jennie, born September 1863, in British Columbia. She was eighteen to his forty at the time. Jennie, no last name given, was a First Nation's-Canadian Indian on her mother's side and her father a Scotsman. It's likely they were married in the British Dominion, as no record of marriage was recorded in Washington Territory. That same year the couple moved to Avon, just north of Mount Vernon, where she was left alone while Gorsage took a job at the Upper Skagit logging camp of Matherlett MFG of Seattle. Gorsage would refer to himself as an engineer. Although he lacked the intellect of a building engineer, he might have found a job running one of the logging company's locomotives.

By May 1885, Jennie had given birth to two daughters: Nina three-years-old and Mabel eight-months. Sometime during those early years, she had lost an infant, possibly during childbirth.

In 1887, life took a sudden turn for the family. Like so many in the logging industry, Gorsage was injured on the job, becoming a "busted logger." On October 4, 1887, he filed for his soldier's pension as an invalid. This was possible even if injuries were not war related. There was also the matter of another mouth to feed, as Jennie had given birth to a son, Delber, in November 1886. Perhaps the only positive thing that year was Gorsage now had a son.

Unable to hold a job in logging, Gorsage turned to farming on his little Avon spread. Gorsage knew nothing of farming. He may had relied heavily upon Jennie's knowledge, coming from a farming family herself.

The community of Avon was an important Skagit agricultural center. The village itself was established as a temperance community where no drink or saloon could be found or tolerated. Farming families were tight-knit, who all knew and helped one-another. By 1900 the little village on the banks of the Skagit River had a population of 500. Three churches stood, a hotel, a general merchandise store, blacksmith, two creameries, two sawmills, and two shingle mills. Communities along the river were dependent on steamers to transport their products. Riverboats pulled up to the Avon wharf and loaded hay, dairy, lumber and oats.

It's unknown what triggering factors made William Gorsage beat his wife. But, being physically combative with her didn't end there. From 1887 onward, he was at odds with anyone and everyone in Avon, and nearby Mount Vernon. He argued and fought with his neighbors and was quick to ostracize himself from the community. He had no friends. He took up heavy drinking, which wasn't tolerated in Avon. He drank away the family savings, and profits from the small farm. Fights ensued in Mount Vernon saloons, ending with Gorsage being thrown out.

An inept farmer, Gorsage sold the Avon property. It's conceivable Avon's governance approached him regarding the village's temperance laws, pressuring him to leave. Gorsage purchased a tiny wood frame house with two bedrooms, a sitting area, kitchen and pantry in the newly acquired Riverside Addition to Mount Vernon. With no job, he lived off the proceeds from the farm sale and his meager pension.

Closer to the city's drinking establishments, and flush with cash, Gorsage started coming home intoxicated each night to beat his wife. A miserable being to begin with, Gorsage was increasingly taking his failings and frustrations out on Jennie. Words no doubt were exchanged over money to feed the children, while he spent the last of the family savings getting drunk. Gorsage didn't want to hear this, and Jennie took a beating for raising her voice to him. Gorsage soon found it acceptable to beat his wife even if not drunk. Jennie's "nagging" as her husband would say, would bring down his wrath, and a severe beating. The fact there was nothing but potatoes in the house demonstrated a lack of nutrition. The children were obviously hungry. It's conceivable Jennie would take a thrashing for being unable to provide a decent meal for her husband.

As Gorsage deteriorated further into his depraved drunken abyss, the heinous beatings of Jennie eventually became routine. There is no evidence of the children being physically abused, but the beatings and ruin delivered upon their mother created suffering torment, and mental abuse on them daily. As the children grew into teenagers the girls retreated into silence, absorbing what was happening, but incapable of doing anything about it. Delber found sanctuary by running about the town, and staying out all night.

As Jennie became an unrelenting punching bag for her husband's amusement, she also retreated into dark depths. She withdrew in self-worth and spirit, but tried to hold on for her children's sake. She had no money to escape her husband, and no means to take her children if she could. Her plight wasn't unknown. Although she never went to the county sheriff or the city marshal, they would come to her. Unwilling, or incapable of protecting herself, Jennie reframed from pressing charges for fear of matters becoming worse. In return, there was little the law could do. When they could, the sheriff or marshal would pull Gorsage out of the house to cool off, or if seen on the street they could detain him overnight until he sobered up in the city jail. Even these meaningful gestures Jennie would pay for later.

It wasn't just the law who attempted to intervene. Men in the community ridiculed Gorsage, branding him as a good-for-nothing wife-beater; a coward of a man. On occasions when an enraged drunken Gorsage left a saloon, and trouble at home was certain, patrons followed making sure Gorsage had an accident along the way, giving Jennie a nod and a reprieve for the night. The law would look the other way on such occasions.

Jennie would later claim as time went, the beatings went from slaps to all night beating affairs. Her husband would pound on her until she caved to the floor. Unable to rise, he would kick her until he tired and went to bed. She would lie still, giving him no pleasure of hearing her moans. After a beating, Jennie wasn't seen in public and when she emerged her face was often bruised, swollen and yellowish. On one occasion, Gorsage split her upper lip up to her nostril, the scar noticeable in photos. Another time, he grabbed hold of Jennie's little finger and snapped the bone in half; the joint ever after enlarged and mending crooked.[90]

The Night the Abuse Ended

Toward the end of 1900, Jennie found the courage to leave her husband on several occasions, for a nearby neighbor's farm. Each time Gorsage sought her out and talked her back, only to repeat the process. On the morning of Friday, December 14, 1900, Jennie claimed Gorsage threatened her life and told her if she ever left him again "human eyes alive or dead would never see her again." The words burned into her memory: "The next time don't leave me. Kill me instead. For if you don't kill me, I'll kill you and I'll put you in the river where they will never find your body."[91]

That night the abuse ended. In her own words, Jennie would tell City Marshal Jasper Hollman and Skagit County Sheriff Edwin Wells:

"My husband came home about 6 o'clock in the evening, intoxicated, and proceeded to abuse me, and finally knocked me down and kicked and beat me. I told him that I would leave him and he answered: 'If you do, I will follow you and kill you. I would rather have you killed than leave me.' The abuse kept up until about ten o'clock, when he went to bed and kept up the quarrel. I was sitting in the next room. He had been in bed about half an hour when the sudden impulse to kill him came over me. I went and got his pistol, and, reaching into the room, the bed being so close to the door, I shot him. He is better off than to live the way he did, and I am not sorry for it."[92]

After ten o'clock, Friday night, twenty-eight-year-old City Marshal Jasper Hollman stepped inside the Hayes & Fergusons Saloon (sometimes called Hickey's Saloon) and sat down; his back to the door. He had just walked a beat and was chilled to the bone by the damp December air alongside the Skagit River. He hadn't taken his coat off yet when Delber Gorsage came to the saloon door and called out, "Jap." Delber was a minor and not allowed inside the drinking establishment. Hollman turned around to see young Gorsage standing there. He wanted to see him. Hollman knew what it was about. Billy had beaten Jennie again.

The city marshal stepped outside into the cold again. Delber said his moth-

---

[90] State of Washington vs. Jennie Gorsage, Testimony.

[91] Skagit County Record of Inquisition, December 14 (filed Dec 7), 1900.

[92] State of Washington vs. Jennie Gorsage, City Marshal Jasper Hollman testimony.

er wanted to see him. "Where is she?" He asked. Delber pointed across the street. Hollman could see two women in the shadows. He walked over to where Jennie stood with her daughter, Mabel at the corner of Laughlin's Furniture Store. He greeted them with a tilt of his hat, "Good evening," but Jennie didn't speak. She walked away over toward Moldstad's Corner with her head hung low. Hollman, sensing something amiss, followed her. She turned around to face him and in a firm voice stated, "I have taken Mr. Gorsage's life and I have come to give myself up."

Hollman, a little thrown back asked if this was truly so, and she affirmed that it was. "Yes, I have," said Jennie staring into the marshal's eyes, "I had to." Hollman was sympathetic towards Jennie, but not her husband. She said, "I couldn't stand it any longer—He was abusing me; beating me." She showed Hollman the side of her face and ear and again said, "I can't stand it any longer." The side of her face was deeply bruised with her husband's heel marks. The imprint was such that Hollman could see the outline in near darkness.

"She commenced to cry and I told her to be quiet," said Hollman later. The city marshal needed to think over his options. "She said she shot him. I asked her where was the gun." Jennie was wearing her kitchen apron, with her hand all balled up underneath it. Hollman thought she was protecting her hand from the cold or perhaps covering a wound, and then she pulled out a .32-cal Iver Johnson revolver. "Here it is." And Jennie handed the pistol over to the marshal. Hollman opened the gun just enough so it wouldn't throw the shells out of the cylinder, to see how many cartridges was in it—and how many had been fired.

Hollman then led Jennie and Mabel down to the courthouse to call Skagit County Sheriff Edwin Wells, but found the door locked. Delber walked off in a different direction once hearing his father was dead. Hollman thought for a moment then led them up to the Grand Central Hotel.

Taking the women into the hotel lobby Hollman told them to please take a seat and wait. He took aside desk clerk "Doc" Miller and told him Jennie shot her husband. Miller didn't act overly surprised to hear the news. Hollman asked if he would watch over them while he went to the Gorsage home to check on Billy. Meantime, he said he would send for the sheriff. Miller was very sympathetic, agreeing to watch over the women. He provided a sitting room and had coffee brought.

As Hollman left the hotel he noticed 60-year-old Irishman, Tom O'Keefe walking away from Hickey's Saloon. He called the old man over, O'Keefe declaring he had enough to drink for one night and was piloting himself home.

Hollman assured O'Keefe it wasn't why he called him over. The marshal passed on the worst, asking the Irishman if he would send for coroner Dr. James Vercoe, who was also a practicing physician. O'Keefe said he would, mumbling something to the effect that death couldn't have come for a better man.

Walking south toward the Riverside Addition, Hollman met Fred Carlini, a big Swede who worked a saloon. Again, he repeated Jennie's story and asked if he wouldn't mind sending for Sheriff Wells to come down. He suggested Wells might retrieve Jennie from the hotel first. Carlini had to contend with the drunken Gorsage on several occasions and knew of the abuse. He showed no sign of distress if the man was dead, but asked the marshal about the wife. Hollman declared she had some injuries, but seemed fine.

The marshal proceeded toward Riverside where the Gorsage house stood. Isaac (Ike) Orcutt was just going into his home with a lantern in hand. Hollman had no matches and couldn't remember whether there was electricity at the house or not. He hollered for Ike to come over with his lantern. The door was locked, the thumb latch being on. Hollman placed his knee against the door and easily pushed it in. The men noticed a light burning bright in the main room. Stepping into the house, newspapers were found scattered over the floor. Hollman heard a low gurgling sound off to the right were the bedroom was. The room was dark, but the bed was visible less than two feet from the door frame. Orcutt was holding his lantern high, as there was no light in the bedroom.

"The next thing I saw was Mr. Gorsage covered up as though he just went to bed. I expected to find him on the floor."[93] Hollman went in and saw Gorsage lying in his bed. "He was making a good deal of noise, and I tried to see if he would speak, but he didn't. He may have rolled his eyes a little…I said 'Hello Billy!' He didn't say anything. I said, 'What is the matter?' He didn't speak. His eyes kind of rolled a little."

Hollman made an examination without moving Gorsage. "I put my hand on his heart to see how that was running and it was beating rather slow, and I began to see where he was hurt. I couldn't see where he was shot until I saw the powder burn on the pillow sham, and then I saw the range the shot was fired from and knew in my own mind the course it took."

Holman had held the position of city marshal for three years, and had been acquainted with Jennie for at least 13 years. He knew, as well as many folks in town knew, that this day would come. The only question was which Gorsage would be found dead. Most assumed it would be Jennie who would be found

93 Ibid

beaten to death, and William Gorsage would hang for the offense. It was also agreeable if Jennie were found with a smoking gun over her husband's corpse, most in the city would turn a blind eye. The law, although never acknowledging it, felt those same sentiments.

But when Jasper Hollman discovered Jennie had shot her husband in the head during his sleep, he was in distress for her. No one would have blamed her for shooting such a heinous man. And over the years there were countless circumstances for a case of self-defense, but it would be with great difficulty for the court to help her under these circumstances. Hollman admitted to himself, this was going to go hard on Jennie. If only she had seized the moment to kill him at any other time that night, no one would care.

Hollman asked Orcutt if he would stay with the dying man, as he would fetch a doctor. He knew Dr. A. C. Lewis was presently at the opera house, but Lewis had to retrieve his bag. He must have taken his time getting to Riverside, as it was thirty minutes before Lewis arrived. The coroner was present, waiting for the man to die. Coroner Vercoe, although a practicing doctor, did nothing for the dying man. Gorsage was still alive, but died shortly after.

As the last breath left the body, Dr. Vercoe preceded to call an inquest.[94] Jurors were chosen from a rapidly growing crowd inside the small house who had come to watch Gorsage die. Word had spread of the shooting and by the time Sheriff Wells appeared with Jennie a mob had assembled outside her home. Respect was shown, as Jennie was led inside.

The inquest was swift. Over a dozen men crammed into the tight 10 x 12-foot bedroom already filled by the bed and a few pieces of furniture. Orcutt, now a juror, held his lantern for Vercoe's examination. Lewis assisted. Gorsage's head was rolled over for a better look. Blood had soaked into the pillow. After a quick examination Vercoe wanted out of the stuffy room, relocating the inquest to the larger front room. He questioned Jennie as to the events that night. In a very composed manner, she related how her husband came home and commenced arguing with her. He was continuing their morning quarrel over her threat to leave him. His anger had obviously stewed throughout his drunken day and into evening. He had beaten her until she could no longer lift herself off the floor. And when he could no longer strike her with fists, he kicked her.

By 2 a. m., the inquest ended. Vercoe and the jury decided, "William Gorsage came to his death by a gunshot wound inflicted by Mrs. Jennie Gorsage between

---

[94] Inquest panel: William E. Williams, H. E. (Gene) Hutchison, John Cleary, C. R. Rings, John Hatter and Isaac (Ike) Orcutt.

ten and eleven p. m., December 14, 1900 in their residence in South Mt. Vernon."
Jennie was given over to Sheriff Edwin Wells. As for the body, Vercoe decide it

MURDER AT MT. VERNON.

Killed Her Husband and Surrendered to the Authorities.

William Gorsage was shot through the head at his home in Mount Vernon Friday evening by his wife and died a few minutes later. Mrs. Gorsage then went into town and told the authorities what she had done. Coroner Vercoe immediately held an inquest, at which Mrs. Gorsage told the story of the trouble as follows:

Murder at Mt. Vernon.
Weekly Anacortes American, December 21, 1900

was fine where it lay and could be retrieved later in the day.[95]

Her Day in Court

Jennie Gorsage was given a preliminary hearing on Monday, December 17, before the Justice of the Peace of South Mount Vernon, Oscar C. Sturgis. Skagit County Prosecutor Maynard P. Hurd filed information stating "Jennie Gorsage...did purposely and of her deliberate and premeditated malice kill one William Gorsage... shooting and mortally wounding William Gorsage with a revolver..."[96]

The attorneys for the defense, John F. Dore and Henry McLean offered no testimony, and the accused was committed to the county jail without bail. Jennie was charged with the crime of murder in the first-degree. Sheriff Wells told the court he had no place to keep a female prisoner as the jail was full of men. He further claimed he had no place to separate the prisoners so Jennie could have a private cell. In order to keep her safe, Wells asked he be permitted to take the

[95] Skagit County Coroner's Warrant, Dec 15, 1900.
[96] State of Washington vs. Jennie Gorsage, Skagit County Criminal Case No. 3695 Warrant, Dec 15, 1900.
[97] Petition to move Gorsage to King County, Edwin Wells. Dec 15, 1900.

The Skagit County Courthouse, 1893. Not a soul in Mount Vernon didn't know of Jennie Gorsage's plight. Skagit Prosecutor Maynard P. Hurd pushed for a verdict of first-degree murder, but did so halfheartedly. Courtesy of Whatcom Museum

prisoner to the King County Jail until her trial. The request was granted.[97]

On Monday, February 18, 1901, jury selection began with the case ready to be heard the following day. Skagit Prosecutor Hurd pushed for a verdict of first-degree murder, but did so halfheartedly. By all accounts he had to make a good appearance for the state, but seldom would he pressure witnesses. In the questioning of Mabel Gorsage of the night's events leading to the shooting, he could hardly extract anything of value. Mabel, protecting her mother, played dumb and hardly admitted to knowing anything at all. Her testimony would shut down the frustrated prosecutor, who finally gave up on the girl.

Defense Attorneys Dore and McLean gave little evidence, letting William Gorsage's actions speak for them. They would paint Jennie Gorsage as a battered woman whose spirit was shattered by her abusive husband.

Newspapers were having a field day with the story, reporting Gorsage as a violent brut and the murderer should be pitied. The *Anacortes American* described Jennie as a "half-breed" with three children, but taking the side of the murderess. "Until about a year ago," said the *American*, "the family lived on a farm about two miles above Mount Vernon, when the farm was sold and a home bought in town. Gorsage had been drinking up the proceeds of the sale of the farm, and quarrels were frequent."

The most imaginative stories came from the *Seattle Daily-Times*, and those reported on the front page of the *San Francisco Call*. Both claimed Jennie Gorsage was encouraged and inspired by the writings of famous British novelist, Marie Corelli.[98] Defense attorney Dore in his opening statement to the jury claimed Corelli's novel, Thelma (1887) was found open on the table in the front room when authorities arrived.

"Gorsage," said Dore, "according to the testimony of all who knew him, was a surly and altogether unlovable character, harsh and exacting toward his wife and ready with a curse or a blow, especially when in liquor....those who will testify for the defense had witnessed several stormy scenes between the alleged murderess and her husband."

Dore claimed Gorsage was maddened by liquor that morning when he warned Jennie: "The next time don't leave me. Kill me instead. For if you don't kill me, I'll kill you and I'll put you in the river where they will never find your body."

Dore told the jury once Gorsage retired for the night Jennie sat down to read Corelli's novel. "Her heart was full of the wrongs that she suffered and as she turned the pages of the book the following paragraph burned itself into her brain." Dore then read a passage from page 77, the page open when the book was found:

"Thus it is, Mon Errington. This gentleman named Güldmar had a most lovely wife, a mysterious lady with an evident secret. The beautiful one was never seen in the church or in any town or village; she was met sometimes in the hills, by rivers, in valleys, carrying her child in her arms. The people grew afraid of her, but now see what happens.

"Suddenly she appears no more. Someone ventures to ask this Monsieur Guldmer 'What has become of Madame?' His answer is brief, 'She is dead.' Satisfactory so far, yet not quite; for Madame being dead, then what has become of the corpse of Madame? It was never seen—no coffin was ordered—and apparently, it was never buried.

"What follows? The good people of Bosekop draw the only conclusion possible—Monsieur Güldmar, who is said to have a terrific temper, killed Madame and made away with her body."

After reading the passage, Dore closed his copy of *Thelma* letting what he

---

[98] Born Mary Mackay (1855-1924), she was a successful novelist of romance and gothic fantasy, but was criticized as being "overly melodramatic." Her works are now considered as part of the foundation of New Age religion.

had just read sink into the minds of the jury. Then he added, "With a sudden resolution, the accused rose from her seat, went to the place where her husband kept his revolver, took it and going to the door of the room where he slept, placed the muzzle of the weapon close to his head and fired."

Testimony

Coroner James Vercoe was the first witness called to the stand giving evidence as to how he had found William Gorsage and the particulars of the inquest he convened at the murdered man's home. Vercoe explained he was at home when Tom O'Keefe came to his window about eleven o'clock that night, stating the marshal had sent him. "Gorsage wasn't quite dead when I got there."

Hurd asked if he had done anything to relieve the suffering of the man during the half-hour before Dr. Lewis arrived. Vercoe gave a simple, "No."

Vercoe went on stating, "I formed an inquest and formed a panel. Mrs. Gorsage testified at her own free will. She said she shot him while he was in bed. As near as I can remember it was like this. I may not have it exactly right. But she said 'He abused me and got me down on the floor and pounded me and kicked me and afterwards I said I would leave him in the morning. He said I will follow you up and kill you if you leave me. You had better kill me first, and I did. He is better off as he is.' She killed him about half an hour after he went to bed. He was fully undressed."

Hurd asked if in his questioning of Jennie if he "observed her manner, demeanor, looks and conduct" while giving testimony:

"She seemed to be pretty perfectly cool and composed. She wasn't agitated particularly. I think possibly she didn't realize the magnitude of the offense. She made statements of the trouble they had before that. I didn't make an examination of her."

On cross-examination by Henry McLean for the defense, Vercoe was asked if he had done anything to help when Dr. Lewis arrived. "I found the pulse very feeble. There were blood stains on the pillow that we didn't see until after Dr. Lewis turned the body over. There were both powder and hair on the pillow."

"In the inquest, what was her general manner and demeanor?"

"She seemed like a desperate woman."

Mabel Gorsage told the prosecution she was 15 years old. She claimed to have been in the barn feeding their colt for about 15 minutes when her father was shot. "I heard the shot fired and ran right in. Mother told me she shot him." Beyond this testimony, she added little.

"Did you know she was going to shoot him before?"

"No, sir." (The question was repeated twice.)

"Do you remember…testifying (at the inquest) that you had an idea your mother would kill him; that she was going to shoot him that night?"

Hurd kept grilling Mabel, repeating the same lines over and over, but continued to receive a mystifying look from the girl with a curt "No, sir" each time. The question was repeated so many times Judge Sturgis finally told Hurd to move along. Hurd switched his line of questioning to why it was she was in the barn.

Mabel remained evasive throughout the questioning. She didn't know where in the house her parents were when she went out to the barn. She was adamant that she had no idea where her father was or whether he was up, in bed or even in the house. She gave various answers to Hurd's questioning. Frustrated, Prosecutor Hurd asked, "Can you give me somewhere near the time? Was it twenty minutes? Give us somewhere near the time after you came in until your brother came home?"

"I don't know."

"Was there any conversation at all? Didn't you have any conversation with your mother and brother? Didn't your mother and brother come up town?"

"No, sir."

"Didn't your mother and brother come up town after your mother had shot your father—come up town here and see the marshal?"

"I suppose they did."

On cross-examination with Henry McLean.

"Isn't it a fact that when you met your mother at the door, that shortly after you and she came up town together…?"

To which Mabel smiled and answered, "Oh, yes sir. We first went to the Rings Saloon and from there to the bank, where we met my brother at the Brooklyn Hotel. From there we went looking for the marshal."

Mabel continued to testify to the numerous times her father had beaten and even attempted to kill her mother, even the time he had chased her mother with a knife, her mother locking herself up in the kitchen. She spoke as to the last quarrel, corroborating her mother's testimony. At a little after ten o'clock she went to the barn to look after the colt, and while there heard the pistol shot. Running to the house, she met her mother at the door, who exclaimed: "I have shot him." Her mother was excited and attempted to shoot herself, but was prevented by the daughter.

Thirteen-year-old Delber Gorsage testified he wasn't running around town all evening:

"I met mamma and my sister right by the Brooklyn Hotel. She wanted me to find Jasper Hollman. She didn't say the reason why. I forget whether she told me what she wanted him about, but I believe she told me she shot father. I walked back a little way with her and I saw Jasper going into Hickey's Saloon. I hollered for him to come out, I wanted to see him. (We) went across the block towards the post office and walked down on the opposite side of the street. I heard her tell Jasper she killed my father and gave Jasper the gun."

Delber didn't follow Hollman to the courthouse. He needed time to think about what he had just heard.

Court recessed for the day.

The following morning Jasper Hollman related to the court all the events up to the death of William Gorsage, as have been already told. The questioning soon turned to Jennie's demeanor after the shooting. Was she excited or cold? Did she seem to comprehend the magnitude of the offense? What did she say besides what you have mentioned?

Hollman declared Jennie didn't seem to be very much excited. She seemed relieved in the sense she had gone through a long ordeal and was now exhausted from it. The marshal was asked what he had done after bringing Dr. Lewis to the crime scene:

"When Lewis and I got there, there was quite a crowd of boys 10 or 15. The coroner was there and called a jury. They made an examination. I went up and notified the undertaker and got him to go down and take charge of the remains. Wells was there when I returned. Coroner Vercoe and Wells, I believe, came to the conclusion they would leave him (Gorsage) there until morning. So, we locked up the house and left him in the same position until morning. It was about two or three o'clock then. We left him alone."

Dr. A. C. Lewis followed Marshal Hollman to the stand.

"What did you find when you went to the Gorsage residence?" asked the prosecution:

"I found him lying in bed and shot in the head. The ball entered the back part of the head and a little to the left. From the position he was lying in I judge it passed forward and to the left, downward. It didn't pass through. He was lying on his back, slightly to the left, with his head turned toward the wall, toward the left. He was shot in the back of the head. There was black powder marks or powder burns on the pillowcase within a few inches of his head. He wasn't dead when I arrived, but died in 10 or 15 minutes."

"In your opinion, what was the cause of Mr. Gorsage's death?"

"I think the shot was the cause of his death."

The sole question now at issue was whether Jennie Gorsage was insane when she committed the terrible deed. Was she mentally irresponsible? "The quandary for jurors," newspapers would state, "she had been in the past, dozens of times placed in positions where she could have killed her husband and been abundantly justified on the grounds of self-defense." Would shooting a man in his sleep constitute self-defense?

Testimony ended, followed by only a few closing remarks. Predictably, the state claimed there could be no self-defense if the abuser was asleep. The moment of abuse had past, and Jennie could have run away. The defense declared years of abuse left her a beaten down woman incapable of escape. Jennie was only safe to defend herself when her husband's guard was down. Sympathy ran high in the courtroom; it was just the manner in which Jennie attained justice for herself that left the law having to justify her actions. Sentiments were even felt in Judge Sturgis' instructions to the jury.

Instructions with Empathy

"You are instructed that the word "purposely" in the law means with a purpose...that is, to kill being the purpose of the person charged with the offence...Before this woman can be said to have done a thing purposely she must have been in a condition and have been able to have formed a purpose. If the defendant in this case was not able to have formed a purpose to kill...you must give the defendant the benefit of that doubt and acquit her of the crime of murder in the first degree.

"The defense of insanity has to be considered...that the mind of one may be shattered, her reason overthrown or destroyed as the result of suffering, mentally. Or physical...One is not to be punished or found guilty of any offense in doing an act...if compelled to the commission of it, or to the commission of which she was driven by the goading of insane desperation brought on by abuse received by her at the hands of the deceased.

"...the same weight of circumstances that one woman might bear under and survive depresses and destroys others, and the same circumstances which some women's minds may survive and live under, will wholly destroy and render powerless the minds of others. This being so, it is to the facts of each case, considering the individual, her physical condition, her former mental strain the individual may have been subjected to, the inability to resist…The true test is, how was the defendant situated; what are the facts that surround her; what were they at the time and before; what condition of mind did she have previous to the alleged killing; what was the weight of her mental strain produced by the abuses she was compelled to bear or which was forced upon her; how would they… affect her at the time when the fatal shot was fired?"

After two days of testimony, statements and instruction, the jury went into deliberation. On Thursday, February 21, they returned a verdict finding the defendant guilty of the crime of manslaughter. The said verdict being read in court and filed therein by the clerk of court, motion for an arrest of judgment and a motion for a new trial to come on March 13, 1901, was entered.

Having been informed by the court of the verdict of the jury, the defendant was asked if she had any legal excuse to show why the judgment of the court should not be pronounced against her. Jennie answered that she had no reason. Judge Oscar Sturgis ordered Jennie Gorsage to be sentenced to confinement at hard labor in the penitentiary of the State of Washington in the city of Walla Walla for a period of one year and six months, and she would pay a fine of five dollars. Sheriff Wells was ordered the task to directly convey Jennie to the penitentiary forthwith.

On February 27, 1901, The *San Francisco Call* reported in faraway Mount Vernon, Washington, "Jury Convicts Mt. Vernon Husband-Slayer of Manslaughter."

The article stated Attorney John Dore tried to show the abuse Jennie suffered at the hands of her husband had "up seated her reason," but the jury simply took the argument of the prosecution that she had killed a man and ought to be punished. "The verdict was a great surprise to Mount Vernon people, who said that time and time again Mrs. Gorsage would have been justified in killing her husband." Others believed the sentence was fair for killing a sleeping man, but the same folks believed if Gorsage had not been sleeping she should have been acquitted.

Jennie Gorsage entered the prison system on December 11, 1901, nearly a year after killing her husband. Her inmate entrance information is very brief: Prisoner No. 2615 Age: 35. Height: 5-foot 1 and half inches. Hair: Brown. Eyes:

No. 2615	Name Jennie GARBAGE	Marks and Scars	Remarks
Alias		Scar on right upper lip.	
Crime Manslaughter		2nd Joint little finger	
Age 35	Height 5'1½" Weight	enlarged and slightly crooked.	
Build	Hair Brown Eyes Black		
Comp.	Born B. C.		
Occupation Housewife	Nativity Canadian		
Rec'd from Skagit Co	Sentence 1½ Yrs.		
	12/11/01		

Jennie Gorsage (misspelled Garsage) enters the penitentiary at Walla Walla on December 11, 1901. She will serve seven months.
Courtesy of the Washington State Archives, Olympia

Black. Occupation: Housewife. Jennie was discharged on June 12, 1902, after serving only seven months.

During her incarceration, William S. Anable, the court appointed administrator of her husband's estate, did his best to manage her assets, pay bills and help her children. He immediately sold the colt as an unnecessary expense. Gorsage's personal estate value equaled $125.00. The family had little. The estate listed only a bag of potatoes, a horse, a few farming tools and a few pieces of furniture.

The small framed house on the Riverside Addition was "of cheap construction in reasonably good state of repair $250-300." Anable hoped to rent the property long enough to pay court and child care costs.

When Jennie was released the estate was still in litigation. For a short time, Jennie and Mabel lived in Seattle, while Delber stayed in Sumas before they would come together again in Mount Vernon. Nina had been living in Los Angeles. On December 30, 1902, all personal estate items were turned over to Jennie, leaving her the undertaker's bill. Jennie filed for her husband's veteran benefits as a widow on January 24, 1906. It was the end of the trail for the Gorsage family. After 1906, the family disappears from the written record.

Along this peaceful stretch of Cleveland Avenue stood the Gorsage home, where Jennie, in fear for her life, took her husband's life just before Christmas, 1900. The Riverside Addition was the seedier end of town.
Photo taken by the author

Chapter 13
A Deadly Encounter on Blakely Island
by Daryl C. McClary

I am greatly indebted to Daryl McClary for contributing his story of the killing of George Lanterman on Blakely Island, San Juan County. I was introduced to Daryl while writing *Murder in the Fourth Corner*. Since then he has contributed, "Grimm Murders in Sauk Valley" in *More Murder in the Fourth Corner*. Daryl has a vast knowledge of the criminal element.

Daryl has published nearly 200 articles on the HistoryLink.org. He holds two degrees from Western Washington University: Education/English and Anthropology/Sociology. He was a federal investigator for 30 years and for 10 years worked on the U.S./Canadian Border stationed in Blaine, Washington.

Blakely Island looking east, showing the resort site at the northern tip of the island on Peavine Pass. Courtesy of Whatcom Museum

Blakely Island is a private island located directly south of Orcas Island in east central San Juan County (established 1873). With a landmass of 6.61 square miles, it is the sixth largest island in the San Juan archipelago. It was charted in 1841 by the Wilkes Expedition and named Blakely Island in honor of Captain Johnston Blakely, a naval officer who died during the War of 1812 aboard the USS *Wasp*, which sank during a storm. Captain Blakely was awarded the Congressional Gold Medal posthumously for the daring capture of the Royal Navy's 18-gun sloop HMS *Reindeer* on June 28, 1814.

Richard H. Straub (1846-1897) and his wife Jane (1834-1895) had a 143-acre farm located on the southeast tip of Blakely Island. The 166-acre homestead adjacent to the Straubs, belonged to James C. Burns and his wife, Pauline, daughter of San Juan County pioneer George Lanterman. Burns worked for the railroad and was absent most of the time. The homestead was worked by Pauline and her 11-year-old son Percy, with help from her brother, Leone M. Lanterman (1872-1895), and stepbrother, Ralph Blythe. Lanterman and Blythe resided on Decatur Island, a half mile south of Blakely, across Thatcher Pass.

The animosity Straub had for the Burns/Lanterman clan originated over the acquisition of land. Straub purchased his property in 1889 from Edward C. Gillette, San Juan County's first surveyor. He also wanted the adjoining acreage. However, Burns had filed a claim for it under the 1862 Homestead Act. This vexed Straub and over time the antagonism between the neighbors grew.

Prior to settling on Blakely Island, Straub taught school on Whidbey Island. He married Jane Elizabeth Terry, widow of Whidbey pioneer Grove C. Terry, there on July 24, 1883. They moved to Blakely Island in 1889 and took up farming. The handful of families living on the island built a log schoolhouse and elected Straub as the teacher. He became known throughout the island for his irascibility, however, and eventually public sentiment turned against him.

On May 11, 1895, Jane Straub, age 61, died of kidney failure and was buried on the farm overlooking Rosario Strait. In June 1895, the Blakely school committee, at the insistence of members Pauline Burns and Leone Lanterman, decided to dismiss Straub and elect a new teacher. Straub was irate, declaring Lanterman wasn't even a resident of Blakely Island. During a community meeting at the schoolhouse to decide the issue, Straub attempted to provoke a fight with Lanterman, but attendees prevented the confrontation, advising Straub to return home and regain his composure.

Unhinged by the recent death of his wife and the school committee's rejection, Straub became embittered. He decided to kill Burns and Lanterman and finagled 17-year-old Irving S. Parberry, a Blakely Island resident, into helping carry out his revenge.

On Friday, August 30, 1895, Lanterman and Blythe were at the Burns' farm, helping Pauline harvest potatoes. At approximately 5:00 p.m., they were hoeing in the potato patch when Parberry emerged from the undergrowth, approached the split-rail fence and began making himself obnoxious. He taunted Lanterman, calling him vile names and accusing him of deliberately starting forest fires, which had caused considerable damage on the island. Lanterman laid down his hoe and approached Parberry, asking why he was making such slanderous statements. Burns and Blythe stopped working and anxiously watched as the confrontation unfolded.

Parberry suddenly struck Lanterman on the left shoulder with the flat of an ax he was carrying. Taken off guard, Lanterman started grappling with his assailant. Parberry pulled a revolver from his pants and began firing wildly into the dirt. Without warning, Straub suddenly emerged from behind a large tree stump with a .38-55 caliber Winchester rifle and began shooting at Lanterman. When Lanterman fell, Straub turned his rifle toward Blythe and started firing. Blythe immediately dropped to the ground and played dead. Straub then turned toward Pauline Burns and shouted: "Now I will kill you." As he reloaded his rifle, she began running zigzag across the field. Straub loosened a hail of bullets at Burns and one grazed the top of her shoulder, close to the neck. She reached the farmhouse, however, without further injury. Meanwhile, Blythe took the opportunity to crawl under the fence and conceal himself in the underbrush.

The farmhouse was located near the shoreline where Pauline Burns had beached a dinghy. She and her son, Percy, launched the boat and rowed north to Thatcher where there was a sawmill that made apple crates, owned by Theodore W. Spencer. Burns reported that Straub and Parberry had just shot her two brothers and tried to kill her. Spencer organized a posse and proceeded to the Burns farm to investigate. They found Blythe, uninjured, hiding in the underbrush, and Lanterman, dead, near the split-rail fence where he had fallen. Spencer dispatched a mill employee to Friday Harbor to summon San Juan County Coroner Dr. George S. Wright and advise San Juan County Sheriff Newton Jones of the shooting. Lanterman's body was taken to the Burns farmhouse and prepared for Dr. Wright's arrival.

Having failed to eliminate who they thought was the only witnesses to the shooting spree, Straub and Parberry were concerned about the possibility of being lynched. Charles Smith, a neighbor of the Parberrys, took them to Friday

Harbor in his boat where they surrendered to Sheriff Jones upon arrival. He immediately locked Straub and Parberry in the county's ramshackle jailhouse to preclude any vigilantism.

Old San Juan County Jail, 1968. Courtesy of Whatcom Museum

Dr. Wright arrived at Blakely Island early Saturday morning, August 31, 1895, autopsied Lanterman's body and held a coroner's inquest. The postmortem revealed that .38-caliber bullets had struck the victim in the forearm, the abdomen and the head. The coroner's jury determined that Lanterman had died of gunshot wounds inflicted by Straub and Parberry "with malice and without due provocation."

On Sunday, September 1, 1895, a funeral service for Lanterman was held at the Methodist church on Lopez Island, officiated by Reverend Isaac Dillon. He was buried at the Lopez Union Cemetery on Davis Bay Road. Reverend Dillon's fiery oratory about the atrocity stirred up public sentiment and there were rumors about storming the jail and dispensing some frontier justice. On Monday evening Sheriff Newton, fearing trouble from an angry mob, spirited Straub and Parberry out of the jail and hid them in the woods under special guard.

BLAKELY MURDER

Leo Lanterman Shot by
R. H. Straub.

A NEIGHBORHOOD QUARREL.

Indignant Citizens Attempt to
Lynch the Murderer at
Friday Harbor.

Blakely Murder
Anacortes American, September 6, 1895

Since no steamships were due to call at Friday Harbor on Tuesday afternoon, Sheriff Jones arranged with Lieutenant Edmund Cardin, captain of the U.S. Revenue Launch *Scout*, to transport the prisoners to the jail in Whatcom County for safekeeping. The vessel was scheduled to pick up the prisoners at a clandestine location at 6:00 p.m., presumably when most of the mob would be at supper.

At 1:00 p.m., on Tuesday, September 3, 1895, a preliminary hearing was held at the courthouse before Justice of the Peace John C. Werner. Straub was ordered held without bond and Parberry's bail was fixed at $5,000. The defendants pleaded not guilty to a complaint charging the first-degree murder of Lanterman and they were bound over for trial during the October session of the San Juan County Superior Court.

Sheriff Jones and Deputy Sheriff Martin Ruthlefsen surreptitiously moved Straub and Parberry to the waterfront at rendezvous time, but the launch had not yet arrived. A picket spotted the furtive movements and fired his gun as a signal to the other vigilantes who quickly gathered in the street. While Sheriff Jones diverted the crowd's attention, Deputy Ruthlefsen and the prisoners crouched behind a solid board fence. The *Scout* eventually steamed into Friday Harbor, 20 minutes late, and Sheriff Jones ran to the dock and hurried his prisoners aboard. The lynch mob, nearly all armed with rifles, attempted to follow, but Lieutenant Cardin drew his revolver and declared he would shoot anyone who attacked his vessel. The mob withdrew and the *Scout* immediately got underway for New Whatcom (now Bellingham). Afterward, Sheriff Jones told the press that the jail at Friday Harbor was not secure enough to hold the killers and the Whatcom County Jail would be more cost effective for the San Juan County citizenry.

On Tuesday, October 1, 1895, Sheriff Jones returned Straub and Parberry to Friday Harbor for the trial, scheduled to commence on October 9. The San

Juan County Courthouse was far too small to accommodate all the people who wanted to watch the trial, however, so it was moved up the street to the capacious Odd Fellows Hall. On Saturday, October 5, San Juan County Superior Court Judge John R. Winn heard a motion from the defense requesting change of venue. Attorney Emanuel C. Nordyke maintained his clients could not receive a fair trial in San Juan County. Judge Winn heard arguments on Wednesday morning, October 9, and then denied the motion. He held out the possibility of a reversal of his ruling, however, if there was any difficulty in selecting an impartial jury. In a surprise move, San Juan County Prosecutor William H. Thacker filed a motion to have the charge against Parberry dismissed and ordered him held a material witness. Judge Winn granted the motion on condition that Parberry post a $1,000 bond to appear in court. The work of selecting a jury began during the court's afternoon session and was completed late Thursday night.

San Juan County Superior Court Judge John R. Winn. Author's Collection

On Friday morning, October 11, Judge Winn impaneled the jury, composed of 12 men, and the trial began. In his opening statement, Prosecutor Thacker said he would present testimony from witnesses, including a co-conspirator, who were present when Straub deliberately shot and killed Lanterman without provocation. It was clearly an act of premeditated murder for which the defendant should be hanged. The defense reserved presenting an opening statement until later in the trial.

The prosecution's first two witnesses were Ralph Blythe and Pauline Burns who testified in great detail about the ambush at the potato patch. Their testimony was supported by Irving Parberry who claimed Straub forced him to take part in the murder plot with threats of violence toward his family. Joseph H. Prettyman, a member of the Blakely school committee, related the incident at the town meeting in June, where Straub became enraged and threatened to kill Lanterman. Members of the Parberry family testified they had lived in fear of Straub's wrath for some time and substantiated Prettyman's testimony regarding the altercation at the town meeting. Dr. Wright, the county coroner, explained the nature of the victim's injuries, and stated the head wound appeared to have been delivered postmortem.

In his opening statement, defense attorney Charles R. Repath conceded Straub killed Lanterman, but claimed he was defending the life of young Parberry. Lanterman's death, although tragic, was not premeditated and his client must be acquitted of the charge of first-degree murder.

Richard Straub testified in his own defense, giving a detailed account of his movements on Friday, August 30, 1895. In Straub's version of the incident, Lanterman was about to shoot Parberry with a revolver when he happened along. There was a gun battle during which Lanterman was unfortunately shot and killed. Realizing the gravity of the situation, Straub convinced Parberry they should immediately go to Friday Harbor and surrender to the sheriff. Straub declared the testimony of the state's witnesses about the shooting was patently untrue. His story fell apart under cross-examination, however, and attempts by defense counsel to repair damage to his testimony on redirect examination was futile. Previously, Parberry testified that Straub had concocted that story on their long trip to Friday Harbor to surrender to Sheriff Jones.

Most of Saturday, October 19, 1895 was taken up by lengthy closing arguments. Afterward, Judge Winn gave instructions to the jury and submitted the case for deliberation at 4:50 p.m. Shortly after midnight on Sunday, October 20, the jury foreman advised the bailiff they had reached a verdict. The judge was immediately notified and a short while later two armed guards brought Straub, manacled, into the courtroom. Judge Winn reconvened the court and his clerk announced the jury found Straub guilty of murder in the first-degree, which mandated the death penalty. After the verdict was read, the jurors were dismissed and they filed silently out of the courtroom. Defense attorney Repath immediately filed a motion for a new trial based on judicial error, for denying a change of venue, and jury prejudice. After court was adjourned, the U.S. Revenue Launch *Scout* took Sheriff Jones and his prisoner back to the jail in Whatcom County.

Judge Winn heard arguments on Friday, November 15, 1895 and then denied the defense motion for a new trial. When attorney Repath gave notice of appealing the conviction to the Washington State Supreme Court, the judge stayed Straub's execution date until the appeals process had run its course.

On Tuesday, December 8, 1896, the state Supreme Court affirmed Straub's conviction and the judgment in the lower court. An application for a rehearing by the justices was subsequently denied. Straub didn't have the finances to appeal his case to the U.S. Supreme Court and he was referred back to Superior Court for sentencing and an execution date. Judge Winn retired from the bench on January 11, 1897, however, and took up the private practice of law at New Whatcom. He was replaced by Superior Court Judge Jesse P. Houser, who was assigned judicial responsibility for both Skagit and San Juan Counties.

On Tuesday, February 18, 1897, Judge Houser set Straub's execution date for Friday morning, March 26, 1897, at Friday Harbor. The death warrant was drawn up by Prosecutor Thacker, signed by Judge Houser and delivered to Sheriff Jones for implementation. Meanwhile, Straub's attorneys and friends had been busy writing letters and gathering signatures in support of a petition for executive clemency.

Washington State Governor John R. Rogers sent an official letter to Sheriff Jones, dated March 17, 1897, granting a delay of execution until April 23, so that he could review the request for commutation of Straub's death sentence. On April 10, 1895, he stated publicly that the pardoning power of the governor must be used only when there had been a clear miscarriage of justice. Governor Rogers believed the defendant had been given a fair and impartial trial and that his conviction and sentence, affirmed by the state Supreme Court, were just. On April 21, Governor Rogers announced that, after due consideration, he would not interfere with Straub's execution.

Meantime, Sheriff Jones started a crew of carpenters to work constructing the scaffold. The execution was set to take place in the lot between the county courthouse and the jail. To insure privacy, a solid board fence surrounded the area, 16 feet high. The gallows and a new five-inch, hemp rope were thoroughly tested with sandbags and all was in readiness for the execution on Friday, April 23, 1897.

Admission to the hanging was by invitation only and limited to 20 witnesses which included Whatcom County Sheriff Samuel Eastabrook, Straub's spiritual advisor, Methodist minister Theodore L. Dyer, San Juan County Coroner Dr. George S. Wright, a reporter from the *San Juan County Islander* and various county officials. Shortly after 11:00 a.m., Sheriff Jones escorted the condemned prisoner into the enclosure. Straub was positioned upon the trapdoor, his hands, legs and feet were secured with leather straps and was asked if he had any last words. Straub thanked everyone, especially Sheriffs Jones and Eastabrook, for their kindness during his incarceration and then uttered a final farewell. At 11:15 a.m., Sheriff Jones drew a cloth hood over his head, made sure the noose was properly positioned and signaled for the drop. After dangling for 20 minutes, Straub was cut down and Dr. Wright pronounced him dead. His body was placed in a plain, cedar-plank coffin and taken to the 508-acre military reserve at Point Caution (now Point Caution Biological Preserve) for a private burial. With the passage of time, the location of Straub's gravesite has been forgotten.

Irving Sylvester Parberry moved to Whatcom County and became a logger. He married Susie Estella Hobart in Bellingham on July 6, 1903 and over the years they had nine children. Parberry worked in various logging camps in Washington and British Columbia throughout his career, often as camp foreman. Susie died in Sumas on August 17, 1942 at age 56; Irving died in Bellingham on July 19, 1948 at age 70. They are both buried at the Kendall Cemetery in Kendall, Washington.

Following the execution, San Juan County Superior Court issued an order-of-sale for Straub's acreage on Blakely Island to satisfy outstanding debts totaling approximately $1,000. Sheriff Jones held a public auction on Saturday, July 31, 1897 at the courthouse in Friday Harbor, selling title to the property. Unsettled by the hanging, Jones decided not to seek reelection and accepted a position as superintendent of the Seaside Lumber Company, a new sawmill located at Everett in Snohomish County. He supervised several mills during his years in business and served as Everett's mayor from 1907 to 1910. Newton Jones died on May 23, 1922 at age 55 and is buried at Evergreen Cemetery, 4504 Broadway, in Everett.

The first capital punishment statute, enacted by the Washington State Territorial Legislature in 1854, called for the mandatory sentence of death for persons convicted of first-degree murder. Richard H. Straub was the only person to be legally executed in San Juan County. In 1901, the Washington State Legislature amended the capital punishment statute, requiring that all executions take place at the Washington State Penitentiary in Walla Walla.

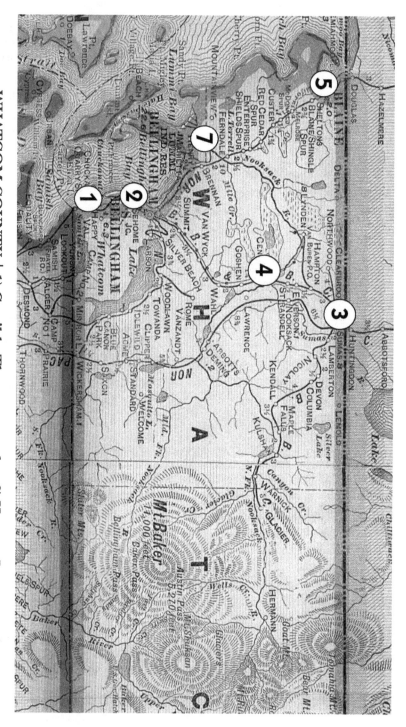

WHATCOM COUNTY | 1) Gunilda Thomas murder 2) Humes-Long murder
3) Jake Terry murder 4) Anna Belle murder & Kerns suicide
5) Emma Pinkerton murder & Shin suicide 7) Nora Gossett murder

282

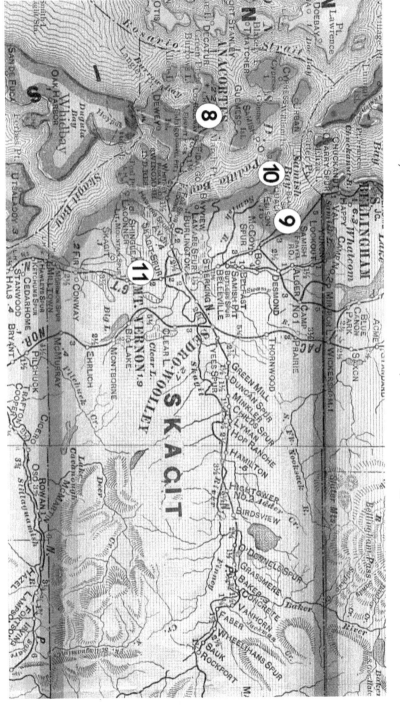

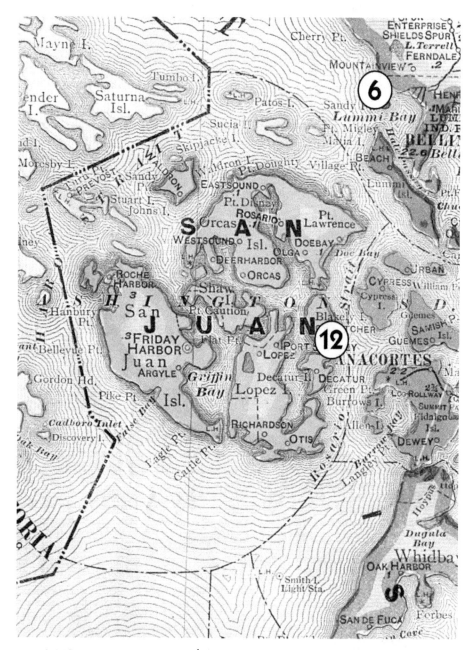

SAN JUAN COUNTY | 6) **John Harris murder (Whatcom)**
12) **Lanterman murder**

ABOUT THE AUTHOR

T. A. Warger is a historian and filmmaker based in Bellingham, Washington. Warger is the recipient of the 2009 Washington State Historical Society's David Douglas Award for the documentary film, *Shipyard* (2008). His latest documentary, *The Mountain Runners* (2012) is an award-winning and Emmy-nominated film about the 1911-13 Mount Baker Marathon. He is the co-author of *Images of America: Mount Baker*, and is a contributor to the *Journal of the Whatcom County Historical Society* as well as The Sea Chest, the journal of the *Puget Sound Maritime Historic Society*. Warger received his B.A. from the University of Nevada and attended graduate studies from Western Washington University. He is on staff at the Whatcom Museum.

Bibliography
PART I

Chapter 1: Mrs. Thomas' Potato Patch
Books/Periodicals

Griffin, Brian L., *Fairhaven: A History*. Knox Cellars Publishing Co., Bellingham, Washington, 2015.

"Insurance Maps of Bellingham, Washington." Sanborn Map Co., 11 Broadway, N.Y. 1913, 1930.

"New Whatcom Directory, 1891." Speirs & Whittier: Speirs; The Printer, Fourteenth St, 1891.

"R. L. Polk & Co's Directory of Olympia, Port Townsend, Fairhaven, New Whatcom and Whatcom," Vol. 1. R. L. Polk & Co., 1891.

Documents

Gruida Thomas v. James K. Thomas, Complaint. Washington State Superior Court, Whatcom County. Undated

Gunilda Thomas v. James K. Thomas, Findings of Fact and Conclusions of Law. Washington State Superior Court, Whatcom County. 9 Feb. 1906.

Gunilda Thomas v. James K. Thomas, Affidavit. Washington State Superior Court, Whatcom County. 9 Feb. 1906.

Gunilda Thomas v. James K. Thomas, Order. No. 7747. Washington State Superior Court, Whatcom County. 27 Nov. 1907.

Gunilda Thomas v. James K. Thomas, Civil Case No. 7435. Washington State Superior Court, Whatcom County. Law offices of Frye and Healy, Lighthouse Block. CPNWS. Undated.

Pierce County, Marriage Certificate, Washington State Digital Archives.

State of Washington v. James K. Thomas, Information for Murder in the First Degree, No. 70. Washington State Superior Court, Whatcom County. 29 Sept. 1908.

State of Washington v. James K. Thomas, Witnesses for the State. Washington State Superior Court, Whatcom County. Undated.

Washington State Penitentiary Biographical Statement of Convict, No. 5340, 12 Apr. 1909.

Washington State Penitentiary Convict Entrance—Medical Examination.

Washington State Penitentiary, Governor's Office, Pardon Case files 1889-1917.

Washington State Penitentiary Inmate Register Identification Record, No. 5340.

Newspapers

American Reveille [Bellingham] 26-28, 30 Sept. 1908.

American Reveille [Bellingham] 3 Oct. 1908.

American Reveille [Bellingham] 6, 10, 11, 13 Dec. 1908.

Bellingham Herald [Bellingham] 26, 28, 29 Sept. 1908.
Bellingham Herald [Bellingham] 1, 5, 9, 16 Oct. 1908.
Bellingham Herald [Bellingham] 21 Nov. 1908.
Bellingham Herald [Bellingham] 7-11, 14, 21 Dec. 1908.
Bellingham Herald [Bellingham] 20, Jan. 1909.
Bellingham Herald [Bellingham] 15, 31 Mar. 1909.
Bellingham Herald [Bellingham] 27 Jul. 1909.
Bellingham Herald [Bellingham] 18 Apr. 1909.

Websites

www.ancestry.com
www.digitalarchives.wa.gov
www.genealogybank.com
www.wagenweb.org

Chapter 2: David Long's Domestic Woe

Books/Periodicals

Ainslee's Magazine, May 1900.

Aiston, Peggy. "Lummi Island Chronological History 1519-1899." Vol. 1. Unpublished.

Edson, Lelah J., *The Fourth Corner: Highlights from The Early Northwest.* Whatcom Museum of History and Art, Bellingham, Washington, 1968.

"Insurance Maps of Bellingham, Washington." Sanborn Map Co.,
11 Broadway, N.Y. 1913, 1930.

"New Whatcom Directory, 1891." Speirs & Whittier: Speirs; The Printer,
Fourteenth St, 1891.

"R. L. Polk & Co's Directory of Olympia, Port Townsend, Fairhaven, New Whatcom and Whatcom, Vol. 1." R. L. Polk & Co., 1891.

Roth, Lotte R., *History of Whatcom County.* Pioneer Historical Publishing Co., Seattle, Washington, 1926.

Documents

Census: 1889
Marriage Certificate Return, Washington State Digital Archives.
State of Washington v. David H. Long, Information for Murder in the First Degree, No. 1355. Washington State Superior Court, Whatcom County. Undated.

Newspapers

Bellingham Bay Reveille [New Whatcom] 15 Jan. 1891.
Bellingham Bay Reveille [New Whatcom] 4, 11, 18, 25 Dec. 1891.

Bellingham Bay Reveille [New Whatcom] 12, 19 Feb. 1892.
Bellingham Bay Reveille [New Whatcom] 4, 25 Mar. 1892.
Bellingham Bay Reveille [New Whatcom] 1, 8, 15 Apr. 1892.
Bellingham Bay Reveille [New Whatcom] 19 Jun. 1892.

Fairhaven Herald [Fairhaven] 25, 26, 29-31 Mar. 1892.
Fairhaven Herald [Fairhaven] 1-3, 5 Apr. 1892.

Websites

www.ancestry.com
www.digitalarchives.wa.gov
www.digitalhistoryproject.com
www.genealogybank.com
www.wagenweb.org

Chapter 3: "Terrible" Jake Terry and the Siege of Sumas

Books/Periodicals

Jones, Roy F., *Boundary Town: Early Days in a Northwest Boundry Town.*
Fleet Printing Co., Vancouver, Washington. 1958.

Documents

Territory of Washington v. John Terry, King County, Warrant. 21 Jul. 1873.

Territory of Washington v. John Terry, District Court for the Third Judicial District
of Washington Territory holding Terms at Seattle in and for the branches of King,
Kitsap and Snohomish, Case file No. 993. Aug. 1873.

Territory of Washington v. John Terry, King County, Motion to Arrest Judgment and
Set Aside Verdict. 9 Aug. 1873.

Territory of Washington v. John Terry, King County, Verdict. 7 Aug. 1873.

M. S. Kenyon v. Annie L. Kenyon, Decree. Civil Case No. 5593. Washington State
Superior Court, Whatcom County. 10 Mar. 1898.

M. S. Kenyon v. Annie L. Kenyon, Findings of Fact and Conclusions of Law. Civil
Case No. 5593. Washington State Superior Court, Whatcom County. 10 Mar 1898.

M. S. Kenyon v. Annie L. Kenyon, Stipulation. Civil Case No. 5593. Washington
State Superior Court, Whatcom County. 28 Mar 1898.

M. S. Kenyon v. Annie L. Kenyon, Motion to Require Plaintiff to Make His Complaint More Definite and Certain. Civil Case No. 5593. Washington State Superior
Court, Whatcom County. Mar. 1898.

M. S. Kenyon v. Annie L. Kenyon, Action for Divorce and to Vest Title to Property in
Plaintiff. Civil Case No. 5593. Washington State Superior Court, Whatcom County.
11 Apr 1898.

A. L. Lindey vs. Gust Lindey, Complaint. Civil Case No. 7728. Washington State Superior Court, Whatcom County. 23 Dec. 1905.

A. L. Lindey v. Gust Lindey, Order. Civil Case No. 7728. Washington State Superior Court, Whatcom County. Undated.

A. L. Lindey v. Gust Lindey, Affidavit. Civil Case No. 7728. Washington State Superior Court, Whatcom County. Undated

State of Washington v. Gust Lindey, Affidavit. No. 753. Washington State Superior Court, Whatcom County. 5 Oct. 1907.

State of Washington v. Gust Lindey, Affidavit of Mrs. Lindey. No. 753. Washington State Superior Court, Whatcom County. 5 Oct. 1907.

State of Washington v. Gust Lindey, Affidavit of Mr. D. B. Lucas. No. 753. Washington State Superior Court, Whatcom County. 5 Oct. 1907.

State of Washington v. Gust Lindey, Affidavit of Virgil Peringer. No. 753. Washington State Superior Court, Whatcom County. 5 Oct. 1907.

State of Washington v. Gust Lindey, Motion to Dismiss. No. 753. Washington State Superior Court, Whatcom County. 5 Oct. 1907.

Gust Lindey v. Annie L. Lindey, Complaint. Civil Case No. 8883. Washington State Superior Court, Whatcom County. Sept. 1908.

Gust Lindey v. Annie L. Lindey, Summons. Civil Case No. 8883. Washington State Superior Court, Whatcom County. Sept. 1908.

Gust Lindey v. Annie L. Lindey, Affidavit for Default. Civil Case No. 8883. Washington State Superior Court, Whatcom County. 23 Sept. 1908.

Gust Lindey v. Annie L. Lindey, Affidavit. Civil Case No. 8883. Washington State Superior Court, Whatcom County. 8 Jan. 1909.

Gust Lindey v. Annie L. Lindey, Finds of Fact and Conclusion of Law. Civil Case No. 8883. Washington State Superior Court, Whatcom County. 15 Jan. 1909.

Gust Lindey v. Annie L. Lindey, Decree. Civil Case No. 8883. Washington State Superior Court, Whatcom County. 15 Jan. 1909.

Gust Lindey v. Annie L. Lindey, Affidavit. Civil Case No. 8883. Washington State Superior Court, Whatcom County. 15 Jan. 1909.

Gust Lindey v. Annie L. Lindey, Order Of Default. Civil Case No. 8883. Washington State Superior Court, Whatcom County. 16 Jan. 1909.

Gust Lindey v. Annie L. Lindey, Motion of Default. Civil Case No. 8883. Washington State Superior Court, Whatcom County. 16 Jan. 1909.

State of Nebraska, County of Douglas, (Notary Public residing at Omaha) Undated.

Newspapers

American Reveille [Bellingham] 7 Jul. 1907.

Bellingham Bay Express [Bellingham] 30 Jul. 1891.

Bellingham Herald [Bellingham] 27-28 Dec. 1905.
Bellingham Herald [Bellingham] 9-17 Jan 1906.
Bellingham Herald [Bellingham] 1-2, 5, 9, 20, 22 Feb. 1906.
Bellingham Herald [Bellingham] 5 Jul. 1906.
Bellingham Herald [Bellingham] 6, 8 Jul. 1907.
Bellingham Herald [Bellingham] 25 Sept. 1908.
Bellingham Herald [Bellingham] 18 Jan. 1909.
Bellingham Herald [Bellingham] 4 Jun. 1937.

Bellingham Reveille [Bellingham] 26-28 Dec. 1905.
Bellingham Reveille [Bellingham] 9-14, 17 Jan. 1906.
Bellingham Reveille [Bellingham] 3 Feb. 1906.
Bellingham Reveille [Bellingham] 8, 18-19, 22 May 1906.

Morning Reveille [Bellingham] 6-7 Jul. 1907.
Morning Reveille [Bellingham] 16 Jan. 1909.

Seattle Post-Intelligencer [Seattle] 7-8, 21 Oct. 1888.
Seattle Post-Intelligencer [Seattle] 11 Oct. 1889.
Seattle Post-Intelligencer [Seattle] 29 Jan. 1890.
Seattle Post-Intelligencer [Seattle] 26 Feb. 1890.
Seattle Post-Intelligencer [Seattle] 5, 8 Mar. 1890.
Seattle Post-Intelligencer [Seattle] 26 Apr. 1890.
Seattle Post-Intelligencer [Seattle] 23 May 1890.
Seattle Post-Intelligencer [Seattle] 3 Jun. 1890.
Seattle Post-Intelligencer [Seattle] 23 Aug. 1890.

Chapter 4: All Night Wrangle
Documents
Census: 1910

Newspapers

American Reveille [Bellingham] 15 Dec. 1909.
Bellingham Herald [Bellingham] 14, 15 Jan. 1909.

Websites

www.ancestry.com
www.digitalarchives.wa.gov

www.genealogybank.com
www.wagenweb.org

Chapter 5: Mrs. Pinkerton
Newspapers
American Reveille [Bellingham] 17, 18 Oct. 1916.
American Reveille [Bellingham] 10 Aug. 1917.
Bellingham Herald [Bellingham] 17 Oct. 1916.
Berkeley Daily Gazette [Berkeley] 17 Oct. 1916.
Blaine Journal [Blaine] 10, 20 Oct. 1916.
Blaine Journal [Blaine] 10 Aug. 1917.
Daily Capital Journal [Salem] 17 Oct. 1916.

Websites
www.digitalarchives.wa.gov
www.wagenweb.org

Chapter 6: Altercation on Point Roberts
Books/Periodicals
Clark, Richard E., *Point Roberts, U.S.A.: The History of a Canadian Enclave*.
Textype Publishing, Bellingham, Washington, 1980.

Jeffcott, Percival R., *Nooksack Tales and Trails: Historical Stories of Whatcom County*.
Sedro-Woolley Courier-Times. Ferndale, Washington, 1949.

Documents
Whatcom County Census of 1870, p. 3, #17.

Whatcom County Census of 1880, p. 12, #180.

Whatcom County Probate Court, Appts of Executor's Journal, p. 29.

Whatcom Genealogical Society, Bulletin, #7, #4, June 1977.

Territory of Washington, Whatcom County, Affidavit for Warrant. Roger S. Greene, Chief Justice of W.T., 18 Apr 1883.

Territory of Washington v. Mitchell, Affidavit for Warrant. 1883.

Territory of Washington v. Mitchell. Burke and Jacobs Charge. 1884.

Territory of Washington v. Mitchell, Verdict. 1884.

Territory of Washington, Whatcom County Probate Court, Harris estate. 1883.

Whatcom County Orders and Decrees, Harris Estate. 1878-1907.

Newspapers
Bellingham Bay Mail [Whatcom] 12 Jul. 1873.

Bellingham Bay Mail [Whatcom] 9 Aug. 1873.

Blaine Journal [Blaine] 12 Dec. 1889.

La Connor Mail [La Connor] Feb. 1883.

Northwest Enterprise [Anacortes] 27 Jan. 1883.

Whatcom Reveille [Whatcom] 15 Jun. 1883.
Whatcom Reveille [Whatcom] 21 Mar. 1884.

Websites

www.digitalarchives.wa.gov

www.wagenweb.org

Chapter 7: "I Held Her Too Long!"
Publications

"My Wife Was My Best Neighbor," Actual Detective Stories, Actual Detective Stories Co., 731 Plymouth Court, Chicago, Ill. Vol. V., No. 12., April 1942.

Newspapers

Bellingham Herald [Bellingham] 21-23, 26 Apr. 1941.
Bellingham Herald [Bellingham] 6, 19 May 1941.
Bellingham Herald [Bellingham] 2 Jun. 1941.

Documents

Nora E. Gossett v. Berton L. Gossett, Suit for Divorce Subsequently Reconciliation. Civil Case Pen Entry No. 18794. Washington State Superior Court, Whatcom County. 1930.

Nora E. Gossett v. Berton L. Gossett, Finding of Fact and Conclusions. No. 21505. Washington State Superior Court, Whatcom County. May 1932.

Nora E. Gossett v. Berton L. Gossett, Restraining Order. No. 24695. Washington State Superior Court, Whatcom County. Sept. 1937.

Nora E. Gossett v. Berton L. Gossett, Interlocutory Decree: Property Award. No. 24695. Washington State Superior Court, Whatcom County. 2 Jul. 1938.

Nora E. Gossett v. Berton L. Gossett, Finding of Fact and Conclusions of Law. No. 24695. Washington State Superior Court, Whatcom County. 16 Jul. 1938.

Nora E. Gossett v. Berton L. Gossett, Order of Show Cause. No. 24695. Washington State Superior Court, Whatcom County. 3 Jul. 1939.

Nora E. Gossett v. Berton L. Gossett, Order of Modification of Interlocutory Decree of Divorce. No. 24695. Washington State Superior Court, Whatcom County. 1939.

Nora E. Gossett v. Berton L. Gossett, Clerk Civil Case Files. No. 24695. Washington State Superior Court, Whatcom County. 18 Oct. 1940.

Chapter 8: Dead Man Walking:
The Story of Alfred Hawkins, Scene II
Books/Publications

Hastie, Thomas P., *Illustrated History of Skagit and Snohomish Counties* (Chicago: Interstate Publishing Co., 1906), 168-69.

"Insurance Maps of Bellingham, Washington." Sanborn Map Co., 11 Broadway, N.Y. 1913, 1930.

Documents

State of Washington v. Alfred Hawkins—alias—Alfred Hamilton, Appellant No. 3566, Supreme Court of Washington, 23. Wash. 289 P. 258, 19 Nov. 1900, Decided.

Newspapers

Anacortes American [Anacortes] 23 May 1902.

Bellingham Bay Reveille [New Whatcom] 21-24 May 1901.

Blade [Whatcom] 23, 25 May 1901.

Fairhaven Evening Herald [Fairhaven] 23 May 1902.

Fairhaven Herald [Fairhaven] 22, 24 May 1901.

Seattle Star [Seattle] 16 Aug. 1901.
Seattle Star [Seattle] 18 Feb. 1902.

Seattle Times [Seattle] 20-21, 23-24 May 1901.
Seattle Times [Seattle] 16, 25 Jul. 1901.
Seattle Times [Seattle] 17-19 Feb. 1902.
Seattle Times [Seattle] 18 Apr. 1902.
Seattle Times [Seattle] 19-20, 22-23 May 1902.

Weekly Blade [Whatcom] 7 May 1902.
Weekly World-Herald [Fairhaven] 23, 30 May 1902.

Publications
"Alfred Hamilton Shoots and Kills Attorney David M. Woodbury in Anacortes on September 7, 1899." HistoryLink.Org Essay 10004. Daryl McClary, January 18, 2012.

PART II - Skagit & San Juan Counties

Chapter 9: Dead Man Walking:
The Story of Alfred Hawkins, Scene I
Documents

State of Washington v. Alfred Hawkins—alias—Alfred Hamilton, Appellant. No. 3566. Washington State Superior Court, 23. Wash. 289 P. 258, Decided. 19 Nov. 1900.

State of Washington v. Alfred Hawkins—alias—Alfred Hamilton, Order. No.1355. Washington State Superior Court, Skagit County. 25 Feb. 1901.

State of Washington v. Alfred Hawkins—Alias—Alfred Hamilton, Transfer of Evidence. No. 3536 from Skagit to Whatcom County. 8 Mar. 1901.

Whatcom County Superior Court Civil Case Journals: 27 Nov 1900-21 Jul 1901. Hawkins, Alfred—Alfred Hamilton, Case No.188. Pages: 298 Order, Arrangement, 23 Mar 1901; 385 Order, Subpoenas, 25 Apr 1901; 391 Order, Subpoenas, 29 Apr 1901; 458-459 Order, Subpoenas—Jury Selection, 20 May 1901; 560 Order, Second Viewing; 461-465 Order, Third Viewing Returnable, 21 May 1901; 472 Order and Verdict, 23 May 1901; 474 Order, Motion, 24 May 1901 (550 Order, Judgment; 552 Order, Death Warrant, 16 Aug 1901—Signed 17 Jun 1901.

Newspapers

Anacortes Weekly American [Anacortes] 14, 21 Sept. 1899.

Anacortes Weekly American [Anacortes] 16, 19 Nov. 1899.

Bellingham Bay Reveille [New Whatcom] 8-9 Sept. 1899.

Seattle Post-Intelligencer [Seattle] 8 Sept. 1899.

Seattle Star [Seattle] 8-9, 11 Sept. 1899.

Skagit County Times [Sedro-Woolley] 14 Sept. 1899.

Websites

"Alfred Hamilton Shoots and Kills Attorney David M. Woodbury in Anacortes on September 7, 1899." HistoryLink.Org Essay 10004. Daryl McClary, January 18, 2012.

Chapter 10: Train Ride to Hell: The Great Northern Massacre

Books/Publications

Willis, Margaret, Editor, *Skagit Settlers Trails and Triumphs 1890-1920*. The Skagit County Historical Series, Vol. 4, McCallum Printing Group Inc. Edmonton, Alberta Canada. 1975.

Newspapers

American Reveille [Bellingham] 21-22, 24-27 Feb. 1914.

American Reveille [Bellingham] 3, 27 Mar. 1914.

American Reveille [Bellingham] 8, 12 Apr. 1914.

Bellingham Herald [Bellingham] 21, 23-25, 27-28 Feb. 1914.

Bellingham Herald [Bellingham] 2-3, 20, 27-28 Mar. 1914..

Bellingham Herald [Bellingham] 2, 10-11, 14, 16, 20 Apr. 1914.

Bellingham Herald [Bellingham] 8,12, 16-18 Jun. 1914.

Seattle Post-Intelligencer [Seattle] 21-23 Feb. 1914.

Seattle Post-Intelligencer [Seattle] 26, 28-29 Mar. 1914.

Seattle Post-Intelligencer [Seattle] 11, 26 Apr. 1914.

Seattle Post-Intelligencer [Seattle] 6-7, 12, 16 Jun. 1914.

Chapter 11: Battle of Samish
Books/Periodicals

Hastie, Thomas P., *Illustrated History of Skagit and Snohomish Counties* (Chicago: Interstate Publishing Co., 1906) p. 163-64.

Lang, H. O., *History of the Willamette Valley*. Portland, OR; 1885 p. 663.

Miller, Fred and Susan, *Samish Island: A History: From the Beginnings to the 1970's*. Mount Vernon, Washington Copy & Print Store. 2007. p. 96, 99-100, 107, 117, 149-50.

Pike, Irene, "An Early History of Samish Island and its Pioneers." *Burlington Journal*. 12 June, 1952.

Seattle Directory 1890 and 1891.

Wetherell, Nelle v. The Confederate Colonel Who Had a Novel Rehabilitation Plan, 19 May, 1949.

Willis, Margaret, Editor, Chechacos All: The Pioneering of Skagit. The Skagit County Historical Series, Vol. 3, McCallum Printing Group Inc. Edmonton, Alberta Canada. 1973.

Documents

Census 1860.

State of Washington Plaintiff v. Baldwin, Perkins Loop and Worden: Defendants Justice Court. Washington State Superior Court, Skagit County 17 Aug. 1895.

State of Washington v. Edwin Baldwin, Ozro Perkins and Ulysses Loop, Information. No. 2804. Washington State Superior Court, Skagit County. 11 Oct. 1895

State of Washington v. Edwin Baldwin, Ozro Perkins and Ulysses Loop, Judgement. No. 2804. Washington State Superior Court, Skagit County. 23 Oct. (2 Nov. 1895)1895.

Probate file 8209, Box 7 Alonzo Wheeler.

Petition for Letters of Administration, Judge Henry McBride. E. C. Million appointed by Attorney J. P. Houser as administrator. 28 Sept. 1895.

Probate File No. 8208, Box 6, Rebecca J. Wheeler.

No. 127, Petition of Augustus Ray Lewis of Edison.

Final Account and Distribution. No. 127. 3 Nov 1900.

Washington State Penitentiary, Governor's Office, Pardon Case files 1889-1917. Perkins Correspondence 31 Mar 1898 writes Governor John R. Rogers that his wife has filed divorce and wants to children and begs for release. Recommendation by Board of Pardons. 20 Jun. 1897.

Myrta Maud "Inman" Perkins v. Ozro Lambert Perkins Complaint in Divorce.

Washington State Superior Court, Skagit County. 11 Apr. 1898.

Newspapers

Daily Journal [Corvallis] 23 Oct 1902.

Daily Reveille [Bellingham] 17 Aug 1895.

Daily Reveille [Bellingham] 30 Oct 30 1895.

Daily Reveille [Bellingham] 2-3 Nov 1895.

Polk County Itemizer [Corvallis] 14 Nov 1902.

Weekly Anacortes American [Anacortes] Undated.

Weekly Anacortes American [Anacortes] Undated.

Weekly Anacortes American [Anacortes] Undated.

Oral History

Skagit County Oral History Project: 1962-1979. Interviews: Roland Lewis; Helen Loop, Maud Dever Hopley, Viola Dolittle Cameron.

Chapter 12: Bloody Revenge at Mount Vernon
Books/Publications

Hastie, Thomas P., *Illustrated History of Skagit and Snohomish Counties* (Chicago: Interstate Publishing Co., 1906).

Documents

Census: 1860 NY, 1880 WT, 1885 WT, 1900 WA.

Skagit County Record of Inquisition, Dec. 14 (filed 7 Dec.), 1900.

Justice Court, South Mount Vernon Precinct: Complaint Dec. 15, 1900.

Skagit County Coroner's Warrant, Dec 15, 1900.

State of Washington Death Return Records.

State of Washington v. Jennie Gorsage, Warrant. Washington State Superior Court, Skagit County Criminal Case No. 3695. 15 Dec. 1900.

State of Washington v. Jennie Gorsage, Petition to move Gorsage to King County. Washington State Superior Court, Skagit County Criminal Case No. 3695. 15 Dec. 1900. Print.

State of Washington v. Jennie Gorsage, Testimony. Washington State Superior Court, Skagit County Criminal Case No. 3695. Undated.

State of Washington v. Jennie Gorsage, Instructions. Washington State Superior Court, Skagit County Criminal Case No. 3695. Undated.

State of Washington v. Jennie Gorsage, Judgment of Verdict. Washington State Superior Court, Skagit County Criminal Case No. 3695. 13 Mar. 1901.

State of Washington v. Jennie Gorsage, Order Overruling Motion for Arrest of Judgment and Motion for New Trial. Washington State Superior Court, Skagit County Criminal Case No. 3695. Undated.

State of Washington v. Jennie Gorsage, Supreme Court No. 4075. Judgment in the Appellant, session. 3 Oct. 1901.

State of Washington Wills and Probate No. 287.

United States Civil War Pension records.

Washington State Penitentiary Record Inmate No. 2615.

Newspapers

Anacortes American [Anacortes] Dec. 1900.

San Francisco Call [San Francisco] 21, 27 Feb. 1901.

Websites

www.ancestry.com

www.digitalarchives.wa.gov

Chapter 13: A Deadly Encounter on Blakely Island
By Daryl C. McClary

Books/Publications

Edmund S. Meany, *Origin of Washington Geographic Names* (Seattle: University of Washington Press, 1923) 22.

David Richardson, *Pig War Islands* (Eastsound, WA: Orcas Publishing Company, 1971) 218-224.

Newspapers

Daily Journal [Corvallis] 23 Oct 1902.

San Juan Islander [Friday Harbor] 5 Sept 1895.
San Juan Islander [Friday Harbor] 17 Oct 1895.
San Juan Islander [Friday Harbor] 24 Oct 1895.
San Juan Islander [Friday Harbor] 7 Nov 1895
San Juan Islander [Friday Harbor] 18 Mar 1897.
San Juan Islander [Friday Harbor] 15 Apr 1897.
San Juan Islander [Friday Harbor] 29 Apr 1897.
San Juan Islander [Friday Harbor] 13 May 1897.
San Juan Islander [Friday Harbor] 22 May 1897.

Morning Olympian [Olympia] 5 Sept 1895.
Morning Olympian [Olympia] 14 Oct 1895.
Morning Olympian [Olympia] 8 Dec 1896.
Morning Olympian [Olympia] 10 Apr 1897.
Morning Olympian [Olympia] 13 Apr 1897.
Morning Olympian [Olympia] 20 Apr 1897.
Morning Olympian [Olympia] 21 Apr 1897.
Morning Olympian [Olympia] 23 Apr 1897.

Tacoma Daily News [Tacoma] 21 Oct 1895.
Tacoma Daily News [Tacoma] 16 Nov 1895.
Tacoma Daily News [Tacoma] 19 Feb 1897.

Tacoma Daily News [Tacoma] 24 Apr 1897.

Tacoma Daily News [Tacoma] 8 May 1897.

Websites

ancestry.com

Washington State Archives (http://www.digitalarchives.wa.gov)

CPSIA information can be obtained
at www.ICGtesting.com
Printed in the USA
FSHW020245050821
83614FS